Research and Development Management: From the Soviet Union to Russia

Contributions to Economics

Albrecht Ritschl
Prices and Production
- Elements of a System - Theoretic Perspective -
1989. 159pp. Softcover DM 59,-
ISBN 3-7908-0429-0

Arnulf Grübler
The Rise and Fall of Infrastructures
- Dynamics of Evolution and Technological Change in Transport -
1990. 305pp. Softcover DM 85,-
ISBN 3-7908-0479-7

Peter R. Haiss
Cultural Influences on Strategic Planning
1990. 188pp. Softcover DM 65,-
ISBN 3-7908-0481-9

Manfred Kremer/Marion Weber (Eds.)
Transforming Economic Systems: The Case of Poland
1992. 179pp. Softcover DM 69,-
ISBN 3-7908-91415-3

Marcel F. van Marion
Liberal Trade and Japan
1993. 298pp. Softcover DM 90,-
ISBN 3-7908-0699-4

Michael Carlberg
Open Economy Dynamics
1993. 203 pp. Softcover DM 75,-
ISBN 3-7908-0708-7

Hans Schneeweiß/
Klaus F. Zimmermann (Eds.)
Studies in Applied Econometrics
1993. 238 pp. Softcover DM 85,-
ISBN 3-7908-0716-8

Gerhard Gehrig/Wladyslaw Welfe (Eds.)
Economies in Transition
1993. 292 pp. Softcover DM 90,-
ISBN 3-7908-0721-4

Alfred Franz/Carsten Stahmer (Eds.)
Approaches to Environmental Accounting
1993. 542 pp. Softcover DM 178,-
ISBN 3-7908-0719-2

János Gács / Georg Winckler (Eds.)
International Trade and Restructuring in Eastern Europe
1994. 343 pp. Softcover DM 98,-
ISBN 3-7908-0759-1

Christoph M. Schneider

Research and Development Management: From the Soviet Union to Russia

With 46 Figures

Springer-Verlag Berlin Heidelberg GmbH

Series Editor
Werner A. Müller
Peter Schuster

Author
Christoph M. Schneider, Ph. D.
International Institute for Applied
Systems Analysis (IIASA)
Schloßplatz 1
A-2361 Laxenburg, Austria

ISBN 978-3-7908-0757-8

CIP-Titelaufnahme der Deutschen Bibliothek
Schneider, Christoph M.:
Research and development : from the Soviet Union to Russia /
Christoph M. Schneider. - Heidelberg : Physica-Verl., 1994
(Contributions to economics)

ISBN 978-3-7908-0757-8 ISBN 978-3-662-30372-6 (eBook)
DOI 10.1007/978-3-662-30372-6

Originally published by Physica-Verlag Heidelberg in 1994

88/2202-543210 - Printed on acid-free paper

Preface

In the past, intensive interest in Soviet research and development has been sporadic both in the West and in the USSR. The end of the 1980s coincided with the demise of the Soviet model of economic development. As a result, a surge of attention has been given to the factors driving the motor of Soviet growth and development, as well as R&D. The opening, first, of the Soviet and, subsequently, of the Russian economy, finally exposed it to global standards. The long period of international isolation with respect to scientific and technological exchanges made it difficult for scholars and policy makers at home and abroad to measure the status of Soviet advances. Consequently, some overrated the levels, while others underestimated them. Now it comes to light that, although the Soviets put the first satellite in space (*Sputnik*) and developed their own hydrogen bomb, these were more the exceptions of innovation from research results rather than the rule. Therefore, as the management of the entire economy increasingly malfunctioned, so did the management of R&D in contributing to economic growth and development.

There is no denying the incredible investment of the former Soviet state in domestic science and research. The R&D community was one of the largest, if not the largest, in the world during the second half of the twentieth century. Now, Russia has inherited not only this enormous resource, but also the inadequate organization, management, and structure. There is a fear of losing some of the valuable potential but a need to rationalize, increase productivity and efficiency, and reorient according to market signals. Russia is in a unique position. The transition to a market economy at a time when research and technological processes are becoming more international than ever provides great opportunities for reorganizing and restructuring the R&D sector to be representative of and conducive to such a transformation. The impact on economic benefits for the domestic and world economies could be substantial, and should not be underestimated.

The purpose of this study is to provide a clear picture of the R&D resources and management that were created under the former Soviet-style system and of the roots and prospects of the present reform movement.

Contents

Abbreviations

AIK	Advances in Knowledge
CEE	Central and Eastern Europe
CMEA	Council for Mutual Economic Assistance
COCOM	Coordinating Committee on Multilateral Export Controls
CPE	Centrally Planned Economy
CPS	Centrally Planned System
EME	Emerging Market Economy
FDI	Foreign Direct Investment
FZU	Factory training schools, USSR
GERD	Gross Expenditure on Research and Development
GFCF	Gross Fixed Capital Formation
GKNT	USSR State Committee for Science and Technology
GDP	Gross Domestic Product
GNP	Gross National Product
GOSKOMSTAT	USSR State Committee for Statistics
GOSPLAN	USSR State Planning Committee
GOSSTANDARD	USSR State Standardization Committee
JV	Joint Venture
KGB	USSR Committee for State Security
MIC	Military Industrial Complex
MNTK	Inter-sectoral scientific and technical complex, USSR
NIC	Newly Industrialized Country
NPO	Scientific Production Organization, USSR
NSB	National Science Board
OECD	Organisation for Economic Co-operation and Development
PTU	Technical trade school, USSR
R&D	Research and Development
R&T	Research and Technology
S&E	Scientists and Engineers
S&T	Science and Technology
SEL	State Enterprise Law, USSR (1987)
SPTU	Secondary technical trade school, USSR
SSUZ	Secondary specialized school or technicum, USSR
TNC	Transnational Corporation
VINITI	All-Union Institute of Science and Technical Information
VUZ	University, USSR

List of Tables

List of Figures

Chapter 1

Introduction

An excerpt from a book on the logic of a planned economy illustrates how the author, Pawel Dembinski, interestingly formulates the perception of the average man in the street in a centrally planned economy:

> There's no unemployment, and yet nobody works.
> Nobody works, and yet the plan gets fulfilled.
> The plan gets fulfilled, and yet there's never anything in the shops.
> There's never anything in the shops, and yet every fridge is full.
> Every fridge is full, and yet everyone complains.
> Everyone complains, and yet the same people keep getting elected.
> [Dembinski, 1991, p. xiii]

This statement has become more than just an anecdote; particularly toward the end of the Soviet-style of government, it became indicative of the system's functioning and finally synonymous with the definition of the system. The problems described in this quote became systematic, actually rooted in the politico-economic structure of the Soviet system. No sector of the economy was spared, including research and development (R&D). The management, organization, and motivations of the R&D sector led to a confusing situation with its very own logic. The same quality scientific resources that launched *Sputnik* satellites into space were simultaneously incapable of incorporating sufficient technological potential into the production process in order to progressively improve consumer welfare.

Such paradoxes combined with other more basic issues such as linguistic problems inhibiting personal contacts and knowledge of foreign scientific literature have led Western experts to perceive certain gaps in the Soviet R&D or the more general scientific and technological system. Despite these gaps, Westerners often underestimated Soviet scientific performance in specific fields.

Indeed, today little doubt remains that the size of the scientific community in the former Soviet Union was enormous. The size was a function of the resources devoted to its development based on the status of science perceived by members of society and politicians. The incredible and consistent ideological commitment over the decades, since the birth of the Soviet Union, gave the region potential beyond that recognized by foreign analysts. Although this sector has been inbred with the customary problems associated with Soviet Communist economics, and the resolution of some of these problems may prove painful, the R&D sector is much more a blessing than a burden in the transition to a future market economy in the successor republics of the former USSR.

Reforms introduced to realize the transition to a market economy have opened the door to bring the largest successor republic, the Russian Federation, back onto the world stage as a major player in science and technology. In order to be in a position to best consider the alternatives, a thorough analysis of the Soviet R&D sector is required. This book undertakes to show how the Soviet model of scientific and technological development serves as a case study of the influence of the management of R&D on past and future economic and social factors of the region.

1.1 The Topic

1.1.1 Research and development

Over time, *research and development* has become an almost superficial description that appears to indicate a single activity. It is, of course, much more. In fact, these words represent complex processes that are the basis of technological change, which is, in turn, essential for an improvement in our well-being. Investment in and management of research and development are crucial factors in determining the style of economic growth and development a nation will follow.

Although the elements of research and development support one another, some fundamental characteristics are different between them: namely, the objectives, the relationship to the needs of society, and the viewpoint and intellectual characteristics of the practitioners (O'Brien, 1964, p. 659). Even in a planned economy, where the policies concerning the R&D sector originate almost solely in state priorities, the distinctions are upheld.

In this study, the often imprecise terms of science, research, engineering, development, and technology conform to the following generally accepted definitions:

- *Science:* The accumulated knowledge of the physical world and the process of extending this knowledge.
- *Research:* The process of investigation and experimentation aimed at the discovery and interpretation of new facts and relationships for practical and theoretical application.
- *Engineering:* The process of utilizing the results of science and research to design, develop, and build specific equipment and systems.
- *Development:* The phase in which the objective sought is beyond the current state of the art and in which new design concepts are evaluated and improved by experimentation, usually guided and evaluated by analysis.
- *Technology:* The product of the cumulative means employed to provide objects necessary for human sustenance and comfort.

Essentially, each factor contributing to technological advance has direct or indirect links with all of the others. Technological advance is the key catalytic factor to raise productivity and spur the economic growth process. Implicitly or explicitly it is assumed that there is a *production function* relating the input of the resources applied to R&D to the output of technological advance (Nelson *et al.*, 1967, p. 23). The production function for technology is actually a combined product curve, incorporating numerous factors including those listed above.[1] It was, after all, Friedrich Engels, close friend and colleague of Karl Marx, who pointed out that: "Technology depends to a considerable extent on the state of science, science depends to a far greater degree on the state and requirements of technology" (cited by Lane, 1985, p. 298).

The management of R&D refers to the style in which R&D is structured, organized, operated, and governed in the science and technology (S&T) community. Any particular method of R&D management attempts, in some manner, to find a balance between two main objectives:

1. The risks associated with investing human and capital resources for the production of innovations and technological change.
2. The benefits that accrue to individuals and to the system as a whole depending on the effectiveness of the R&D investment (referred to as *commercialability*).

The system of R&D management in the former Soviet Union is the focus of this study. It was one in which the management, like in other sectors of the economy, was centrally organized on a planning basis influenced in part by various, often unclear, bargaining procedures between components of the hierarchy. The basic environment was not a market economy; there was no consumer-originating demand and no democratic decision-making process like that which occurs in many Western countries.

In a general sense, economists have long neglected the crucial relationship between technological advance and economic growth and development. Nor have the components of technological change, such as science and research and development, been accorded their actual importance for the expansion of output and the improvement in universal social well-being. Of course, since Robert Solow's influential 1957 article calling attention to the importance of technological change in American economic growth, attitudes and emphases have been modified. Today the topic continues to be of leading interest, and many issues remain controversial. Nevertheless, there is agreement that economic analysis of this source of growth can provide an indication of the implications and effects of the public policy toward R&D in a particular economic system.

1.1.2 R&D and growth in the Soviet/Russian context

The analysis in this paper provides evidence of the critical need for modifying Soviet-style science and technology management in order to foster modern economic growth. This study depicts the *mismatch* between new technology and the old institutions in the USSR (and now the Russian Federation) as one of the main reasons for the productivity slowdown and one of the key impediments to economic growth and development in the second half of the twentieth century.

The USSR possessed many of the requirements to facilitate a move away from the stubbornly adhered to paradigm of old-style growth. The country has vast amounts of natural resources, generous stocks of human capital, a highly developed educational system, an enormous market size, and many other beneficial attributes.[2] Thus, it is to some extent incomprehensible (other than due to the obviously different political denomination) why the Soviet Union did not achieve over the past few decades a level of development or modern-style growth that would more adequately resemble its potential.

The problems lie in the Marxist legacy persevered in the USSR and modified to fit the Stalinist approach to extensive economic development; this legacy resulted in an emphasis of scientific rather than technological advancement in all sectors except the military sector. Under the shrouds of strict socialism that ensured the forced continuation of a planned market economy, the system led to a complete distortion of incentives, focused production on specific industries (many of which have become unimportant for modern development and reduced the requirements for more advanced research and technological standards), gave quantity priority over quality, and made productivity a secondary goal. The accompanying isolation removed the influence of foreign competition, restricted technology transfer, and led to a policy of importing capital with embodied technology rather than knowledge upon which future economic progress could be based. The imported technology was used until it became obsolete; further domestic development to improve the national technology base and its international status was not encouraged. The whole system lacked proper management of research and technology (R&T) at the foundation; it was inefficient, sometimes even unproductive, and generally far from being market determined, particularly with respect to consumer products.

After the breakup of the Soviet Union in 1991, Russia inherited both the great resources invested in R&D during the Soviet Communists' rule and the problematic organizational structure that did not fit into a country attempting to undergo the transition to a market economy. In the future, change to modern-style economic growth could lead to rapid development and great growth in the Russian Federation. Bridging the technology gap by beginning an energetic catch-up that effectively uses inherited resources could be one of the paths to economic growth and development. If this should take place, it may influence the overall situation in world markets.

The growth and development characteristic of the Japanese economy since World War II is an example of the realization of economic potential given certain prerequisites. Japan had been devastated by World War II. In 1950, agricultural production and industrial production were still below the levels of the early 1930s – a perilous situation in light of the rapidly expanding Japanese population at the time (Denison and Chung, 1976). Credit was being freely extended by the government in hopes of expanding production, and inflation was a high three-digit number. The introduction of a well-defined market system facilitating competition (not just allowing but simultaneously encouraging participation in the world market), emphasis on technology and knowledge versus capital equipment, and application of R&D to a strong domestic base led the way to social prosperity and economic and technological leadership.

Whether a similar potential destiny might take place in the former USSR remains to be seen. The history, developments, and issues concerned with R&D management within the science and technology sector and how these affected the Soviet past and how they may influence the Russian future is the topic of this study. The more precise objectives are reviewed in detail in Section 1.2.

1.2 The Study

1.2.1 Major objectives

The objectives of this study treat the practical issues that have arisen during the discussions on the reorganization of the science and technology establishment, or more narrowly the research and development sector, as it existed in the former Soviet Union. This sector, now essentially existing within the Russian Federation, must be reformed to accommodate the changes throughout the country in its effort to develop a market economy. Due to its impact on technological advances and consequent influences on economic growth and development, research and development has an important role in securing the potential of the emerging market economy at home and internationally. In the Soviet/Russian case this role may prove to be even more pivotal due to the fundamental position these factors had in the former centrally planned economic system. So, as often happens in history, the past has become consequential for the future.

Discussions with previously Soviet and presently Russian scholars and policy makers reveal the extent of the problems caused by decades of intellectual isolation and adherence to the Soviet way of doing things. Namely, substantial deficiencies seem to exist with respect to the knowledge of the Soviet scientific community's true standing in relation to those of the leading Western industrialized nations that Soviet politics professed to be superior to. In addition, already in the final years of the Brezhnev era and more vigorously during Gorbachev's *perestroika* period, issues arose questioning the productivity and efficiency of the enormous investment in basic and applied R&D. Indeed, some experts queried whether the rate of return had not fallen too low (or even became negative) to warrant continuing in the existing fashion. Thus, the need for reorganizing and restructuring the management of R&D is obvious. But how, if one knows not one's position with respect to the rest of the world, and especially to those nations one *thought* one was competing with?

While these questions provide sufficient reasons for a detailed review of Soviet research and development, the treatment of the topic in Western literature, which has been politely described as less than exhaustive, emphasizes this need. Whether the problems lie in the inaccessibility and/or lack of consistent, reliable data or, perhaps, simply in a lack of researchers in the field, there is still much that can be done.[3] It is difficult to make good judgments about the depth and potential of Soviet/Russian R&D from a Western (and, for that matter, from an Eastern) perspective. Many of the predictions and reviews of the past have been revealed as not completely reflecting reality.

Today, in light of the dramatic political and economic transition to a market economy, an up-to-date, comprehensive, and comparative account of the R&D sector is more important than ever and can be a valuable contribution to decision-making materials. Even in an established market system, the precise contribution of R&D to economic growth remains an unresolved issue; during the transition from a centrally planned economy to a market economy one can imagine how contentious the arguments for and against R&D may become. The situation in Russia and other Central and Eastern European countries is more crucial as they have begun to feel the budget crunch and are searching for places to cut government spending – in many cases, R&D is high on the budget-cutting list. Consequently, the future looks precarious.

These immediate needs are addressed in this work. This study provides important material, much of which has not yet been published in Western sources, to interested parties in Russia, other formerly planned economies in Central and Eastern Europe (CEE), and the West, where experts aspiring to assist frequently lack adequate background information. Of course, due to the organizational and structural similarities inherent in sharing the same Soviet-style central planning system, policy makers from the smaller CEE nations could gain valuable insights from this study. Although it is impossible to cover all aspects, the goal here is to fill in as many pieces of the puzzle as possible and advance the work on this topic.

Therefore, it is in this spirit that a great effort is made in this book to describe and compare the Soviet R&D sector. Much is made of the comparative aspect throughout the work. The relative perspective is often presented in a thorough manner in which it has not been done before. In summary, the main objectives of this study can be stated as follows:

- To offer an up-to-date review of the status of Soviet research and development and its position in the Soviet-style economic system, using previously unpublished Soviet sources (including interviews) and existing Western literature concerned with Soviet science and technology.
- To provide a historical and international comparison of the resources available to the Soviet R&D community and of its output with those available to other developed nations and newly industrialized nations.
- To emphasize the valuable elements of the R&D establishment and accompanying components created under the former Communist regime in Russia's bid to rejoin the world scientific and economic communities.

- To discuss the requirements for a new style of R&D management to complement such a formidable goal.

1.2.2 Organization of the book

The analysis is carried out using a descriptive and international comparative approach. Most of the book is devoted to a historical analysis, but efforts are made to link this historical analysis with potential implications for the future.

Chapter 2 deals with theoretical considerations related to research and development. Emphasis is given to the catalytic character of R&D for economic growth, development, and improvement of social welfare. There are two parts to the chapter; the first part reviews the relevant theory, and the second part covers the empirical evidence – that is, the studies that have already been conducted in the West to provide numerical evidence of the R&D contribution to the level and style of growth.

Chapter 3 treats technological development, growth, and R&D management and is also divided into two parts. The first part discusses how R&D management can make a difference and ties this impact to technological progress and subsequently growth prospects. The second part is concerned specifically with these factors within the setting of the former Soviet Union. It begins with a general introduction to the economic and technological standing of the Soviet Union and then turns to the specifics of the R&D sector including the actors, organization, and background ideology. The chapter concludes with a two-phase review of science, research, development, and technology in the Soviet Union before 1985 and in the turbulent period after 1985 until the dissolution of the USSR in 1991.

Chapter 4 focuses on the inputs to the Soviet R&D sector. The three essential components crucial to any R&D community are education, R&D personnel, and R&D financing. The chapter reveals the enormity of the Soviet R&D sector and the special emphasis accorded it by central policies that resulted in the dependence on the generous state resources. The three factors described at length and in the international perspective reveal the interdependence upon one another and simultaneously the inherent difficulties arising in the attempts at total central management.

Chapter 5 concentrates on the internationalization of Soviet research and technology. The chapter looks at foreign direct investment, transnational corporations and joint ventures, involvement in international scientific activities, technology gaps and trade, domestic and foreign government barriers, and several other points. Comparisons are drawn whenever possible to the Soviet system, where the presence or lack of particular international aspects directly influences the techno-economic growth and development.

Chapter 6 is not exactly specific to the R&D issue, but a somewhat more general problem is discussed that has in no small part affected the style of management of Soviet research and development. It addresses the influence of the central planning system and the bargaining, which was characteristic of the Soviet-style system, on R&D. Basically, the chapter attempts to reveal the extent of the ample supply of natural and human resources at the disposal of Soviet planners and how these may have actually been burdens of abundance to a more productive R&D sector.

Finally, Chapter 7 discusses R&D management in transition, implying the conversion of the R&D sector governed by the rules of the former Soviet-style system to an integrated component of the emerging market economy in the Russian Federation. This chapter reviews potentially valuable elements of the R&D sector created under the former regime that, under new circumstances, could contribute to growth and development. The chapter closes by discussing the requirements of a good R&D organization and how it could contribute to economic growth.

The study ends with a summary of the main findings of each chapter and some final conclusions.

Notes

[1] For example, the rate of advance of technical understanding has probably been related to the number of educated employees engaged in R&D (Nelson *et al.*, 1967, p. 17). In a more specific example of the manufacturing industry, Nelson (1980, p. 146) found that the differences in the pace of technological change responsible for productivity growth reflected disparities in R&D spending and R&D effectiveness. This subject is discussed further in Section 2.1.

[2] These resources, however, could have been a critical part of the reason why the old path was so fondly maintained; see discussion in Chapter 4. They may remain obstacles to rapid change in the future.

[3] Stephen Fortescue has just made a recent bibliographical review of pertinent material covering science and technology in the Soviet Union. His essay and lists, which are divided according to topics such as history, ideology, structure, behavior, and the future, are presented as an article in the *Soviet Studies Guide* (1992).

Chapter 2

Research and Development and Economic Theory

The optimal organization of research and development (R&D) in a market economy is one of the unsettled questions of economics. R&D has great externalities that make its support more complicated than the support needed for most goods. In a market system the private benefits and private costs are contrasted to approximate the social welfare. Thus, the organization of R&D has become a key issue in the transition to a market system of the former centrally planned economies. This is particularly true for the former USSR, which has been a major source of science and technology.

The phenomenon of technological change and the need to keep up with that change are not new. The impact of improved production and new invention and thus increased productivity, efficiency, quality, comfort, and real output per capita have, in the past, had important economic (in industry and commerce), social, and political consequences. Technology has facilitated the inception of solutions to pressing economic problems (i.e., hunger, disease, working conditions), and is paving the way to answers that are required to deal with the continual flow of today's urgent issues such as sustainability of development, economic reform, conservation of resources, environmental issues, and the "quality of life" (which includes value of leisure time and time allocation). In addition, technological change transforms the structure of firms and industries and the basic nature of competition in an economy (Rosegger, 1980, p. 3). Thus, it is the technological change that causes changes in productivity that influence the progress and style of economic growth.

In general, technology consists of research, development, and related investments in new technology. Technological change is described as being either disembodied or embodied.[1] Disembodied change happens automatically; that is, it requires no investment in plants and equipment. The isoquant curves of the production function shift toward the origin with time, independent of changes in the factor inputs (Stoneman, 1983, p. 4). On the other hand, embodied change is introduced into the productive process by being inherent in new investments of either capital or labor (i.e., as machinery, equipment, or personnel with new skills). The rate and direction of, and inevitably the influence on, related economic factors (such as growth and standard of living) of embodied technological advance are functions of the economic environment in which the change occurs.

The results of numerous studies on the private and social rates of return on agricultural and industrial research and development (in some cases this included extension or diffusion assistance) in a market-oriented economy show that the rates are not only positive, but also quite high. Therefore, based on the consensus that productivity growth is largely determined by the pace of technological progress, it is actually the underlying spending on and effectiveness of research and development activity, which is at the heart of technological change, that directly influence the progress and style of economic growth.[2] Overall, technological progress is inhibited via social, institutional, and economic difficulties.

Economic and technological advantages depend on changes in management organization and behavior. These exist most beneficially as dynamic processes and not in static states. According to most of the studies to date, the rate of technological change is by no means constant. It occurs in what Joseph Schumpeter referred to as creative gales of destruction. Schumpeter also emphasized that this process of change is characterized by *both* organizational innovations and technical innovations (originating in applied R&D) and their interdependence. Therefore, modern-style growth and, consequently, development of a national economy result in part when individuals and firms (in particular, private ones) commit resources to search for ways of doing things better, usually in the form of new institutional or technical technology. The critical point is that these economic agents primarily act in this manner because they expect future economic gains.

2.1 Characteristics of R&D: The Theory

More than two centuries ago, Adam Smith, the father of economics, identified the division of labor, free markets, and technical change in the form of new machines as the three important causes of increasing incomes (Coombs *et al.*, 1987, p. 138). Until the 1950s, there appeared to be a relative neglect of the issues associated with technological change. Since then there has been a surge of interest in this topic, and, today, technological progress has been generally recognized and subsequently verified as a key driving force of long-term economic growth and development. Economic growth indicates simply more output, while economic development implies the alterations of the technological and institutional establishments that make more output possible. Technical innovation, namely, research and development, is a crucial source of dynamism in capitalist economies. However, science and technology alone confer no economic benefits. Achieving economic benefits requires commercialization, which takes production and marketing skills.

Numerous theoretical and quantitative studies by scholars, such as Joseph Schumpeter early on and later Robert Solow, Edward Denison, Edwin Mansfield, and Zvi Griliches, have on the whole, supported this thesis.[3] Technological progress is an essential element that facilitates development simultaneously with growth and not just growth in an economy. This means that growth and development are to a certain extent dependent on science and technology policy and, more specifically, on the management of research and technology. The effects of reasonably successful management influence the incentive structure and motivation as well as the welfare of society, and inherently also influence national and international competition.

The organization of science and technology often reflects the organization of the economy. Changes attributed to a modernizing world require nations to appropriately and rapidly adjust their efforts in science and engineering research and development to secure a basis for improving the standard of living.

A thorough investigation of the management of the factors of technological change and the inevitable importance of and need for an optimal organization of research and development to achieve modern-style economic growth reveals that pure economic analysis, by itself, is inadequate. As a result of the nature of R&D activities, which are variable, disorderly, uncertain, often unpredictable, and nonuniform, scholars agree that conventional, or orthodox, economic theory cannot clearly explain the reality of R&D processes.[4] Nevertheless, a review of the literature covering the relevant theory is essential to obtain an understanding of the influence of R&D on the productive process and thus on the development of living standards.

In a market economy, fluctuations in the *inventory of technical knowledge* are the result of changes in expenditures on R&D by private firms, by the government, and by groups or individuals in universities and other nonprofit and nongovernmental research institutions. This inventory is cumulative; therefore, what may often appear as an impressive new technological

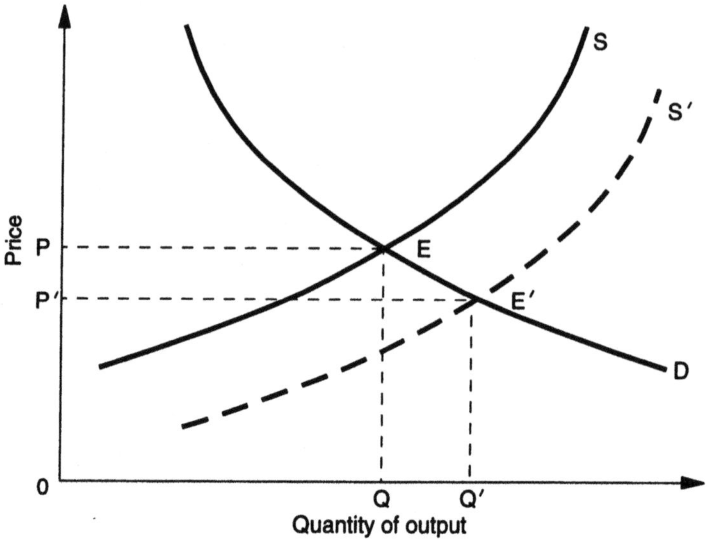

Figure 2.1. R&D-induced technological change shifts the supply curve.

advancement is usually the result of countless smaller advances of related research and development.

Evidence indicates that the majority of the research undertaken results in returns in excess of costs to the firm (profit) and that, in general, the benefits to society are greater than the benefits to the firm (Braunstein *et al.*, 1980, p. 19). Under conventional market conditions, R&D expenditures are the main contribution that ensure the availability of technology as a good that is introduced into the market because it appears profitable to do so. Profit incentives are themselves affected by many aspects of the economic climate. Thus, productivity and growth, as well as development, may improve, become stagnant, or decline depending on the incentives to invest in R&D.

Today, as never before, it is necessary for producers to find ways of modifying their products or introducing new products, in each case reducing the costs of and improving the methods of production to remain competitive. Investments in research and development of technologies in any industry – medical, electronics, chemical, automotive, aeronautics – facilitate lower costs of production, higher quality, and new products. At a given price, a change in technology that decreases production costs will increase profits. This profit incentive tends to result in increased production, shifting the entire supply curve(s) to the right (see *Figure 2.1*).

This complete shift of the supply curve indicates a change in the quantity supplied at each price (P) of that quantity (Q). Due to this shift, the area under the demand (D) curve and above the new price P', known as the consumers' surplus, has increased by the area $PEE'P'$ (E equals equilibrium). Thus, the difference between the total value consumers place on all units consumed of a particular commodity (produced better, cheaper, or at all due to the technological advance) and the actual payment for the purchase of the same amount of the commodity has increased in their favor. In the presence of competitive market conditions, economists have used the area under a product's demand curve between the original curve and the shifted supply curve S' to measure the social benefits from an innovation (Braunstein *et al.*, 1980, p. 29). *Ceteris paribus*, these benefits are a combination of the social value of the additional quantity of the product available and the social value of the resources saved as a result of the successful innovation. Consequently, if the contribution of R&D and other inputs relating to the innovation are compared with the related accruing social benefits measured in the way described here, it is possible to estimate the social rate of return from the investment in the innovation for a selected time interval. Economists like Griliches and Mansfield have made significant contributions in this field. Some of their work is reviewed in Section 2.2.

Another method of demonstrating the influence of research and development (via technological change) on the economy is with the production function. It can be represented graphically as a series of isoquants called iso-product curves. This function shows the relationship between the maximum level of output that can be achieved by each and every combination of inputs. For example, in the iso-product curve in *Figure 2.2*, Q indicates a given level of output that is produced using various combinations of capital (K) and labor (L) based on the existing state of knowledge in technology (Freeman and Soete, 1987, p. 40). Under completely competitive market conditions, the location of the curve depends on the particular production method and the relative prices of the inputs. Generally, the curve is convex to the origin and downward-sloping implying that both factor inputs are subject to the law of diminishing returns and that each has a positive marginal product.

If capital becomes relatively more expensive, then more labor will be utilized, indicating a movement along the curve down and to the right; an increase in the relative cost of labor will force movement up and to the left along the curve. Therefore, a change in the relative prices of the inputs will cause movement along the curve Q. In contrast, a useful technological innovation should shift the entire curve toward the origin to a new position Q^1. From *Figure 2.2* it can be seen that the successful implementation of a technological innovation resulting from R&D activities makes it possible to

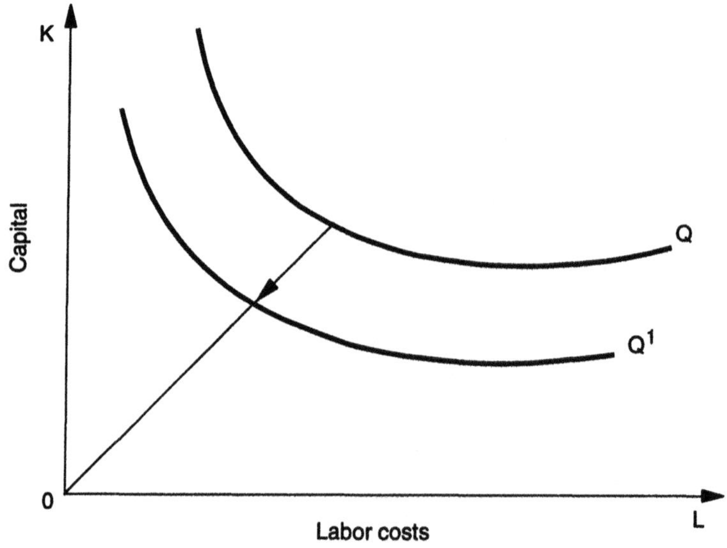

Figure 2.2. The iso-product curve.

produce the given level of output with less inputs. This process can also be represented by an upward shift of the conventional production function (the Cobb–Douglas style) from P^{t1} to P^{t2}, where P^{t1} is the level of production at the original state of knowledge and P^{t2} is the level with the technological innovation (see *Figure 2.3*).

The technological change illustrated by the parallel shift of the iso-product curve, or production function, toward the origin in *Figure 2.2* is characteristic of the neutral type of technological change. Previously in this chapter we have alluded to the term biased technological advance, which, unlike the curve in *Figure 2.2*, is a non-neutral shift of the curve. If the new technical change, considered to be disembodied and at constant prices, is expected to require proportionately more capital than that which is needed at the original level (Q^1), the new relevant production function isoquant moves to Q^3; if proportionately more labor is required, a shift to Q^4 will be the result (see *Figure 2.4*).

Following Stoneman (1983, p. 4), *Figure 2.4* can also be shown mathematically. The traditional production function, where output is a function of factor inputs, capital (K) and labor (L), for a given time period (t), is written as

$$Q = F(K, L; t) \ .$$

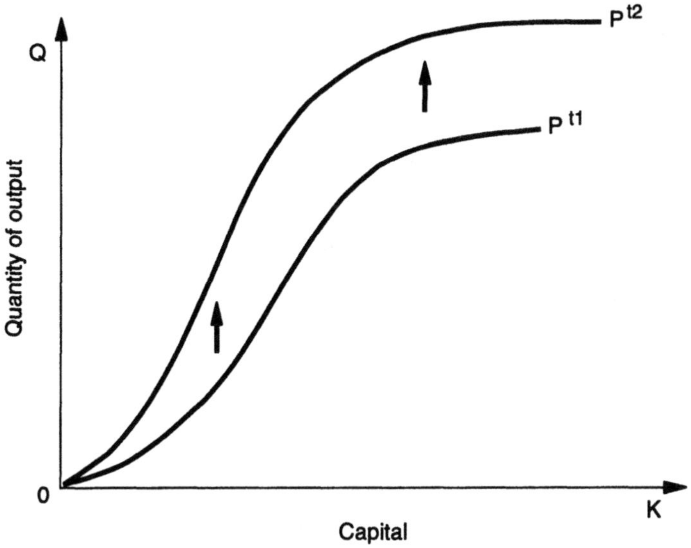

Figure 2.3. The traditional production function.

Assuming that the function has positive first-order and negative second-order derivatives with respect to the inputs and that it can be rewritten in per capita form, it can be rearranged to explicitly account for factor-augmenting technological advance:

$$Q = F(K, L; t) = G\{b(t)K, a(t)L\} \ .$$

Placing a dot ($\dot{}$) above a particular variable to indicate the derivative with respect to time, $\dot{b}(t) = \dot{a}(t)$, which is the shift $Q^1 \rightarrow Q^2$ in *Figure 2.4*, represents a neutral change also referred to as Hicks's neutral technical change. In this case, the efficiencies of both inputs have increased so that the capital-labor ratio remains unchanged – the marginal rate of substitution between K and L does not change with a change in technology. In other words, the new iso-product curve, Q^2, uses the same *optimal* combination of inputs as Q^1:

$$Q^2 : \dot{a}(t) = \dot{b}(t) \ ,$$
$$Q^3 : \dot{b}(t) = 0 \text{ and } \dot{a}(t) > 0 \ ,$$
$$Q^4 : \dot{b}(t) > 0 \text{ and } \dot{a}(t) = 0 \ .$$

The shift from $Q^1 \rightarrow Q^3$ is an example of labor-augmenting or Harrod's neutral technological change and occurs when $\dot{b}(t) = 0$ and $\dot{a}(t) > 0$. This so-called labor-saving advance is a substitute for labor if, at a constant level

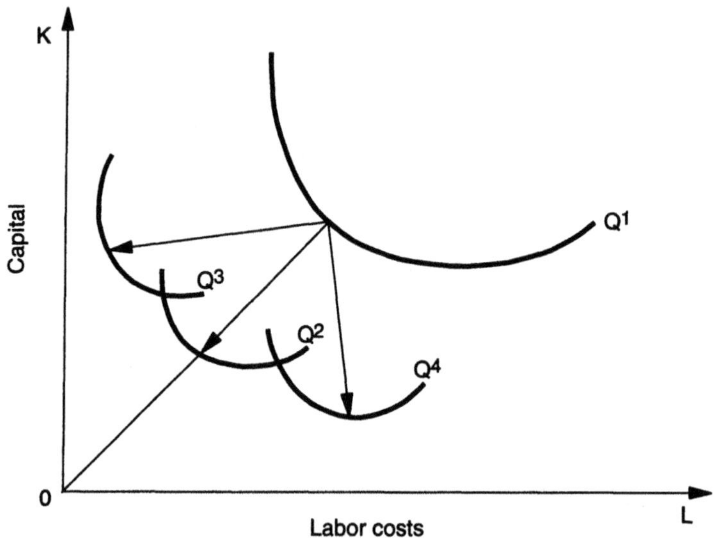

Figure 2.4. Different forms of technological change.

of capital productivity, output will be raised at a given labor input (Freeman and Soete, 1987, p. 36). The shift $Q^1 \rightarrow Q^4$, referred to as capital-augmenting (or Solow's neutral) technological change, occurs when $\dot{b}(t) > 0$ and $\dot{a}(t) = 0$. This so-called capital-saving technical progress acts as a substitute for capital; in the presence of a constant level of labor productivity, output can be increased at a given capital input. Only the Cobb–Douglas type of production function is consistent with all three concepts of technical change.

Thus far, the theory has concentrated primarily on how technological change as a whole fits into the production picture. Technological progress is traditionally divided into three activities: invention, innovation, and diffusion. Investments in research and development are the basic inputs that produce technological advance. In general, economic theory suggests that R&D will be undertaken by a particular individual, group, or firm if the expectation to generate profits with the investment in R&D exists. One would assume that the level of R&D expenditure is somehow proportional to the extent and speed of technological change, thus influencing economic growth and development. The measure to which this is true depends on the economic forces present.

At the firm level, the profits from R&D depend on the costs required to facilitate the advance and on the revenues from the use or marketing of the changes (Stoneman, 1983, p. 30). Of course, profits vary depending on

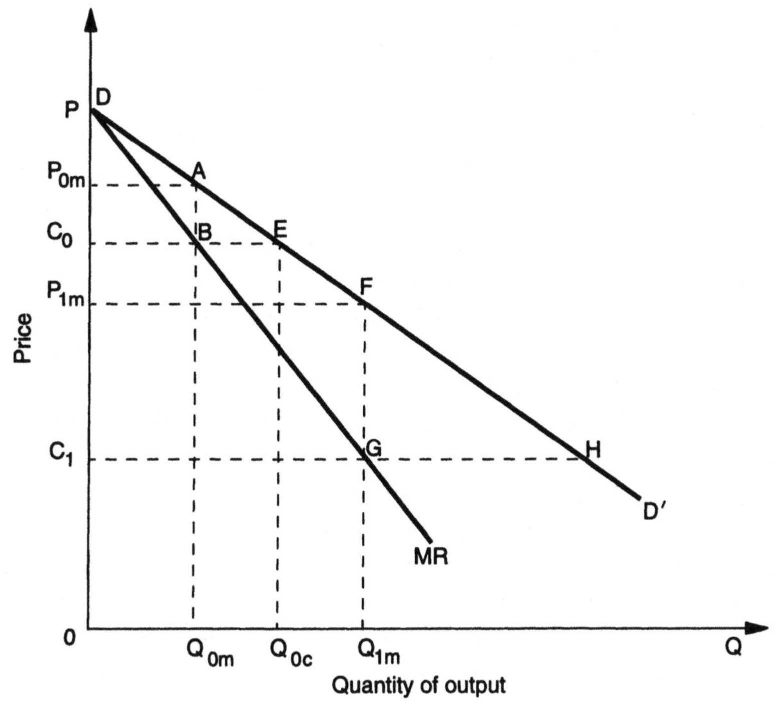

Figure 2.5. The profits to R&D investment.

the success of the technological change. A special characteristic of R&D spending as an investment to generate a future flow of benefits is its uncertainty. At the outset of a new R&D project, whether a stock of knowledge exists in the field or not, it is extremely difficult to accurately predict the costs required to achieve the objective. Consequently, a prediction about the amount and timing of a future stream of benefits, especially under competitive conditions, would appear to be even more uncertain.

Despite the fact that the conventional theory often seems insufficient to thoroughly explain empirical results, no account of the influence of R&D on economic processes would be complete without a review of the Arrow model.[5] The incentives to engage in R&D in monopolistic, competitive, and socially managed economies prove to be very revealing and have considerable implications. In this book actual R&D situations in market economies are compared with the situations in planned economies.

Figure 2.5 depicts an industry facing a demand curve, DD', and a marginal revenue function, MR. Assuming profit maximization and initial costs at c_0, the competitive market price would be at c_0 and the quantity at Q_{0c}, while the monopoly would produce at P_{0m} and Q_{0m}, respectively. Consequently, the monopoly profit (π_0) is $P_{0m}ABc_0$.

On the presumption that R&D has resulted in a new technology facilitating a drop in unit costs of production to c_1, the monopoly figures for price and output change to P_{1m} and Q_{1m}, respectively. Now monopoly profits are $P_{1m}FGc_1$, an increase of $(P_{1m}FGc_1 - P_{0m}ABc_0)$. In a competitive situation, Arrow contends that the inventor controlling the new technology will sell it in the market charging a royalty, the level of which will be between $c_0 - c_1$ and $P_{1m} - c_1$. He further asserts that the competitive profits from a new technology are greater than those in a monopolistic environment, concluding that a competitive market provides the greatest incentives for a firm to invest in R&D. There are conflicting opinions among scholars of economics of technological change with respect to this conclusion.

Nevertheless, reasonable consensus does exist with respect to a subsequent point made by Arrow. Namely, the incentives to both competitive and monopoly industries are less than the potential social benefits (Stoneman, 1983, p. 32). The socially managed market would generate social profits equivalent to the area c_0EHc_1 in *Figure 2.5*: larger than the potential profits under either competitive conditions or monopolistic conditions. This would indicate a tendency to underinvest in a purely market economy and that a socially managed or planned economy should be most capable of achieving the optimal (meaning most profitable and least wasteful to maximize social benefits) level of returns for society using the optimal level of investment in R&D. Base on this theoretical rationale, the planned societies should reach far superior levels of economic growth, development, and living standards than those nations with market-oriented economies.

The theory doesn't stop there. Much theorizing has been done to understand the importance of the market structure to be conducive to high returns from R&D. To procure such benefits, some experts have hypothesized that certain structures are more encouraging for firms to undertake research than others. For example, only large firms with large profit potential, high market shares in large secure markets, and the possibility of achieving economies of scale in their R&D departments will engage in the risky operation and financing of R&D (Stoneman, 1983, p. 46).[6] Too many firms doing research may generate unnecessary repetition and a low productivity research process at the industry level. Of course, the market structure varies to some degree depending on the industrial sector.

So, considering the theoretical perspective, a country like the former Soviet Union possessed many prerequisites for economic success. It was a completely managed economy on the basis of achieving the social optimum, there were the mega-enterprises that enjoyed monopoly power and extensive vertical integration, and the economy was supposedly being spared the *wasteful competition* characteristic of Western economies. In textbook terms, these elements should have created an environment especially favorable for investing in factors, such as R&D activity to facilitate technological advance and, consequently, modern economic development and improved social welfare. At least, this is the normative interpretation. But, where are they now?

These theoretical suggestions have *not* been verified; the course of history, particularly recent decades, has actually proved the contrary. This issue is addressed in the following chapters. The second part of this chapter reviews the results of empirical work on the understanding of the role of R&D in the development of the national economy.

2.2 Characteristics of R&D: The Empirical Evidence

Sixty years ago, Schumpeter emphasized the importance of endogenous and exogenous technological change as a key force behind economic growth. He further suggested that investments in innovation will be made in expectation of earning existing monopoly benefits while being protected by proprietary knowledge and/or other advantages such as patent rights (Schumpeter, 1943). In the early 1900s, Schumpeter asserted that innovation requires resources such as R&D and design, which themselves abide by basic economic principles.

In the late 1950s, other economists began turning their attention more intensively toward the previously neglected field of empirical investigations concerning the actual influence of R&D on output and growth. The number of studies has grown as quickly as the popularity and importance of this subject. The earlier works, completed approximately a quarter century ago, form the foundation of further study and continue to be the most frequently cited.

The economic analyses of the effects of research and development in a market economy have covered more than just an appraisal of the costs and benefits of R&D activities; these analyses have gone so far as to make estimates regarding the rates of return on investments in R&D to individual firms, in selected economic sectors, and to society at large. In addition, the practical application of econometric methodology to actual data has been extended to estimate the share of technological change (the product of R&D and other inputs) in the growth of per capita output over time.

Table 2.1. Early studies on technological change and GNP growth.[a]

Author	Approximate share of technological progress in a 1% increase of GNP	Data period
Solow[b]	0.875	1909–1949
Fabricant[c]	0.90	1871–1951
Denison[d]	0.345 (0.50)	1929–1969
Griliches[e]	0.20	1973
Denison[f]	0.226 (0.363)	1929–1982

[a]All estimates are from studies based on the US economy. The estimates vary quite widely due to the different industries, sectors, or number of firms; the alternative definitions of technological change and GNP; the various time periods; and differing methods of calculation. However, the important point to recognize is that each study, regardless of its differences to the others, revealed a crucial role for technological change in output growth.
[b]See Solow (1957). The study is restricted to private non-farm economic activity.
[c]See Fabricant (1954). The figure is based on the standard output-per-unit-of-input calculation.
[d]See Denison (1974). The values account for the proportional share of Denison's measure for technological change in a 1% increase in national income and not gross national product, though both move in a very similar fashion. The value in parenthesis includes the contribution of rising educational attainment.
[e]See Griliches (1973).
[f]See Denison (1985). The first value represents the portion that *advances in knowledge*, Denison's measure for technological change, contributed to the 1929–1982 growth rate of total actual national income. The value in parenthesis includes the contribution of increased educational attainment. If the focus were only on the growth rate of total actual national income in nonresidential business during the same period, then the values would be significantly higher at 0.31 and 0.50, respectively.

The studies in this field have utilized alternative and related measures. The list began with only the explanation of the residual in the Cobb–Douglas production function as the component representing the contribution of technological change to economic growth (as in Solow, 1957). Since then, the list of measures for technological change has expanded to include: public expenditure on R&D, private investment in R&D, R&D expenditures to sales ratio, number of scientists and engineers employed, number of patents, number of innovations, capital vintages employed, and new capital investments to name a few. More recently, the work has primarily focused on the industrial manufacturing sector,[7] though the other sectors of the economy have also been analyzed. In fact, the earliest studies were carried out concerning the agricultural sector (Griliches, 1958 and 1964).

The figures from the studies presented in *Table 2.1* seem to undoubtedly indicate that technological change not only has an influence, but is the single most influential factor determining the total growth of the market economy's output. Although the results of the investigations vary, they coincide with respect to the positive and substantial contribution of R&D-based technological advance to increases in national product and/or income. This conclusion gives support to the theory that technological change is one of the key motors driving economic growth. Therefore, if this concept is extrapolated to encompass the inputs generating technological progress, it appears that the emphasis of the effort in R&D is a component which, to a large extent, determines the style of economic development, the standard of living, and, consequently, the level of welfare in an economy.

Solow's contribution to this theme in 1957 was a milestone in attempting to generate empirical evidence for the theoretical concepts. Assuming that factors of production (capital and labor) are paid their marginal products in the presence of neutral technological change and constant returns to scale, Solow developed an elementary way of segregating variations in output per head due to technical change from those due to changes in the availability of capital per head. The results show that, for the 40 years between 1909 and 1949, the average rate of technological change was about 1.5% per year, and during this period that 87.5% of the increase in output per man-hour could be credited to technical change and only 12.5% to increased capital employed per man-hour. Solomon Fabricant (1954) has achieved a similar result (though with a different method): he attributed 90% of the increase in output over an 80-year period ending in 1951 to technical progress.

While subsequent studies have reinforced the clear positive trend of these early findings, the influence of technological advance on the rate of output growth was determined to be somewhat milder than previously estimated (*Table 2.1*). Griliches began with the assumption of a Cobb–Douglas production function and used the rate of total factor productivity growth and rough estimates for the rate of return to research expenditures and the net investment in R&D divided by total output. He concluded that approximately 20% of the growth rate of US output was caused by R&D expenditures.

Denison, an expert analyst of economic growth and its sources, postulates that, as knowledge relative to production advances, the output that can be obtained from a given quantity of resources rises (Denison, 1967, p. 267). Thus, he identifies technological change as *advances in knowledge* (AIK), which encompass knowledge of the technological and the managerial and organizational types, so long as they permit reduction in unit costs (Denison, 1974, p. 112). Denison has made repeated studies using different time periods and concluded that advances in knowledge significantly contribute to the growth of the whole economy; 35% in the 40 years from 1929 to 1969 and 23% in the 53 years between 1929 and 1982. As noted in note *f* to *Table 2.1*, these shares would prove to be substantially higher (between 10 and 15 percentage points more) if the influence of AIK on only the growth of the total actual national income in nonresidential business were considered. In addition, moving the contribution of increased educational attainment from the general labor category to the AIK category would further enhance the share of the latter as a determinant of growth – in Denison's experiment by about 15 percentage points to reach 50% for the 40-year period and 36% for the 53-year period.[8]

The work of Denison and his colleagues demonstrates that advances in knowledge, or technological change (primarily based on the investment in R&D), have been the largest single source of long-term growth of total output in the USA.[9] A 20% share in the rate of sector growth has been the lowest estimate. To justify the enthusiasm surrounding the empirical results that permit an endorsement of the importance of technological change and consequently the appropriate management of R&D for economic growth, a comparison is made between the US values (upon which the discussion has been based until this point) and those for 10 other nations (see *Table 2.2*). Other than two rather low, but not disturbing, values for Canada and the former West Germany, the evidence shows that the contribution of AIK to the rate of growth is consistently high for all the countries. Across the 11-country sample, advances in knowledge singly account for an average of almost one-quarter (between 23% and 24%) of the increase in the output over the 20-year period. While Norway, Italy, Japan, and Denmark hovered around the average, it was clearly exceeded in the UK, France, the USA, and Belgium, and not quite attained in the Netherlands, former West Germany, and Canada.

The reasons for these discrepancies are many. The authors of the relevant studies have identified several weaknesses in the analysis. Aside from the general difficulties associated with the accurate measurement of input and output variables attributed to inconsistent and creative data collection, management, and analysis, some factors remain unaccounted for. The most significant of these are the improvements in the quality of goods and services provided, which do not normally contribute to growth as conventionally measured; such improvements that offer the final user a wider range of choice and may enable him to more cost-effectively or conveniently meet his needs are an important result of research and development. In addition, the relationships between output and inputs may be misspecified, variable definitions and concepts of R&D expenditures may prevent meaningful comparability over time or among firms and industries; and there is no unanimous consensus with respect to the depreciation rate for R&D, the length of relevant lags, the nature of interfirm or interindustry technology flows, and so on (Mansfield, 1984, pp. 105–106).

Table 2.2. Shares in the growth rate of national income (selected countries over various periods, 1948–1971).[a]

Country	Labor[b]	Capital[c]	Advances in knowledge and n.e.c.[d]
Belgium	0.25	0.14	0.28
Canada	0.37	0.23	0.13
Denmark	0.16	0.26	0.21
France	0.10	0.17	0.32
Italy	0.17	0.13	0.23
Japan	0.21	0.24	0.22
Netherlands	0.21	0.26	0.18
Norway	0.04	0.26	0.26
United Kingdom	0.25	0.21	0.33
United States	0.32	0.20	0.30
West Germany	0.22	0.23	0.14

[a]This table is an adaptation and a summary from Denison's work on the sources of growth in 11 countries. See Denison (1976, pp. 39). The rows do not add to one because of the exclusion of factors other than the *advances in knowledge* from Denison's category of output per unit of input, standardized.
[b]Labor includes employment, hours worked, age–sex composition, education, and unallocated employment.
[c]Capital includes inventories, nonresidential structures and equipment, dwellings, and international assets.
[d]n.e.c. indicates not elsewhere classified.

Nevertheless, all the values illustrating the contribution of advances in knowledge to economic growth, shown in *Table 2.2*, are conclusively positive, significant, and confined to a relatively narrow range. Although the contributions to the growth rate appear rather evenly split between labor, capital, and AIK at first glance, a close scrutiny of the notes to *Table 2.2* reveals that the first two categories are a conglomerate of sources. Therefore, even in an international sample, advances in knowledge prove once again to be the single most important source of growth for the whole economy.

Soon after economists began studying the general concept concerning the influence of technological change on economic growth, their interest turned toward a more intensive investigation of the components responsible for technological advance. This process has traditionally been defined to include research, development, and diffusion. Schumpeter's words were invention, innovation, and diffusion, while Scherer (1965, p. 165) split the grouping into still more categories to include invention, entrepreneurship, investment, development, and diffusion. Essentially, and throughout this paper, R&D are considered the main inputs for technological production and, consequently, any change therein.

R&D is broken down into three main elements: basic research, applied research, and development. In most market economic systems, basic research is primarily financed by the government, usually localized in only a few industries of national interest, such as electronics, chemicals, and aerospace, and is mainly conducted in higher educational institutions. In a market economy, resources for applied R&D are, in principal, allocated by the market mechanism in a decentralized manner responding to market forces (Schneider, 1991, p. 9). Thus, the private sector is chiefly responsible for funding and conducting applied R&D. It is increasingly difficult to draw a clear distinction between research and development. Nevertheless, development typically refers to routine as well as not so routine changes or improvements in existing technology or organization.

Depending on prevailing economic conditions, the organization and management of these three elements can play a crucial role in determining the style, extent, and pace of growth in an economy. This management will influence not only the behavior of producers with respect to the manner in which they operate their facilities to reduce costs, allocate resources, increase efficiency and productivity, enhance quality, and offer new products, but also the behavior of consumers. Inevitably, appropriate management of R&D can render a substantial contribution to the rate of growth, the standard of living, and a generally higher level of welfare.

After the initial interest in the field began in the 1950s, the main surge of studies that attempted to show the relationship between R&D expenditures and the rate of productivity change came in the late 1960s and continued throughout the 1970s (refer to *Table 2.3*). The results were favorably persuasive for the industries, firms, innovations, and time periods selected. The statistics in *Table 2.3* illustrate that R&D expenditures are consistently related to a positive private rate of return, and a very high one at that. In the cases where the social rates of return from investment in R&D were also calculated, the results usually proved to be substantially above the private levels. On the whole, the studies indicate the highest returns to R&D expenditures were in agriculture and more variable (though generally lower) in other sectors or groups of enterprises.

Griliches (1964) added expenditures on extension to those on research and included the average level of education (among other inputs as land, labor, fertilizer, and machinery) in his study on farm output. In his study he found that the marginal rate of return from R&D expenditures to be 53%. The results of other studies in the agricultural sector (i.e., by Schultz, Evenson, and Peterson) consistently revealed a rate of return to agricultural R&D of close to or more than 50%. In manufacturing, scientists found the rates of return to be lower, but the statistically significant effect of R&D on the

Table 2.3. Studies on productivity increases and R&D expenditures.

Author	Approximate marginal rate of return from R&D expenditures (%)	Year published
Schultz[a]	42	1953
Griliches[a]	53	1964
Mansfield[b]	40+/30	1968
Evenson[a]	57	1968
Minasian[c]	50	1969
Peterson[d]	50	1971
Terleckyj[e]	30	1974
Griliches[f]	17	1975
Mansfield *et al.*[g]	25/56	1977
Mansfield[h]	25/70	1989

[a] Agricultural sector.
[b] Petroleum/chemical industries.
[c] Chemical industry (17 firms from 1948 to 1957).
[d] Poultry industry.
[e] 33 manufacturing and nonmanufacturing industries from 1948 to 1966.
[f] Manufacturing industry (only the private rate of return from R&D expenditures of 900 manufacturing firms).
[g] The private/social rate of return from 17 industrial innovations in a variety of industries (refer to Mansfield *et al.*, 1977, for further details).
[h] The private/social rates of return for 37 innovations in a variety of industries (see Mansfield, 1989, pp. 133–136).

rate of productivity increase remained unquestionable. R&D expenditures were related to the rate of productivity change (Mansfield, 1968) and value added (Minasian, 1969) in the petroleum/chemical industry and chemical industry, respectively, to discover a similarly high rate of return.

In the 1970s Griliches also turned his attention to the industrial sector, but focused on the firm level. He conducted an econometric study to find that in a sample of 900 firms, the amount spent by a firm on R&D was directly related to its rate of productivity growth. The results also implied a private rate of return from R&D expenditures of 17%. Terleckyj's study, also based on economic production functions, revealed a 30% rate of return in manufacturing from an industry's R&D. With the inclusion of interindustry technology flows, Terleckyj demonstrated the presence of a substantial effect of an industry's R&D on the productivity in other industries, which would imply a social rate of return higher than 30% for the industry itself (see Section 2.1). Mansfield *et al.* (1977) has gone a step further. This study investigated the private and social rates of return from the investment in 17 industrial innovations, which are 25% and 56%, respectively. Again, the social rate clearly exceeds the private. In his most recent work, Mansfield

(1989) has increased his sample to include 37 innovations. While the private rate of return has remained in the vicinity of 25%, the social rate has climed as high as 70%. Such results have induced economists to warn policy makers of a continuing underinvestment in civilian research and development.

The studies reviewed in this section have substantially contributed to the understanding of the relationship between research and development, on the one hand, and productivity changes and economic growth, on the other. Although the work has often been based on different types of methodology and data, the results are remarkably consistent. The various investigations indicate that the level of R&D expenditures has a considerable effect on the magnitude and style of economic growth. Investments in new technologies lead to changes in productivity that will influence both producers and consumers in the market. The rates of return from investing in R&D have been positive and impressively high, with the social rate always considerably surpassing the private rate.

Notes

[1] Further distinctions are made with respect to the direction of the technological advance; whether it is seen as neutral or biased with respect to the capital-labor ratio. This phenomenon is explained in greater detail in Section 2.1.

[2] Economic growth can be either modern-style or old-style. The latter is characterized by the traditional method of continually adding capital and labor to the production cycle (also known as extensive growth strategy). This is contrary to the modern-style economic system based on improved productivity, efficiency, and quality of output (including diversity), in that strong biases in traditional growth create an inflexibility with respect to changing resource requirements, technologies, and demands. Modern-style economic growth is distinguished not only by an increase in output (positive growth), but also by a change in the composition of output. Numerous economic catalysts drive this process; R&D expenditures are one important example. Refer to Section 2.1 for further discussion.

[3] The works of these noted economists are listed in the References.

[4] This term is used in the evolutionary approach to economic change described in the work of Nelson and Winter (1982, p. vii.)

[5] An excellent overview of the concepts underlying the Arrow model can be found in Stoneman (1983).

[6] This hypothesis was originally put forward by Schumpeter (1934) and Galbraith (1952). However, since studies have begun to recognize the importance of R&D in the market, the role of monopoly (and more prevalently firm size) in the initiation of R&D has remained a contentious issue. For a complete review of this topic (including alternative views) and related empirical studies, see Kamien and Schwartz (1975).

[7] These studies include Mansfield (1968 and 1989), Minasian (1969), Terleckyj (1974), Griliches (1975), and Mansfield *et al.* (1977).

[8] This would seem to be an appropriate adjustment as a conceptual exercise, particularly, if one agrees that educational attainment could, *de facto*, be considered knowledge relevant to production advances, therefore, yielding supplementary interesting results. Clearly, all known advantages of a larger well-educated and well-trained work force would warrant such a reclassification for experimental purposes.

[9] Many of the studies have been conducted using very similar data sources. Over the years, for example, much has been taken from the output and productivity work of John Kendrick, which constitutes a large portion of the basic material used for the studies. Often, the methods of analysis were also quite similar.

Chapter 3

Technological Development, Growth, and R&D Management in the USSR

Both policy makers and scholars from the East and West have expressed a need for an up-to-date and comprehensive account of the actual state, structure, and progress of research and development management and organization in, what was until recently, the Soviet Union. Certain aspects of R&D in the USSR have been reviewed and analyzed in the literature, but a thorough overview from Western sources supported by actual Soviet data would be beneficial to gain an understanding of this complex system during the time of economic transition. This study aims to provide this understanding.

Many economists and additional experts from other fields are now involved in attempts to provide alternative approaches to resolve the difficulties and determine the origins associated with a rate of technological development that has increasingly been unable to offset the effects of the growing resource scarcity and increasing demand for consumer goods. The dilemma is intensified by the desire to maintain the verified potential of the largest scientific establishment in the world that is, at the same time, plagued by enormous inefficiencies and has been relatively isolated from market activities and production techniques, to say nothing of the international community. In order to approach the existing problems in a suitable manner, the research requires an analysis of the conditions or circumstances that brought about the unique characteristics of the Soviet economy.

3.1 Technological Development, Growth, and R&D Management

3.1.1 Technological development

Technological progress has been generally accepted to be a major engine powering economic growth and development; it has been acclaimed as one of the most influential forces in the transformation not only of productive relationships, but also of whole cultures (Rosegger, 1980, p. 1). Proof of this has been evident since the Industrial Revolution in the eighteenth century.

In the past, changes in the management and development of technology have by no means taken place in a smooth fashion. Although technological advance appears to occur at a continuing rate, transitions in technological development amplify or reorient the process of change. Schumpeter uses the phrase "creative gales of destruction." Three such transitions have molded modern technological development and influenced the importance and management of factors supporting R&D:

1. In the late eighteenth century and early nineteenth century, new production techniques emerged and the need arose to rethink the organization of labor and other factors of production to adequately fulfill the growing significance of efficiency and utility as goals.
2. Late in the nineteenth century, rationalization occurred by integrating scientific advances and modification of techniques into what today is termed technology with the development of comprehensive organizational strategies for production and processes. Close ties between production and R&D, as well as its benefit-oriented management, were becoming necessary. The result was organized innovation: a process of moving away from the inventor-entrepreneur. Those who were originally individual inventors became employed as researchers, while managers, systems engineers, and financial experts took over the entrepreneurial role in innovation.
3. In the second half of the twentieth century, the third transition was under way: the reorientation from energy toward information and communication. More than the technological transitions before it, the third is as yet the most demanding with respect to a need for strategic thinking, planning, and policy development (following Rip, 1989, p. 142). To be successfully competitive in an open environment most favorable for economic growth and development that will result in a higher standard of living, production must be characterized by diffusion and utilization of technologies based on R&D management that reflects changes in the expectations of profits and alterations in demand.

A distinguishing feature of technological progress is its classification as one of the essential elements that facilitates development simultaneously with growth and not just growth in an economy.[1] Therefore, it is the advantage that modern-style growth has over old-style economic growth.

3.1.2 Growth and development

For one reason or another, national economic policies emphasize either old-style economic growth, in which the fundamental goal is to increase output by simply increasing the level of the traditional inputs of capital, labor, and raw materials, or modern-style economic growth, where the goal is to improve productivity, efficiency, and the quality of output (including diversity), though not at the expense of a simultaneous increase in output.

Therefore, basic economic growth is simply associated with an increase in output, while its counterpart, economic development, also incorporates a change in the composition of output that arises as a result of the diffusion of technologies that influence the methods of production (productivity), productive capacities (efficiency), and quality of output. Old-style growth then, by definition, is equivalent to economic growth which encompasses the growth of production as a whole or of manufacturing, in particular, specialization, allocation of resources, the extension of the division of labor, and so on. Modern-style economic growth is consequently associated with the tendency and motivation to transform production in the direction of greater efficiency utilizing any number of potentially available means, of which many have been related to changes in applied technology. These changes are driven by, among other factors, *ex ante* expectations of monetary and nonmonetary benefits and *ex post* alterations in demand.

Growth may be achieved with or without development, but development will not occur without growth. The most successful economies in providing a high standard of living for the population within their borders – basically the industrialized, market economies – prove that both are prerequisites for a robust and hardy economic environment. Growth is a necessary, but not sufficient, condition for development.

In his time, Adam Smith already alluded to the characteristics indicative of modern growth. The cornerstone of his theory was the belief that economic agents will act rationally in order to attain the highest possible benefit for themselves. This meant that the producers would use the means personally available to them to specialize their efforts to maximize their profit and productivity. Ideally, this forces other producers to follow similar paths depending on their respective talents, which directly leads to the inherent need for a market where the fruits of the labor can be exchanged.

The competition arising from the demand for inputs and the desire to attain individual efficiency resultingly improves the efficiency of the economy as a whole. In order to be successful in the race for individual and aggregate economic gain, producers must continually seek to reduce expenditures by further specialization, accumulation, and innovation.[2] Although this statement does not describe a new phenomena, it does emphasize the need for an appropriate economic environment in which the actors have both motivation and opportunity to support the ongoing growth of an economy.

For the market mechanism to function well, the economy to grow, and development to be sustained, the producers need to have certain freedoms and incentives to allocate resources and implement innovations, to appropriate the full returns of investments, to commoditize their output in response to the possibility of trade, and not to have potential improvements in individual productivity and efficiency explicitly prohibited or strictly controlled by political institutions (Chirot, p. 17). It appears that not only trade, but also technology, based on both dedication to domestic R&D and active technology transfer, have jointly become the source of the *wealth of nations.*

The paradigm and policies of old-style growth have persisted to varying degrees in more or less internationally prominent and/or seemingly economically successful nations. Until recently, the traditional method of continually adding capital and labor to the production cycle in order to directly promote growth was a principal component of Soviet-style, centrally planned economic policy. The obsession to increase output in existing industries was most easily and directly achieved with increases in the basic inputs. As time, resource requirements, technologies, and demands change, strictly adhering to this procedure inevitably retards the necessary development needed by an economy in order to maintain an appropriate standard of living for its citizens. Thus, not only is the development in favor of greater productivity and efficiency inhibited, but the sustainability of production, society, and environment, and unavoidably political institutions consequently becomes vulnerable to deterioration and finally to collapse. Such situations become increasingly prone to a misallocation of resources and static inefficiencies that unavoidably drive nations into socioeconomic and often political crises.

The majority of Eastern Europe is faced with such a predicament.[3] In the former Soviet Union, for example, shortages of bare necessities, poor-quality consumer goods, and an incompetence of dealing with disasters drew attention to the dismal economic situation. The roots of these problems can be traced to the socialist dedication in the USSR to policies that have, to a considerable extent, preserved old-style economic growth based simply on capital accumulation. Biased research, development, and diffusion of technological innovation stand out as factors that have led to economic decline in the long run – a predicament aggravated in certain political environments such as that of an administrative command-type system. In Soviet ideology, which for the most part spilled over to its immediate western neighbors (welcome or not), science was certainly the key to national prosperity, but actual implementation was not. There is something fundamentally wrong with a system in which the fairly high-quality innovations of many sciences generally do not diffuse or translate into satisfactory or marketable (particularly consumer) products.

Considerations arise whether the problems can be traced back to the Marxist theory or, probably more correctly, the Stalinist legacy at the foundation of Soviet-style central planning, and if the transition to a new market system will bring the opportunity for engaging in modern-style growth. If so, policy makers and scholars are induced to ponder the potential implications of a move from such a threshold level to economic takeoff – particularly, with respect to the effects on the domestic sectors and (in a large country example) on the regional or, more importantly, world market. Uncertainty will continue to revolve around whether these countries could in any way achieve the relative levels of prosperity of those typified by modern-style economic growth if they would continue on their traditional policy trajectories and were to remain in self-inflicted technological isolation.

How have countries that have emerged from difficult situations, such as post–World War II Japan and Germany, established economies which generate development that leads to a genuine increase in the standard of living? Many of these countries have been forced to artificially acquire advantages because they do not have the good fortune to be blessed with abundant natural resource reserves. In fact, a significant number of industrial countries, which have begun to exhibit distinctly different economic growth patterns in the recent past, have originally exhibited relatively similar situations albeit not at the same time in history.

If a nation possesses certain selected resources (such as a complete social infrastructure, human capital, cultural strength, and political stability) that are just waiting to be efficiently harnessed, then there exists an incredible potential for growth and development. These properties, combined with a deleterious lack of natural, material resources and very thoughtful utilization of policy measures designed to circumvent such real physical disadvantages,[4] released forces into the market that ignited the spectacular growth of Japan's economy for decades and laid the foundation for the current global microchip revolution, which originated in Japan.

So, what might be some of the reasons that a nation as rich in natural resources and cultures and traditions, and among the world leaders in literacy rate and scientific achievement in various sectors as the Soviet Union, becomes such a deteriorating socioeconomic monolith? Was there a lack of appropriate, market demand-and-supply-influenced, foresighted strategies for the management of research and development? If so, can this lack be made significantly responsible? Should a remedy be found and implemented, how will domestic and foreign economies respond?

3.1.3 Research and development management: Does it make a difference?

If technological advance influences the path of growth and development, then it follows that these two latter factors are dependent on science and technology policy and, more specifically, on the management of research and development. The effects of reasonably successful management influences the incentive structure and motivation as well as the welfare of society, and inherently national and international competitive status.

Without question, economic and technical advantages depend on changes in the management organization and technical innovativeness of research and development. Appropriate management is the art of dealing intelligently with uncertainty. Successful management of innovations requires an active commitment to R&D and often a long time horizon (Mansfield, 1989, p. 132).

In the field of economics and technological change, many studies have been performed in an attempt to determine the percentage of successful R&D projects from a certain level of investment in research and development of products and processes. While the wide range of results do not warrant the choice of any specific number in favor of another, various points have generally been accepted:

- R&D activities can be an economically beneficial use of resources.
- The private rate of return on investment in R&D is not only positive, but respectably high; the social rate has been estimated to be even higher.
- The production of innovations is closely related to the amount spent on R&D.
- If there is early, competitive, and discriminatory evaluation of R&D projects, the success rate will increase and resources will be utilized more efficiently.
- Rewards from R&D investment may be fully realized only over the long term; however, short-term fluctuations also occur.
- Productivity increase is related, though with a time lag, to the amount spent on R&D.
- Investing in R&D is accompanied by variable degrees of economic risks.

- Investment and the role of auxiliary activities that link production and marketing are essential to achieving the potential benefits of R&D.

Given the premise that R&D is instrumental in generating long-term profitability and success in the market place as well as a higher standard of living, then the payoff from investing in innovation should not be inversely correlated with the associated risks. In a market economy, R&D projects aiming to make moderate advances are usually identified with low risk and produce only moderate returns. Projects that are characterized as very risky with respect to their technological and subsequent sales success are alluring due to the great potential return on the innovation.

In the Soviet-style system, firm managers were averse to any kind of innovation whether associated with low or high risks because their bonuses were tied to fulfilling the plan determined by the center – any innovative activity was perceived to thwart such goals at the factory level. Therefore, the expectations were rather of losses than of gains, which are the standard incentive to innovate. Risks were apparently interpreted solely as costs, particularly within the managers prescribed planning horizon, and thus had a negative relation to investments.

Paradoxically, scientists at the research institutes faced practically no risks in terms of consequences of success or failure of research projects. They often initiated enormous and expensive research activities with potentially spectacular results as the lure for appropriate financing from the relevant government agency. In this case, high risks were interpreted as a great asset to obtain financing. Thus, inconsistencies arose where primarily research, but also development, was often undertaken irrespective of true market demand and supply impulses that influenced the national standard of living. A void existed between users and producers. Scientists and engineers may have been dealing in their own best interest, but were unaware of business objectives. The lack of diffusion in the industrial and commercial sectors was *de facto* a lack of managerial links and coordination. The outcome has been some very novel results with ambiguous commercial value – a stock of white elephants, interesting but unproductive.

Fittingly, a well-managed research and development portfolio should consist of some equilibrium mixture of projects with either low risks and moderate payoffs, or high risks accompanied by correspondingly high potential profitability. The risks associated with R&D investment have been classified as technical and commercial (Mansfield, 1989, p. 128). The former constitutes the probability of whether or not a project will meet its objective in producing a new and/or improved product or process. An increase in the share of development relative to the share of research indicates less

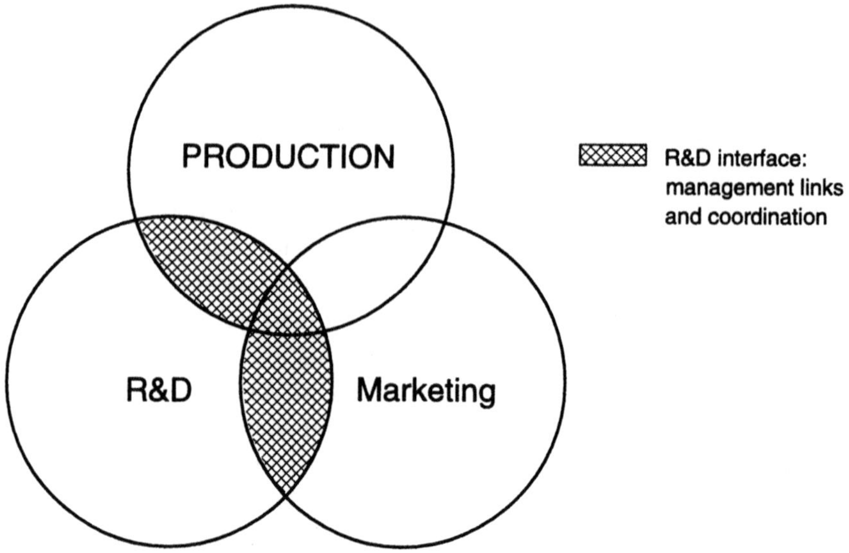

Figure 3.1. Integration of R&D with production and marketing.

risk. The commercial risk reflects the possibility that a technological innovation will permit commercial diffusion (introduction and application). Under conditions in which R&D projects are regularly reviewed and economically evaluated from the proposal through to the application, the probability of technical and economic success will certainly increase.

In addition to the need for an effective organization and management devoted to techno-economic analysis, success is further enhanced if management of R&D includes a systematic search for ideas with technical and commercial potential. Mansfield (1989) names three factors that together determine the economic success of an R&D project:

1. The probability of technical success.
2. The probability of commercialization (given technical success).
3. The probability of economic success (given commercialization).

These factors imply a need for close integration of R&D with production and marketing in order to optimally exploit the potential of resources allocated to R&D (as demonstrated in *Figure 3.1*). Actual integration is more efficient, less time dependent, and managerially more effective than the standard feedback mechanism. Proper management of R&D promotes and accomplishes this integration and reduces the associated risks.

An active commitment to R&D pertaining to economic goals results in new products and processes that lead to technological progress and social

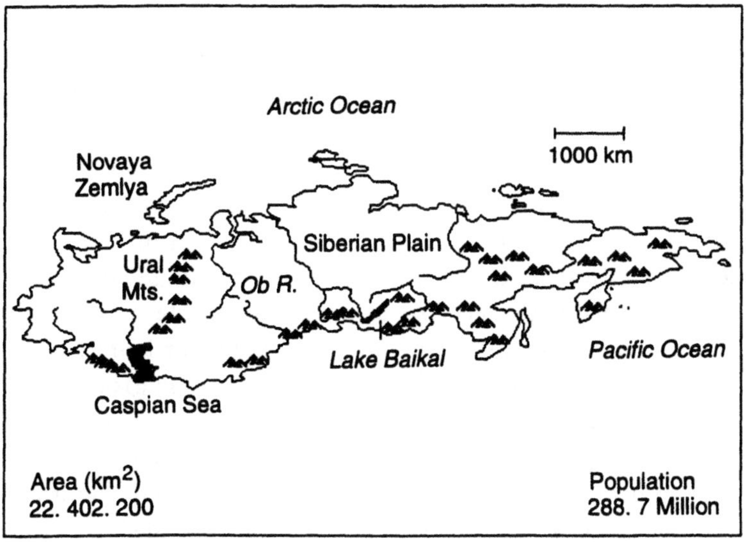

Figure 3.2. The former Soviet Union.

development. Optimal organization of research and development activities can facilitate substantial collective benefits for society from investment in R&D (far in excess of those for the private entrepreneur); it is essential to laying the foundations for securing a comparative advantage that can fuel gains in the present and future standard of living. In pedestrian terms it means jobs, salaries, and tax revenues.

3.2 R&D in the Soviet Centrally Planned Economy

3.2.1 An introduction to the Soviet Union

The former Soviet Union was unique in many ways. Its enormous size (16% to 17% of the world's land area) dwarfed that of all other countries; Canada, the world's second largest nation, has only 45% of the area within former Soviet borders. This vast expanse accounts for a wide variety of geographic and climatic environments. The nation stretched from the tundra north of the Arctic Circle to the arid areas 40° north latitude, spanned more than 8,000 kilometers from west to east, bordered 11 nations, and had access to the waterways of the Arctic and Pacific Oceans, the Atlantic Ocean through the Baltic and North Seas, and the Mediterranean Sea through the Black Sea (see *Figure 3.2*).

The vast territory and the tremendous supply of resources produced both advantages and disadvantages for the country. An urbanization ratio of 65.8% and a population density of 13 persons per square kilometer would indicate that most of the almost 290 million inhabitants were concentrated in the cities. Approximately only 16% of the population lived east of the Ural mountains in the Siberian region where most of the natural resource reserves are to be found. The area sown for agricultural production was over 2 million square kilometers; that is, an area the size of Greenland, or four times the area of France. Although the size is again incredible, the arable land is dispersed and, apart from some exceptions, usually far from the population centers. The population comprised more than 12 ethnic groups, and over 15 different languages were spoken within the former Soviet borders.

In order to link people, energy, and food in this unusually large and diverse natural environment, the Communist Party stressed the importance of science, technology, and capital. These elements were major aspects of economic strategy starting already shortly after the 1917 Russian Revolution. The weight of their importance varied, but the emphasis on these fundamentals provided the grounds for building a *superpower* from a feudal empire in less than a century. After making impressive advances in industrial production, expansion of the transportation network, and growth of agricultural production and energy generation based on simple technology, relatively little progress had been made with respect to high technology other than in a few specialized sectors such as the military and aerospace sectors. The management had not successfully oriented or integrated dynamic advances in R&D into the production processes, resulting in a lack of high technology relative to the leading industrialized nations and a technological gap between the Soviet Union and other world powers.

Part of the problem was that, beginning in the early 1900s, the USSR started investing heavily in nonsustainable old-style growth by spending large amounts to purchase physical capital (usually turnkey factories, assembly lines, manufacturing systems, and so on). As a consequence of this, combined with the policies of isolation and self-sufficiency in practically all sectors, there arose a general neglect for the acquisition of knowledge (by way of exchange between individuals, purchases of licenses, and so on) that could be built up and molded to accommodate demand as time passed and preferences changed. This approach did, however, provide some immediate benefits and proved to be reasonably successful in the first half of the twentieth century.

As long as the economy continued to grow at a respectable rate (albeit according to Soviet economic indicators, namely, those based on material product), there was no need to worry unduly about Soviet economic growth and development. Serious problems associated with such policies only began to surface in the second half of the twentieth century and most obviously in the beginning of the 1980s when insufficient adjustments were undertaken to keep up with the technological progress occurring in other industrialized nations of the world. During this time, toward the end of the Brezhnev years and beginning of the Gorbachev era, technology started changing more rapidly than ever.

As a result of these factors many questions arise. How have the alternative paths of development shaped the state of the various economies relative to those in the industrialized West? To what extent did the devotion to the ideology discussed above actually cost the now young emerging market economies (EMEs)? What have been the benefits and costs? If the need arises, can an EME generate modern-style economic growth where success lies in the dominance of dynamic efficiency? These are the critical issues facing many of the EMEs today. It would be too ambitious to attempt to answer all these questions. The aim of this study is to generate an understanding of the predicament in which a country such as the Soviet Union finds itself with respect to its economic development and the potential domestic and international impacts of bridging the gap to modern-style growth based on advances in technological change by modifying the organization of research and development.

A glance at selected socioeconomic indicators can provide a better picture of the Soviet Union in the twentieth century and an understanding of how the process of change has proceeded and resulted in the state of affairs before 1991. If the data are observed in a comparative way, the interpretations are more meaningful.

Due to the difficulty in obtaining reasonably accurate and consistent historical data for a wide variety of socioeconomic indicators in a large sample of nations, the distribution of employment by sector and the gross domestic product (GDP) were selected. These two factors shed light on both the growth and development aspects of economic activity.

The economy of the USSR grew at an impressive annual rate of 2.34% over the nearly 90-year period. In a five-country sample, this is second only to Japan's yearly growth of GDP of 3.11% per capita, while Germany held at 2.16%, the United States at 1.78%, and the United Kingdom at only 1.37%. However, these numbers do not tell the whole story.

In 1900 the level of GDP for both Japan and the Soviet Union was far behind the British and American GDP level, and at barely half the German level (see *Figure 3.3*). By 1987, Japan had surpassed the British in GDP per capita, was on the heels of Germany, and was closing fast on the USA. On the other hand, the Soviets succeeded in achieving a mere 65% of the British,

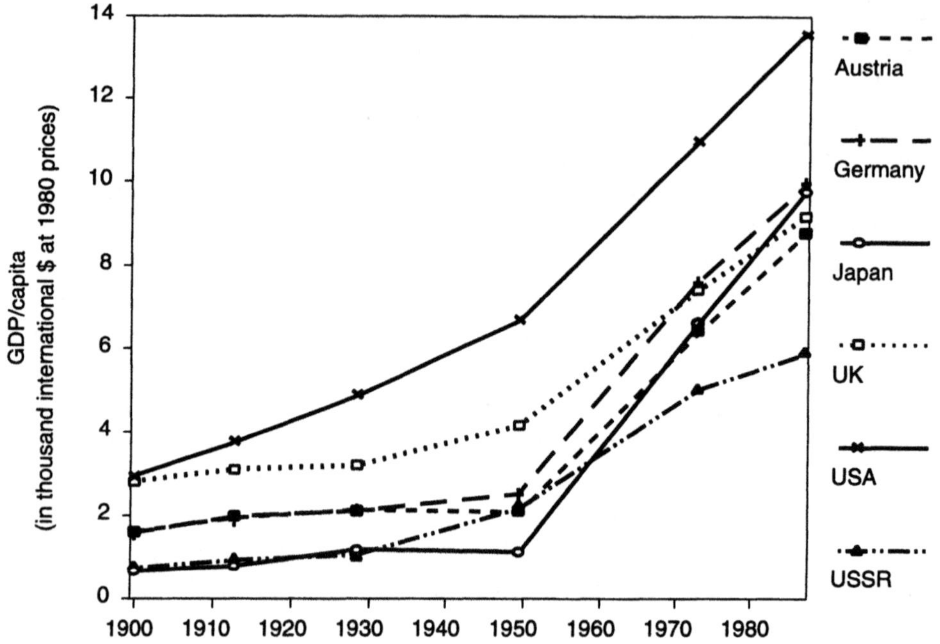

Figure 3.3. Growth of GDP per capita in selected countries, 1900–1987.

45% of the American,[5] and only 61% of the Japanese level; yet, back in 1900, the Soviets were at 118% of the Japanese level. The gap between GDP per capita levels was large 90 years ago and had remained so for the USSR, distancing it further from the old economic powerhouses and from the new world economic leaders.

The distribution of employment by sector allows some conclusions to be made with regard to the development of the economy. The figure for the United Kingdom, the first country to enter the Industrial Revolution in the late eighteenth century, not only show a very clear migration out of the agricultural sector to industry, but already indicate the coming of a new era – the transition to a heavy reliance on and substantial migration of employment from the industrial sector to the service sector in the 1900s. This phenomenon is exemplified by the changes in the shares of employment from 8%, 42%, and 45% in agriculture, industry, and services, respectively, in 1900, to 2%, 27%, and 60% in 1988. The advanced state of British economic development is already visible in 1900 when employment in agriculture was less than 2 percentage points over the current OECD average, and in services it was greater than in industry. The other nations followed in Britain's wake with a time lag and at variable speeds. In fact, British agriculture is credited with contributing as little as 1% to total GDP today.

Since 1900, industrialization has swept more or less strongly throughout various parts of the world. The movement of capital and human resources out of agriculture and into this growing sector was characteristic of this phase of economic development. With the advent of more sophisticated information, technology, and communication, the latter half of the century, particularly recent decades, has seen still another transformation – a type of de-industrialization in the most advanced nations of the world. Ninety years ago, both the USA and Germany had approximately 40% of the total employment concentrated in the agricultural sector and only a quarter in services. Today agricultural employment is below 5% of the working population and employment in services is nearing 60% (this is also true for the UK); in the USA it is well above that, at 68%. The share of employees working in industry rose early in the century, and is now declining. Agriculture contributes 2% to GDP in both nations, industry's contribution is only 25% in the USA and 40% in Germany, and services generate 72% and 59%, respectively.

At the turn of the century, Japan and the USSR were characterized by very similar situations. Both had relatively very low GDP per capita (the Japanese at only 23% and the Soviets at 27% of the US level[6]) and had not yet wholeheartedly entered the industrialization phase as demonstrated by the domination of the agricultural sector with respect to employment – 70% in Japan and 61% in the USSR (*Table 3.1*). Industry and services did not play a major role in the labor market or in output for either of the two countries early in the century. The key point of interest lies in the fact that, from such similar economic origins, the development and growth paths of these two countries have differed substantially. Japan has not only been able to catch-up, but has taken a leading role in the world economy. Employment in agriculture is close to the OECD average, in industry it is at 33%, and in services at 56%.

The Soviet Union did experience growth, but with much less development. In the late 1980s, agricultural employment was still just above 20%, far off the average of the world economic leaders and more in the range of countries like Angola, Kenya, Brazil, and Chile, and above that in nations like China, India, and Cuba. The percentage of the Soviet work force in industry was higher than that in advanced market economies, and the 41% in services was on average about one-third lower. In the USSR, agriculture still contributed over 20% to the gross national product (GNP), industry an imposing 56%, and services only 23% (57% in Japan). These figures verify

Table 3.1. Change in socioeconomic measures, 1900–1988 (in %).

	Employment			
	Agriculture	Industry	Services	GDP/capita[a]
Germany				
1900	38[b]	36[b]	25[b]	1,558
1988	5	39	55	9,964
Japan				
1900	70	12	18	677
1988	8	33	56	9,756
UK				
1900	8[c]	42[c]	45[c]	2,798
1988	2	27	60	9,178
USA				
1900	41	20	25	2,911
1988	3	27	68	13,550
USSR				
1900	61[d]	14[d]	25[d]	797
1988	20	39	41	5,948

[a]1987, in international dollars (1980 prices). [b]1895. [c]1901. [d]1897.
Sources: Compiled from *The Economist* (1985, p. 12; 1990, p. 214), Flora *et al.* (1987, p. 443), ILO (1989, p. 7), Maddison (1987, p. 686; 1989, p. 19), Mitchell (1980, p. 159), and UN (1990, p. 76).

what numerous authors have hypothesized about the growth and development in the USSR during the twentieth century: namely, that the relatively substantial growth was the result of a concerted effort to promote heavy industry and the mass production of technologically less-advanced products. This, as well as the need for a large agricultural sector, was in part the result of the self-inflicted isolation that impeded trade, technology transfer, and participation in the international R&D industry.

In fact, in a sample of both established and newcomer nations in the world market, the path of the former Soviet Union stands out due to its divergence from the common trajectory based on the relationship between labor productivity and GDP per capita (see *Figure 3.4*). Soviet policy was unable to generate the levels of GDP per capita as those achieved in Canada, the UK, and the USA. If a comparison with these nations appears unjust, as they already enjoyed a substantial head start in 1950, then the comparison of the inability to match the 1987 GDP per capita levels of nations of reasonably equal rank in 1950 (such as Japan, Austria, and Germany) is not only fair but very revealing.

In addition, the central planning system could not combine increased GDP per capita with improved labor productivity as other nations had that

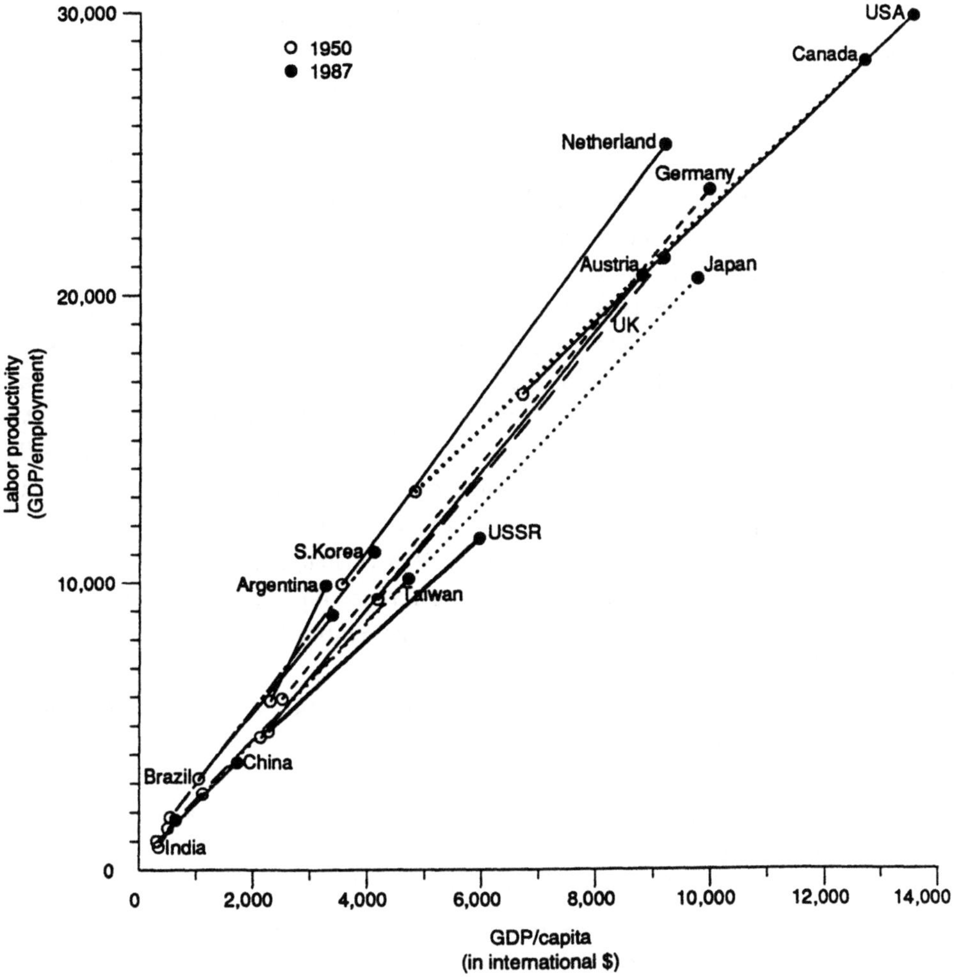

Figure 3.4. Economic growth and development in selected countries, 1950–1987 (in international dollars). Based on data in Appendix 3A.

have already been studied. The Soviets were even ineffectual in realizing the positive development achievements relatively similar to those in nations that were substantially below the Soviet labor productivity to GDP per capita ratio in 1950. These countries (Brazil, Argentina, South Korea, and Taiwan) were close to Soviet GDP per capita levels in 1987, but experience improved labor productivities. The Soviet economy was falling behind in both these factors – a signal of a relative decline in the standard of living on the output side and of a possibly inappropriate policy orientation for R&D management over the years on the input side.

On the surface, current general economic data primarily based on production statistics indicate that the performance of the Soviet Union was excellent well into the late 1980s (*Table 3.2*). It was the world's leading producer of barley, milk, oats, potatoes, sugar, and cotton, and a very close second just behind China in eggs, meat, and wheat. Due in part to rich reserves, the Soviet Union's mining and quarrying sector was one of the top four extractors in the world of dozens of mineral products ranging in diversity from salt to iron ore to gold and diamonds.

The Soviet manufacturing sector ranked among the front-runners in turning out simple products ranging from cigarettes to cement. The first indication of a lack of technological advance based on appropriate integration and management of research and development for the benefit of society can be detected when the Soviet Union dropped out of the list of world's top five in the manufacture of technologically more advanced goods such as radios, televisions, and passenger cars. In fact, the giant passenger car factories in the USSR were at a cumulative fifth position in the world in 1981. By 1989, Italian, Spanish, and British carmakers had surpassed Soviet production levels, and new vehicle producers like South Korea and Brazil were closing rapidly.

Because of the large reservoirs of energy resources, the USSR was a leader in energy production, whether it was from coal, natural gas, or oil, as well as one of the top three consumers of each. On an aggregate scale, the largest nation in the world was complementing its geographic and population size with high output levels.

If the production data are converted from the aggregate to a per capita basis (Appendix 3B), then the Soviet Union drops out of the top five in several categories but the output per person is usually still impressively high with respect to the other nations ranking among the top five in each category. The results indicate that annual yields of basic agricultural crops reached 154 kilograms (kg) of barley, 56 kg of corn, 349 kg of milk (almost one kg per day), 53 kg of oats, and 217 kg of potatoes, and 293 kg of wheat per person. For less basic products the yields are 15 kg of eggs, 67 kg of meat (that is 5.5 kg per capita per month), and 30 kg of sugar per person per year in the late 1980s.

The manufacturing industry also appeared rather diligent with respect to processing food products which resulted in an annual per capita contribution of 6 kg of both butter and cheese, 0.177 hectoliters of beer, and 0.104 hectoliters of wine. In one of the most successful nonfood products achievements, the USSR produced an impressive 1321 cigarettes for every man, woman, and child (smokers and nonsmokers) per year. Although these figures present an impression of plenty and abundance, Soviet consumers

Table 3.2. The former Soviet Union in the world economy.

Item	USSR rank in the world	Item	USSR rank in the world
Agricultural products[a]		*Manufactured goods*[b]	
Barley	1	Beer[1986]	4
Corn	5	Butter[1986]	1
Cotton	1	Cement	2
Eggs	2	Cheese[1986]	2
Meat	2	Cigarettes[1985]	2
Milk[1986]	1	Newsprint	6
Oats	1	Paper & paperboard	5
Potatoes	1	Passenger cars[1989]	8
Sugar	1	Radios[1986]	6
Tea	6	Televisions[1986]	6
Tobacco	3	Wine[1987]	4
Wheat	2	Wool[1986]	2
Mining and quarrying[a]		*Energy*[c]	
Aluminum	2	Electricity capacity	2
Bauxite	4	Electricity production	2
Copper	3	Coal reserves	2
Diamonds	3	Coal production	3
Gold	2	Natural gas reserves[1989]	1
Iron ore	1	Natural gas prod.[1988]	1
Lead	1	Crude petroleum reserves[1989]	5
Magnesium	2	Crude petroleum prod.[1988]	1
Phosphate	2	*Miscellaneous*[d]	
Salt	2	Population	3
Silver	4	Area	1
Zinc	2	GNP	3

[a] In 1988, unless otherwise specified.
[b] In 1988, unless otherwise specified.
[c] 1987 data, unless otherwise specified.
[d] 1990 data.
Source: Calculations based on data from *The Economist Book of World Vital Statistics* (1990), *Motor Vehicle Data* (1991), and *PCGlobe* (1990).

were confronted with shortages of basic necessities throughout a period of apparent ample production.

Manufactured goods were generally produced *both* for export purposes (to procure foreign exchange) and for the domestic market. As a result, low per capita output relative to other products was a cause for concern.

Table 3.3. Soviet productivity in the late 1980s (as a percentage of the average of the top five producers in the world).

Agricultural goods	Labor	Land	Manufactured goods	Labor
Barley	19.2	40.8	Beer	18.4
Corn	5.9	9.8	Butter	54.7
Cotton	48.1	103.3	Cement	68.3
Eggs	28.6	13.8	Cheese	33.2
Meat	25.6	40.0	Cigarettes	52.4
Milk	24.5	39.8	Newsprint	2.0
Oats	33.5	69.3	Paper & paperboard	13.0
Potatoes	40.1	30.8	Passenger cars	6.3
Sugar	8.1	7.1	Radios	1.2
Tea	0.2	1.4	Televisions	20.8
Tobacco	11.6	28.4	Wine	5.7
Wheat	20.3	43.3	Wool	2.9

With regard to Soviet consumer goods, the paradox of seemingly plentiful production and short supply cannot be found as in the agricultural sector. Scarcity of consumer goods can, in part, be traced to the lack of emphasis on their production (though this is not the root of the problem). Although the Soviet Union was rated among the top five manufactures for most products listed in *Table 3.2*, and among the top ten for the rest, the nation's manufacturing sector fell far behind on a per capita basis. Only China, when also in the top five, occasionally had a lower output per individual (largely due to its enormous population). Soviet manufacturing produced only 5.5 kg of newsprint, 22 kg of paper and paperboard, 0.0042 passenger cars (238 persons per car), 0.0278 radios (36 persons per radio), and 0.0334 televisions (30 persons per TV) per person in the late 1980s. This was only 2.9%, 12.9%, 8.1%, 1.1%, and 23.1% respectively of the averages of the other top five nations in each category.

An analysis of the productivities associated with these products sheds more light on the matter (for data and calculations refer to Appendix 3B). In none of the two dozen products listed in *Table 3.3* does Soviet labor productivity even come close to the average of the other top five world producers. On a per agricultural worker basis, Soviets produced less than 2 metric tons of wheat compared with 25 metric tons in Canada; 643 kg of corn compared with almost 37 metric tons in the USA; just over half a metric ton of oats compared with over 5 metric tons in Canada; 3.4 metric tons of wheat compared with close to 35 metric tons in India; only 2.5 metric tons of potatoes compared with as much as 12.7 metric tons in Germany; 345 kg of sugar compared with well over 13 metric tons in Cuba; 775 kg of meat compared with 5.24 metric tons in the USA; and as little as 4 metric tons of milk compared with 22.6 metric tons in France.

The productivity of land was also calculated to study the situation with respect to agricultural production. With the exception of a few products, the productivity of land in the USSR was often appalling below that of the other leading producers. The reason for such paltry levels of output per hectare of arable land could lie in the widespread use of agricultural land that is of only marginal quality; although, inappropriate management, underutilization, and poor levels of organizational, motivational, and technological development are more likely responsible for the particularly poor performance. As a result France produces six times as much wheat per hectare as the USSR, Germany six times as much barley and four times as much meat, China ten times as much corn, Poland almost ten times as many potatoes, and so on.

When studying the Soviet Union, an additional factor cannot be omitted. For many decades, the political orientation led to isolation and a complementary desire, or rather need, for self-sufficiency in the yield of numerous crops that were not especially suitable for Soviet weather and soil conditions or for general farming practices. Consequently, the land productivity of crops like sugar, tea, and tobacco was extremely low. Cuban sugar yields per hectare were 64 times those in the USSR in the late 1980s, Sri Lanka's land productivity in tea production was almost 200 times higher, and China was turning out 12 times as much tobacco per hectare of arable land. This final point on isolation and self-sufficiency had an important and lasting effect on all sectors of the economy from research and development through the producing sectors to services.

The Soviet Union also lagged seriously behind its top five counterparts with respect to the labor productivity of manufactured goods (see Appendix 3B). The figures in *Table 3.3* indicate that, without exception, Soviet labor productivity for the 12 manufactured goods listed was again clearly below the average of the five leading producers in the world. Only in butter, cement, and cigarette production was labor productivity above 50% of the average. Otherwise Soviet output per manufacturing worker was far below that of others: the labor productivity in British beer production was over 8 times as high; South Korea was 13 times higher in television production; Canada's was more than 116 times higher in newsprint and 22 times in paper and paperboard; France was 23 times higher in passenger car production (Japan and USA were 19 and 10 times, respectively); Argentinean wine was produced with a labor productivity 27 times that in the USSR; New Zealand wool was 216 times as high; and Hong Kong labor productivity in making radios was a spectacular 225 times higher.

3.2.2 An introduction to Soviet science and technology

In a setting where events appear to overtake themselves, science and technology in the former Soviet Union is experiencing a revival, or so we are led to believe. Alongside the headlines that publicize economic woes are those that inform readers of a renewed interest in policies oriented toward education, science, and technology. Savior-like characteristics were implied for such a political route in the USSR by countless media endorsements such as: "Soviet Congress Wants Science to be the Savior," "Soviets Pin Economic Hopes on Technology," "Science and the Spark of Perestroika," "Rockets into Ploughshares," and "Science and Social Renewal."[7] Political scrutiny has forced the academic community also to review the requirements, importance, and effects of the research and technology sector during the transition to a market economy. The existence, organization, and integration of this sector has implications not only for the future of the nation as a whole, but also specifically for the personal livelihood of academia.

Today, in order for a country to strive for economic leadership, it must also be at the forefront of the high-technology race. An important cause of difficulties for nations trying to stay abreast of what others are doing is simultaneously one of the most distinguishing features of high technology – the rapidity with which it changes.

The example of Soviet-style socialism has proved to be incompatible with rapid technological innovation. At least five characteristics specific to the Eastern European economies warrant such a generalization.[8] These include:

1. *The considerable effort and motivation of firms to overcome supply difficulties.* In the shortage economy, constraints faced by the enterprise were more significant on the supply side than on the demand side. Enterprises did not create new demand because they were too busy securing input supplies in the mighty vertically integrated industries. Once inventories had been built up, they were a disincentive to innovation because they must be consumed and were used as a bargaining tool by the central planning agency to continue production along established lines. If technological change was implemented, it was primarily to accommodate changes in the demand requirements as designated by the central plan.
2. *Process innovations have dominated over product innovations.* If problems arose during the production process and there was a possibility that the planned requirements would not be met, then adaptations would be made but no genuine alteration would be done to influence the consumer market. In industrial research institutes, the majority of time was utilized to improve existing technologies rather than to develop ideas

that could lead to fundamental innovations. Due to the lure of extra, unplanned income from pseudo-commercial contracts (primarily from state ministries or other state organs), the institutes become flooded with minor projects. Consequently, the proportion of genuine research work done in engineering-oriented institutes had decreased over the past decade by a factor of three (Rich, 1983, p. 464).

3. *Financial incentives for research, development, and implementation have been small, if not negative.* Scientists realized almost no personal monetary reward from developing innovations; the financing alternatives available to enterprises to invest in technological advancements were severely limited (there was no such thing as venture capital or the like); and if innovation resulted in not meeting planned production targets, bonuses were lost.
4. *Enterprises' priorities have been more inclined to emphasize the quantity rather than the quality of output.* The very large, vertically integrated, and highly monopolistic enterprises enjoyed tremendous economies of scale and did not have to compete on the basis of quality (particularly due to the national incentive for self-sufficiency and the shortage aspects faced by the economy).[9]
5. *There has been a long time lag between invention and innovation; subsequent diffusion has also been slow.* Studies have shown that implementation of innovations took three times longer in the Soviet Union than in countries like West Germany and the USA during the same period. Diffusion, even in the high-priority steel industry of the USSR, was a fraction of the rate in other Western industrialized nations, although capacity expansion may have been higher (Gomulka, 1986, p. 48).

The great paradox of the Soviet Union is that some fields of pure science were near the highest standard in a worldwide comparison,[10] but there still appeared to be something fundamentally wrong with the application of science and knowledge because the USSR did not experience an appropriate increase in the productivity and efficiency specific to modern-style economic growth. The diffusion and translation of technological progress into efficient production techniques and products was quite faulty. As a result, the standard of living had not risen with respect to what would seem characteristic of modern development and that which has been realized in many Western, market-oriented nations.

In an environment that simply lacks a competitive and efficient economy, resources are misallocated and static inefficiencies arise. In the absence of dynamic progress, the resources for production are inefficiently allocated because the advances in science are hindered through a much more basic resource misallocation and disincentive system at the research and development level. Both scientific activity and its goal of discovery, which together embody the point of departure for technological change, were generally present in the Soviet Union. It is the next step in this dynamic process, namely, the conversion of technological effort into productive results, that was inadequately achieved.

It appears that science was, to a large extent, detached from the process of technological progress, which itself suffered as a result, inevitably causing deteriorating productivity and efficiency of the overall economic system. The scientific community was an enormous, very hierarchical, and predominantly institutional apparatus that became considerably self-contained; thus, it became remarkably immune to any potential impulses from the market and did not interact with business in questions regarding applied research. Essentially, the scientific community was separated from commercial organizations.

Normally, the effects of skillful management influence the incentive structure and motivation, as well as the welfare, of society and inherently national and international competitive status. The fact that scientific advance has become inseparable from industrial technology in Western economies during the twentieth century implies, to some extent, that Western science has simply made a better organized attack on the secrets of nature and used greater resources in the assault than science in other cultures (Rosenberg and Birdzell, 1990, p. 19). Harnessing scientific activity successfully, which infers rapid and functional conversion into applied technology, continues to increase allocative efficiency that has and will improve human welfare. This activity must be cultivated in the appropriate national environment.

Soviet science certainly presented itself as a unique cultural system. Due to the crumbling and disappearing economic and political system that maintained it, the scientific community of the former USSR is now practically left to fend for itself. Policy makers and scientists in the former Soviet Union must encourage reform of the economy, while simultaneously preventing the collapse of the R&D sector as a result of its own transformation to acclimatize to the new socioeconomic environment. Currently, the growing disproportions in the formerly, solely administrative economic system indicate the urgency to reform the structure of the research and technology sector and the policies that rule it. On the whole, these imbalances arise for the following reasons:

- Concentration of resources in obsolete industries.
- The availability and distribution of financial resources for R&D.
- A large technology gap between military and civilian sectors.

- The relatively small share of the private commercial sector in economic activity.
- Distorted and conflicting incentive structures (i.e., for enterprises, branch ministries, and research institutes)
- High levels of vertical integration in industry, lack of interindustry supply relationships or other cooperation and coordination, and loose economic ties between real technological demand and performed R&D.
- Absence of adequate intellectual property rights.
- Monopolization, barriers to entry, and a lack of participation in the international market with outputs and inputs (i.e., technology).
- Interbranch and interorganizational barriers between research institutes and staff in industry, higher education, and the Academy of Sciences.
- An inappropriate tax system and collapse of the state budget and state promotion of R&D.

Of course, this is not an exhaustive list of problems, but it does indicate some of the immense reconstruction required to promote sustainability of market-oriented technology development and science policy. Existing evidence would seem to indicate that science and technology management inherited from the former USSR will have to change by becoming more responsive to market demand, more flexible and inviting for entry, and profit oriented as reform policies are implemented.

In the past, research and technology has been part of the large nonmarket sector. Due to the alienation from the market process, Soviet R&D was primarily financed by the state in one way or another, while in the United States it is financed, to a large extent (approximately 50%), by the revenue generated from the sale of the product at the market price. Unless the entire system of funding research in the successor republics of the former Soviet Union is changed, constructive reorganization of R&D is practically pointless. Because competition for funding in the former USSR had hardly been based on the research value and the quality of proposals, narrow political interest groups with biased and often inadequately informed ideas on what is useful dominated science policy. Proposals for change are many, but one of the most reasonable seems to involve a peer review similar to that in the West. This would entail research institutes applying for funding of specific proposals, the merits of which should be judged by international referees.

Soviet, now Russian, science must become readily convertible into technology in order to be economically productive. Proper organization and management are crucial. In effect, a new, much more flexible, techno-institutional market structure is required. This structure must introduce competition, stimulate the supply of innovations and their diffusion (while simultaneously allowing demand stimuli from the economy to influence the innovators themselves), allow a blending of domestic and global R&D priorities, and facilitate a longer-term perspective for R&D investors. Russian policy makers and scientists are looking toward Western industrialized countries to gain an understanding of how to deal with research and technology in a modern-style market environment and, still more fundamentally, how to prepare the research and technology sectors in formally command-type administrative economies for the ascent to market responsiveness.

3.2.3 The R&D sector in the Soviet Union: Science and Soviet-style socialism

The problems that plagued the organization and management of the Soviet R&D sector reflect the policies that have directed the whole economy for many decades: R&D was not market oriented. The state determined a set of priority areas within which scientists made proposals that met the planned requirements to ensure funding rather than to break new frontiers in producing "commercializable" research and development results. Scholars were reacting to distorted incentives that were sent not from the market but from the central governing body. The government *was* the market. Consequently, R&D activities and financing were separated from production, other than in cases where such services were requisitioned to fulfill particular orders from supervisory levels of the administrative hierarchy. Universities, generally the centers where scientific interests, business needs, and government policies are often blended to produce useful results in the West, did not have an important role in Soviet R&D. Basic research was conducted in institutes of the Academy of Sciences, and applied research was performed by institutes of the various ministries. In addition, a large percentage of some of the best R&D was done within the secretive enclaves of the military industrial sector, where it often stayed.

As a result, the Soviet Union and its neighbors came to lag behind their Western counterparts. Although Eastern European countries, particularly the former Soviet Union, have been substantial contributors to the world's stock of scientific knowledge in the past, they have been unable to achieve satisfactory conversion into economic productivity; this inability has been a major reason for this gap. Thus, it has become more and more evident that appropriate organization and management of R&D that is inherent to generally implementable technological advance is a true source of the *wealth of nations.*

From its inception until its dissolution, the Soviet Union viewed science as an essential element in promoting growth to attain economic and political supremacy in the world. To achieve these goals, the USSR promoted general and technical education, research and development, and industrial technological advance in an impressive manner during the twentieth century. Therefore, the intellectual potential of this region has dramatically changed since the turn of the last century.

Marxist Theory

The great value attributed to scientific substance goes back to the original ideas of Marxist theory. This concept for economic development and social change conveyed a distinct emphasis on economic efficiency and productivity as fundamental determinants in deciding the outcome of the competition between different forms of organization of economic activity over time. The need to confirm the international superiority of the Soviet economic system, combined with its technological inferiority to Western industrializing nations after the Bolshevik Revolution in 1917, forced science and technology to the top of the party-state central agenda to procure the necessary innovation to catch-up.

The pivotal role of science and technology is an intricate part of classical socialism. It is the instrument for social development and fulfillment. The classics of Marxism–Leninism elaborate an integrated concept of the development of science. These fundamentals present an adequate concept of the nature of science as a cognitive system and a component of society and its position and role in societal life and the basic laws of its development (Mikulinski and Richta, 1983, p. 8). This theoretical approach emphasizes the intricate role of science in socialism and the corresponding scientific advances facilitated by a socialist environment. A socialist system was seen to be a superior basis for scientific activity compared with a capitalist economic system, which had no central planning, promoted wasteful competition, and did not provide sufficient security for the structure and individuals involved in intellectual work such as research and development, where the return on often high investment was risky and gradual.

Under socialism, scientific knowledge mastered by society becomes an integral part of human culture. Some excerpts from Mikulinski and Richta (1983, Chapter 1) reveal what Marx and his colleagues have said about science, research, development, and technology that was consistent with their belief that labor is the most crucial element of the socioeconomic system.

Marx said, "The implements of labor, in the form of machinery, necessitate the substitution of natural forces for human force, and the conscious application of science, instead of the rule of thumb."

Marx believed science (which appears to include both accumulated knowledge and current advances from research and development) to be a universal productive force. In his opinion, socialism unites science and labor, while capitalism makes the worker subordinate to the machine, a product of science. Even the emancipation of labor at the hands of technological advance can be seen positively in Marxist terms, as the increase in free time is to the benefit of the full development of the individual. The feedback of this on the productive power of labor becomes the greatest productive power. Essentially, man, through science, is the wealth of society and fuels its development.

In his extensive works, Marx also made predictions about the future. He wrote that the transformation of science, R&D, and technology into an immediate productive force would shape the development of society.[11] Friedrich Engels, close friend and colleague of Karl Marx, is quoted as saying, "If society has a technical need, this advances science [R&D, and subsequently technology] more than ten universities" (ibid, p. 45). This quote is probably intended to demonstrate the strong influence of society's technological needs rather than to demean the educational institutions.

Lenin generally followed Marxist theories. At the time, these theories did not appear to conflict with the introduction of his so-called New Economic Policies (NEP). Of course, besides being a politician, Lenin was a scholar and extended Marx's ideas by making statements such as, "each step in the development of science adds new grains to the sum total of absolute truth, but the limits of each scientific proposition are relative, now expanding, now shrinking with the growth of knowledge."

Stalinist Legacy

Soviet-style socialism has come a long way from adhering to the fundamentals of Marxist ideology. In fact, some experts contend (probably with good reason) that no member of the politburo in the 1980s had the slightest interest in what Marx actually said on any subject (Nove, 1986, p. 44). The management of the economy took on many different characteristics over the decades, but to its end it remained most troubled by the Stalinist legacy.

Joseph Stalin was a despotic ruler who developed a constitution that carried his own name. He reoriented political and economic priorities, collectivized and centralized the economy leaving no opportunity for any market activity, and subordinated everything to the state, which was the party, which was himself. Terror and strict censorship was used to ensure control and enforce compliance with orders and official ideology. Intelligence, knowledge, and all other traits characteristic of scholars and the scientific community were suspicious. It is well known that an inquiring mind, coupled with intellectual curiosity and an analytical approach, is not easy to discipline. Stalin's great purges of intellectuals were less and less to isolate dissidents or punish specific actions, but more and more for preventive and anticipatory reasons (Nove, 1986, p. 15). For example, Nikolai Vavilov, a great Soviet geneticist and former president of the Academy of Agricultural Science, was persecuted and died in Stalin's Saratov prison in 1943 (Garret, 1989, p. 41).

In recognition of the limited scope of genuine scientific inquiry in fields such as molecular biology and genetics, a whole generation of able young Soviet scholars opted for other fields. The effects can still be observed today in the severe shortage of specialists in the biosciences to help support the present biotechnological program. The social sciences were also victims of a similar history. In addition, the headquarters of the Academy of Sciences was moved from its home of 150 years in St. Petersburg to Moscow in 1934 to allow for improved surveillance and control.

In economic policy, Stalin focused his regime's policies on the development of heavy industry with an increase in physical output as the primary target. A coercive central planning system was the tool implemented to effectively move from a largely agriculturally based economy to one concentrated on expanding heavy and defense industries to promote growth of the whole economy. The emphasis on heavy industrial production was also characteristic of a stage of industrialization in present world leaders such as Japan, Germany, and Britain. Some newly industrialized countries (NICs) in Southeast Asia are now also following this path of development. For some time it was quite successful in the former USSR; as the industrial infrastructure was being built up, leading growth rates for steel production were being achieved. The difference between the former USSR experience and the Japanese or Western European experiences lies in that the latter group was integrated into the world market and responded to changing international demands by moving to a subsequent phase of economic development – often referred to as the new techno-economic paradigm. Interestingly, the emphasis on the expansion on heavy industry continued until very recently and is still continuing in some communist/socialist nations (former Soviet Union, China, Cuba, etc.) as demonstrated by the extremely high shares of investment (often close to 75%) in the energy production, raw material recovery, and defense sectors.

By selecting and overexploiting relatively unsophisticated technologies, the Soviets took advantage of economies of scale (this was also partly due to their dependent neighbors) beyond that normally achieved in Western industry. The large economies of scale, as epitomized by the high degree of monopolization in Soviet industry, and the isolation of the market following Stalin's import substitution strategy reduced the real demand for innovations because enterprises did not have to compete for a share of the market.[12] There was no need to make a product more attractive to consumers – the "no-frills theory." The market was divided, and production quotas allocated. The Academy of Sciences had become little more than a rubber stamp for huge prestigious projects drawn up by the industrial ministries and left many scientists either researching items with little or no commercial prospects or just plain idle.

After Stalin nationalized the means of production and property (completed by 1936), he adjusted the dictated goal for production to the gross ruble value of output, the VAL system (Goldman, 1987, p. 20). Due to a system of pricing on a cost plus basis, producers were actually encouraged to use more and costly inputs to simply increase the value of output. The result was inefficiency, waste, and a strong reluctance to be innovative. As the size, sophistication, and intricacies of control of the planned Soviet economy increased, so did the previously mentioned problems. Furthermore, in the absence of official economic penalties for poor or inadequate work in all sectors, the system was destined to lose its self-correcting mechanisms (which tie quantity and output to quality of work) after a long period of distortion (Goldman, 1987, p. 45).

Post-Stalinist Developments: From Khrushchev to Gorbachev

Unfortunately, many of the characteristics described above continued to hamper attempts to make the system more efficient long after the death of Stalin.

Nikita Khrushchev had a vision that the Soviet Union would match and then supersede American achievements in technology and industry in the long term. He not only reemphasized the importance of research and development, but also stressed the need to link these factors with exploitation of the nation's rich natural resources. Aside from establishing the impressive research center at the Siberian town of Novosibirsk, Khrushchev's attempts to reorganize the management of the national economy and scientific community were primarily tied up by the bureaucrats, administrators, and state planners.

During the extended leadership of Leonid Brezhnev, the already enormous administrative apparatus gained in size and influence. Pure and applied research continued to be generously funded by the state. Institutes paid lip service to the scientific or economic value of their work. Scientists enjoyed great prestige, yet their status has always been uncertain; their privileges made them part of the social elite with a real but strictly contained autonomy (Matcheret, 1987, p. 83).

The Soviet government created new institutes and increased the employment in existing ones, leading to a very large population of institutes, many with employees numbering in the thousands and frequently performing independently of activities elsewhere, consequently, often overlapping. As the size of institutes took on such magnificent proportions, the emphasis was often more on administration rather than on invention. Increasingly, researchers had fewer customers interested in rapidly implementing their ideas, often because this would have interrupted planned industrial or agricultural output. The scientists were hindered rather than encouraged to discuss their work with foreign (especially Western) professional colleagues. Thus, the mammoth Soviet scientific community, already with approximately one-quarter of the world's scientists, was simultaneously deprived of the stimulus of multi-customer demand and of critical international review. Civilian R&D suffered most under these strict conditions; some directed freedoms and incentives made institutes of the military and aerospace sectors relatively productive and successful.

Scientific and technological advances were also portrayed as fundamental to Gorbachev's reform strategies (see discussion in Section 3.2.5). Gorbachev's general economic reform called for cuts in staff in some central ministries and state committees, reductions in state budget outlays, and stricter financial discipline for enterprises. This reform made the survivability of many research institutes as well as their customers difficult, if not impossible, in their then existing form.

From 1985 (the beginning of Gorbachev's ascent to power) until 1991 (the year of his resignation), a number of Soviet politicians including the president made bold statements that science and technology would bring a new economic prosperity to the Soviet nation. Speeding up scientific and technical progress was to be the basis for increasing economic growth. Reports indicated that Soviet academics believed that without rapid scientific advance and the practical application of research in production processes, the government's ambitious program of economic reform was beyond realization.

3.2.4 Actors in Soviet R&D policy

The Soviet Union was characterized by an administrative and hierarchial system. This was also true for planning and managing R&D policy, which was part of the development of science and technology in the national economy.

The entire management process of research, development, and diffusion of innovation began at the top in the Supreme Soviet (see *Figure 3.5*). This, the highest level of government, and the Council of Ministers were the executive bodies that made decisions regarding global questions such as: What are the main priorities and directions of science and technology development? What are the national goals in these fields? How soon should these be realized? What financial and human resources are to be allocated to achieve these goals?

Subsequently, it was the responsibility of GOSPLAN (the State Planning Committee) to elaborate the corresponding short-term (1 year), medium-term (5 years), and long-term (15 years) national plans, which were ultimately adopted by government (the Council of Ministers). GOSPLAN then cooperated with various state committees to set objectives for the management bodies at ministerial, republican, and regional levels. These in turn defined the goals and planning indices for associations of enterprises and single enterprises. This sequence describes the direct, hierarchial planning process which began after the adoption of the national priorities at the national level. During the preparation phase of the plan, there was intensive interaction (negotiations, bargaining, etc.) between all the levels. For example, the State Committee for Science and Technology (GKNT) and the State Standardization Commission were responsible for determining the necessary technical level in a specific branch.

However, the new technological ideas were not simply generated by planning, but were rather results of the efforts of scientific-technological organizations: namely, the research institutes and laboratories of the state committees, the Academy of Sciences, and the industrial ministries. Due to an unclear division of duties between the agencies, conflicts consistently arose between the various organizations with respect to their fields of influence and areas where their activities would complement one another. Unfortunately, the effects of this rivalry were more frequently compartmentalization and isolation instead of healthy competition.

In addition to countless specific departments, most of the state committees had very large, specialized institutes to support their influence on policy. The GKNT had institutes for gathering and analyzing information and data (the VINITI, which employed 26,000 persons), for organization and management, for advanced management education, and so on. The

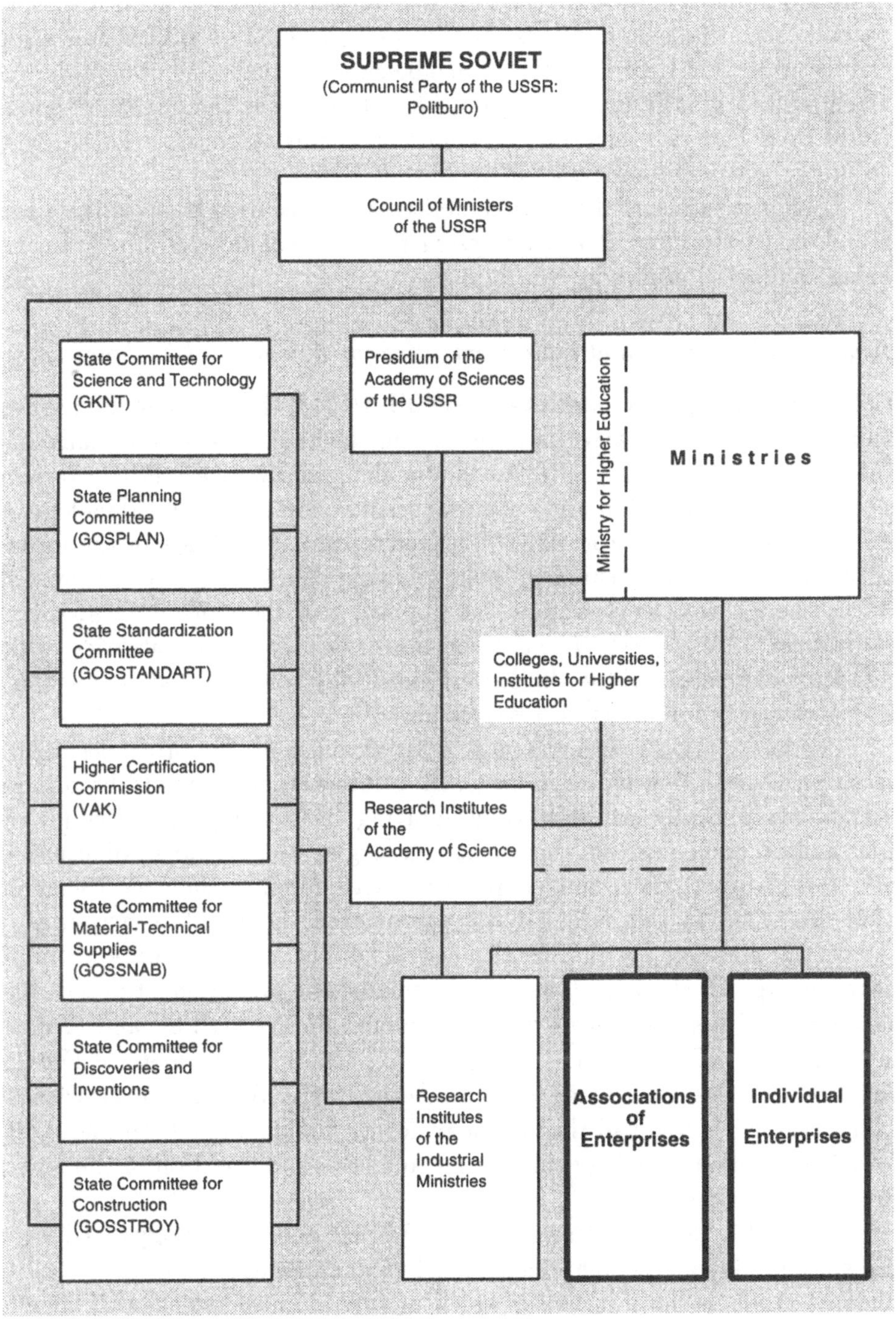

Figure 3.5. Soviet management process of research, development, and diffusion of innovation.

State Committee for Discovery and Inventions supported an institute for patents, scientific examinations, and licenses. GOSSTANDART had a special institute that described the technological conditions and standards, and attempted to modify management systems to improve the quality of goods. GOSPLAN had two scientific, economic institutes responsible for studying economic and social processes in the Soviet Union.

Each institution of the state committees was required to investigate topics relevant to its committee's interests irrespective of any overlap of research being conducted elsewhere.

Academy of Sciences and State Committee for Science and Technology

Other than the specific interests of GOSPLAN,[13] the Academy of Sciences and the State Committee for Science and Technology conventionally had the strongest influences on R&D policy making and were essentially responsible for the organization and output of science, research, and technology, at least in the civilian sector. GKNT played an important part in the formulation of science and technology policy, having coordinating powers over all R&D, though with emphasis on the applied, and therefore branch, sphere (Fortescue, 1987, p. 98). The advisory and executive responsibilities of the Academy of Sciences of the USSR were essentially concentrated on managing and performing fundamental research activities.

Therefore, GKNT was responsible for establishing the principles for directing scientific development, organizing intersectional or interbranch research, economically and effectively applying the results of research (scientific and technological advances), and managing the exchange of scientific and technological data and cooperation with foreign countries (Semeria, 1987, p. 143). In this role, GKNT coordinated the scientific activities of the central planning system, determined the diffusion of information and innovation, approved research budgets, regulated the procurement of scientific and technical literature from abroad, planned S&T activities, and forecast investment in S&T projects. Using its links to the Department of Foreign Relations, to the Committee for State Security (KGB), and to the Defense Ministry, GKNT also had the task of exploring foreign markets (in the West) for leading-edge technology suitable for adoption and insertion in the Soviet production process.

Until 1991, the State Committee for Science and Technology distributed the state funds for research. This giant bureaucratic apparatus allocated its budgets through the ministries, which in turn decided which work should be financed based on recommendations from state committees. As a result, research became tied to the needs of a specific ministry, which may and often did not correspond to the needs of scientific research or industrial technology.

The Academy of Sciences, founded in the early eighteenth century by Peter the Great in St. Petersburg, was the oldest and most prestigious scientific organization in the Soviet Union. This elite scientific community comprised nearly 300 R&D establishments, branches, institutes, laboratories, observatories, stations, libraries, museums, botanical gardens, and the like with a particular emphasis on the basic sciences (Matcheret, 1987, p. 86). Some of the research centers have become quite famous, occasionally for their successful research, but all too often for the size of their colossal staffs, which has been estimated at approximately one-quarter of the world's total scientific personnel. Almost all were located within the borders of the Russian republic, which was the only republic with no Republican Academy to call its own – at least not until late 1991 when the Soviet Academy reacquired the name Russian Academy, its name until 1925.

The Academy of Sciences was governed by an elected Presidium that was responsible for coordinating all basic research in the Soviet Union in accordance with the guidelines adopted by the Council of Ministers. The internal management of the academy proved that some remnants of democracy and autonomy persisted to certain degrees in spite of central planning. Some experts estimate that up to 85% of basic research in the Soviet Union was carried out in academy institutes, leaving only a minor role for institutes of higher education, which had almost solely a teaching function (Matcheret, 1987, p. 87).[14]

In a review of Soviet civil science, Matcheret (1987) gives a comprehensive listing of the tasks of the academy. In addition to those already mentioned, these tasks included defining overall research policy for the scientific disciplines and the social sciences; performing some applied research in laboratories; acting as a key vehicle for technological penetration; training scientific personnel; analyzing and disseminating world scientific and technological findings in relevant fields; publishing journals, reviews, and books; maintaining international contacts; organizing international congresses; representing the Soviet Union in more than 150 international, nongovernmental scientific organizations; and presenting awards for outstanding achievements.

Due to the prestige and to some extent also influence, intellectuals who were members of the academy enjoyed some of the highest salaries in the country, far above those of enterprise managers – a very different picture from that in the West. The general salary level for scientific personnel was markedly higher than the national average for nonscientific workers.

For more than seven decades, science was at the center of Soviet government policy, and the Academy of Sciences was one of the chief instruments

Table 3.4. The age structure of the USSR Academy of Sciences.

Percentage of scientific workers under age 40 in scientific establishments		
Qualification	*1973*	*1983*
Doctors of Sciences	10.7	3.0
Candidates of Sciences	52.4	35.2
All scientific workers	61.6	45.9
Percentage of members of the academy under age 50		
Status	*1976*	*1986*
Academicians	5.8	0.8
Corresponding members	17.8	7.3
Percentage of members of the academy over age 75		
Status	*1976*	*1986*
Academicians	15.3	36.6
Corresponding members	8.1	13.7

Adapted from Kneen (1989, pp. 79–80).

thereof. The academy loyally reconciled its interests to accommodate the interests of government, but usually ineffectually. Yet its mere existence drained support, in the form of personnel and funds, from the universities, leaving it to the Academies of the Republics to amend the balance with respect to the universities in their own territory.

After 1985, the academy itself felt the scouring of reform. It was time for some changes. This giant national think tank was riddled with increasing and an aging bureaucracy and employment. The question where were fresh ideas to come from looking at the age structure of the academy is a valid one. In the categories of doctors of science, candidates of science, and all scientific workers, the share of scientific workers under age 40 shrank from 10.7%, 52.4%, and 61.6% respectively in 1973 to as little as 3.0%, 35.2%, and 45.9% in 1983 (see *Table 3.4*). The statistics for the general members of the academy are even more shocking with over 50% over age 75 in 1986, up more than 27 percentage points from 1976. These circumstances brought about several changes. In academy establishments all managers were to retire at 65, or 70 in the case of a member of the academy, appointments to heads of institutes and their deputies and to heads of laboratories were to be subject to review every five years when an election was to be held, and a director could only be reappointed one additional time by the same procedure, so the maximum consecutive term was 10 years (Garrett, 1989, p. 42).

Unfortunately, some restructuring (*perestroika*) of the scientific community has actually increased the bureaucratic barriers that have proved to be obstacles to productive research. In efforts to democratize (*glasnost*) the hierarchy within the research institutes more tiers were created, adding to the power struggles. The decision to implement a new method for electing the heads of laboratories (subsections of the institutes) lessened the professional character of the research structure. It became more important to gain the support of the relatively larger numbers of nonscientific staff, who were ill-suited to judge the suitability of the candidates professionally.

Finally, some comments regarding the influence of the Supreme Soviet Committee for Defense and State Security on R&D and science. This Committee not only controlled the defense budget (between 10% and 15% of the national budget over the years, including its significant allocation for R&D), but also siphoned some of the country's best scientific, technical, and material resources from the civilian sector. In 1988, about 75% of the budget for R&D went to the defense sector, the results of which hardly, if ever, spilled over to the civilian production sector (Yakovets, 1991, p. 2). Military research was traditionally carried out in *closed* institutes and laboratories. This severely affected the creativity of Soviet S&T development. The secrecy and isolation caused some scientists to inadvertently become victims of the *reinvent-the-wheel* theory and drastically limited contacts with foreign S&T communities. One of the reasons for the relative success of Soviet defense-oriented R&D lies in the extraordinary privileges granted the scientists in these special institutes and towns, and the almost boundless resources available to them.

The quality and potential of the military industrial complex (MIC) of the former USSR is remarkable. Today, there is an urgent need for its conversion to civilian uses before the resources are lost. The MIC is the sector with the highest technological level because noneconomic priorities such as the arms race and the desire for military supremacy have led to a concentration of the most qualified personnel, state-of-the-art machinery and equipment, and enormous investments. This was done at the expense of the nonmilitary industry.[15] Times have changed. Global disarmament and the pressure to restructure the domestic economy have forced decision makers to actively undertake measures to begin conversion of the military industry to civilian uses.

Conversion is a complicated process anywhere; more so, of course, for the former Soviet Union where the defense sector was highly monopolized, isolated from the market, shrouded in secrecy, dependent on generous budget allocations and military orders, and had no independent marketing relations or functions. The transformation of the military orientation is particularly difficult in the case of large, specialized scientific organizations (with a large proportion of fundamental R&D established on an expensive and often unique experimental base), and *closed zones* or *towns* (where an entire locality and its population has been devoted to the research, design, and production of specific military paraphernalia). Conversion of the military sector is of interest to more than just the research community, but it is extremely complicated and should be investigated in detail in a separate study.

3.2.5 Science, research, development, and technology before 1985

The Soviet Union developed the largest scientific community in the world (see Chapter 4). Funding as a percentage of national income was traditionally planned to be relatively high, the facilities were often enormous, and the number of research personnel was awesome. This investment in the Soviet scientific community did not go unnoticed; Soviet scientists had been awarded a respectable number of Nobel Prizes during the 1950s and 1960s.

The origin of the structure of science and technology policy was the same as that of the state which it served. Political goals, which had priority in such a system, caused the evolution of science to be frequently determined by factors of national prestige rather than by the true needs of the economy and society at large. The result was the rise of a socioeconomic phenomenon called *branchdom*: division of the economy into separate, rather isolated, sectors. By the end of the 1930s when the centrally planned system (CPS) was in full operation, all production decisions including R&D and long-term development issues were taken from the authority of industrial enterprises and transferred to higher management levels (i.e., ministries and state committees).

This practice made it difficult for the consumers of R&D products to influence the field, effort, and funding of research through typical channels of a market economy. The scientific community was forever attempting to utilize its bargaining power to influence these elements, though with distorted results. Thus, branchdom cultivated scientific monopolies that distorted the goals of technological progress. This led to a structure in which mainly large-scale R&D institutions, often with many thousands of employees, were most viable. A limited number of rather small-scale institutes, directly serving some ministerial directives, also operated. In the period between 1975 and 1985, while the government imposed strict restrictions on the process of establishing new R&D institutions in fear of losing control, the average size of an R&D institute grew by more than 25%. Furthermore, the centrally planned system (CPS) was in itself a primary cause of strong interbranch and interorganization barriers that prevented information exchange between scientists in research institutes and employees in industry, higher education, and the Academy of Sciences.

Basic research and applied research were separated from one another by the organizational autarky of industrial ministries and the Academy of Sciences. R&D plans for different departments of the CPS were determined by corresponding bodies in the Central Committee of the Communist Party, the State Planning Committee, the Military Industrial Commission, and the State Committee on Science and Technology. With the exception of military industrial R&D, inadequate coordination led to mismanagement and conflicting indicators and objectives.

There was a continual conflict between enterprises' and branch ministries' planning perspectives and the actual duration of technological development from research and development to implementation and diffusion. Additional barriers between the academy, educational institutions, and industry (as well as between industries) split the scientific community into different groups with weak communication and under strict regulation. Therefore, the early 1980s saw the structure of the Soviet R&D sector as extremely monopolized (with discretionary distribution of R&D resources depending on quality) and exceptionally inflexible and unable to respond to new demands of society and science itself.

In general then, the Soviet economy was characterized by profound structural and technological imbalances. Both the substantial discrepancy between administrative management methods (regulation) and the innovation processes and the economic, ideological, and socio-cultural peculiarities resulted in an economic and political system indifferent to innovation and technological change. Excess bureaucracy and ineffective state regulation have been identified as the main obstacles to innovation. The five main factors cited as those most inhibiting innovative ability of the centrally planned system are state control and militarization, waste and shortage economy (including the so-called *anti-innovation branch structure*), monopoly and *monotonous organization* of innovations, economic culture, and technological incompatibility.[16]

The CPS signified total state control of economic life, including science and technology. Success was measured by fulfilling plan assignments and not by making scientific discoveries. The result was a prevalence for short-term interests (to meet the directives) rather than adaptive, long-term commitments that could secure a more certain future. The long-term orientation that existed was one that remained inflexible and concentrated on old problems, thus becoming obsolete in the course of a modernizing world.

In addition, investment, research, and technological policy was essentially dependent on the state budget. Any decisions with respect to these issues had to clear numerous hierarchial levels. Management of R&D financing and selection of particular paths of scientific and technological progress were, until recently, largely beyond the authority of the individual enterprise or association.

In addition, Soviet S&T progress consistently had a substantial military/space orientation.[17] This was accompanied by a lack of devotion to economic development problems (including a disregard for creating national competitiveness) and a severe neglect of the civil sector, which resulted in more direct consequences such as a monopsony situation, distorted prices, and secrecy. The militarization of R&D was a threat to future S&T progress in the Soviet Union due to the significantly weakened channels of converting advanced technology for use in civilian industry and to the rigid command management of enterprises in the military industrial complex.

Paradoxically, the output orientation of the administrative system has, in the long run, led to a shortage economy. In the CPS, science and technological policy was restricted to the framework of the acceleration principle and had no real stabilizing role. Such acceleration was sporadically initiated when central authorities became aware of a widening technological gap between the level in their country and the levels in those countries it was to be competing with.

Of course, the huge shortages characteristic of the Soviet economy directly impeded S&T progress. Physical limitations imposed on the scope of R&D, financial resources became more scarce as the need to generate and implement innovations grew, and efforts to satisfy everyday needs diverted crucial energy and creative potential. A product of such an economic system is the so-called *anti-innovation branch structure*. Its awkward and archaic character is primarily due to a lack of restructuring with respect to changing demands (particularly in the 1970s and 1980s when efforts were made to become more R&D intensive), the inadequate development of various related services, and a high degree of obsolete capital stock.[18]

The artificial type of Soviet monopoly based on administrative principles was clearly an obstacle to innovation and technological change. Insurmountable vertical economic barriers are a direct consequence of the departmental monopoly (*branchdom*). Soviet monopolistic management led to degradation of product quality, lack of competition (especially to spur S&T progress), and a reduction in the choices available to the consumer. Both monopoly and monopsony features bias technological change and impede modern economic growth. Thus, there was little possibility for integration and interdisciplinary activity.

Nevertheless, ministries were required to maintain the given technological level of production according to predetermined state standards and to demonstrate technological achievements to the state authorities. In order to fulfill this purpose, the ministries had a pool that included not only plants and factories, but also research institutes, design bureaus, and laboratories, all somehow linked to industry. These are referred to as science/production agglomerations, which were ignorant of market impulses and processes due to their monopoly positions. Unfortunately, lobbying of the individual elements was strong, coordination between them was weak, and enterprises were generally quite unreceptive to innovations in any case.

Certain features that normally motivate R&D and subsequent technological change and innovation in a market economy were not present in the economic structure of the Soviet Union. These include a functional capital market (as well as venture capital[19]), high labor mobility,[20] and international cooperation in research and exchange of scientists. The closed nature of the centrally planned system and the commitment to secrecy imposed extensive limitations on mobility of skilled personnel and the transfer of information and technology.

The prolonged domination of the CPS resulted in the formation of a special Soviet economic culture. Among the main items influencing successful technological change was the aversion to competition and entrepreneurship and the ignorance of the value of individual innovative spirit. Entrepreneurship was commensurate with exploitation, parasitism, and speculation. The use of ideological regulators of economic development and the existing planning and evaluation system of the results of scientific and technological activities led to an unprecedented *paper entrepreneurship* in the form of exaggeration of quality and quantity of results, and a trend toward spectacular projects with sensational results.

Decades of command control, largely insensitive to changing demands, resulted in incompatibility with technological standards of market economies, with the exception of few selected strategic areas. International R&D cooperation is vital for domestic technological progress and scientific competition that reflect the evolution of demand in a modern society. Reverse engineering was one of the few links that Soviet scientific and technical experts had to the international S&T community. This peculiar research method was most popular in the motor vehicle, aircraft, chemical, and microelectronics industries. It was simply engaged to organize production, not for the long-term improvement or development of technology. Although there has been some trade in licenses, much of Soviet technology imports have been of the turnkey style that limited further domestic development and expansion. The direct import of knowledge and exchange of established or aspiring scientists was minimal.

Overall, the state strategy for S&T development was aimed at achieving international leadership in certain spheres of human knowledge, often at the expense of economic efficiency (Mikerin and Kozlova, 1991, p. 2). There was more emphasis on the support of large-scale technological programs than on creating a favorable economic climate for innovations and technical change. The assessment of the effectiveness of new technology in the Soviet Union revealed contradictory results with respect to contemporary global trends. The causes were the distorted, expenditure-based central pricing system, central distribution of resources, artificially suppressed consumer prices, high taxation of excess profits (practically negating reinvestment possibilities), low wages, and comparatively high prices for new technology. Consequently, it appears that the present and future cost of innovating is far higher than the potential return and an enterprise is better off adhering to the traditional technology. On this premise, enterprises will never be motivated to engage in technologically progressive activities.

Despite periodic showings of scientific achievement, the 1980s were a time of decline for Soviet R&D: stagnation and an ever-widening gap between the rate of *intellectual production* and that in the industrialized countries had become the distinguishing features.[21] Estimates predict that the gap has grown from 10 to 15 years behind in the mid-1950s to 20 to 30 years in the mid-1980s, and is still growing (Motorygin and Glaziev, 1991, p. 8).

3.2.6 Science, research, development, and technology after 1985

Some Soviet experts began to feel that the backwardness in the R&D sector that was characteristic of the technology gap to the Western industrialized countries may acquire a qualitatively irreversible character.[22]

As already mentioned, the Soviet scientific community was faced by what at first glace seemed to be a paradox: questionable performance despite a long-standing scientific tradition, fairly consistent and certainly secure funding (see Chapter 4), a tremendous store of knowledge, and a large number of scientists and engineers. The situation becomes less paradoxical if seen in a different light: namely, the shortage of state-of-the-art scientific equipment that prevented scientists from reproducing world scientific achievements and severely hindered any true pioneering work and the absence of modern communication technology, infrastructure, and ideology that could convey results of work being done in other parts of the world and inform others on those occasions when Soviets did make a discovery. This backwardness in Soviet science was primarily related to backwardness in Soviet industry as a whole, whether in computers, electronics, instrumentation, communication, or other crucial fields.

As a result, the Soviet Union adopted the Comprehensive Program of Scientific and Technical Progress of the CMEA countries to the year 2000 in

1985 (Kneen, 1989, p. 68). This program identified "electronization" of the economy, comprehensive automation, atomic power engineering, biotechnology, and the creation of new types of materials as five areas where accelerated development was considered crucial for the future well-being of the USSR and its socialist partners.

There had been attempts to integrate the research science sector with that of industrial technology to improve interaction with industry. The goal was twofold: to make research more demand responsive and to facilitate technological development. Already late in 1985, a decision of the Supreme Soviet and the Council of Ministers delegated the actual control of several industrial enterprises to Intersectoral Scientific and Technical Complexes (MNTKs). The research and production processes were to be integrated with industry by putting enterprises under the authority of a single body or official for each project. Each MNTK was to be made up of institutes of the Academy of Sciences, branch institutes from the ministries, professorships at institutes of higher education, a project office, and experimental production capacities (Matcheret, 1987, p. 93).

In addition to the MNTKs, Scientific Production Associations (NPOs) had been encouraged at the branch and enterprise levels to further meld together research institutes and production enterprises from different ministries for the purpose of stimulating innovation (Goldman, 1987, p. 81). The essential difference between MNTKs and NPOs is that the former combine research, developmental, and production facilities from *several different branches* of the economy, thus necessitating the cooperation of numerous decision-making bodies. These newly developed establishments were supported by Gorbachev; the twelfth five-year plan was to substantially increase central expenditure for these activities.

The widening technology and knowledge gap to the Western industrialized countries, as well as the disappointing performance of the Soviet S&T community, compelled authorities to introduce *perestroika* in the science establishment with the proclamation of a government decree, "The Transformation of Research Organizations on the Basis of Complete Self-Accounting and Self-Finance," by USSR President Gorbachev in the fall of 1987. This decree gave state research institutes some autonomy with respect to the formulation of research plans and the access to alternative sources of finance. The ministerial organizations and monopolies in the R&D sector were to be abolished, and prices on R&D products liberalized.

If institutes could not procure financing through contracts or continued inefficient or fruitless work they were destined to be closed. Applied research institutes may be able to generate sufficient income on a contract basis, but those concentrating on fundamental research would probably face severe

Table 3.5. R&D expenditures of nonstate organizations (in billion rubles).

Expenditures	1987	1988	1989	1990	1991[a]
Total	0.03	1.21	4.70	6.00	6.15
Including					
R&D cooperatives	0.01	0.17	3.15	3.90	4.00
Youth research centers	0.02	0.85	1.10	1.45	1.50
Permanent research teams of Union of Science and Engineering Society	[b]	0.12	0.35	0.50	0.50
Permanent research teams of All-Union Society of Inventors	[b]	0.07	0.10	0.15	0.15

[a]Estimated.
[b]Insignificant or unavailable.
Source: Motorygin and Glaziev (1991, p. 20).

difficulties. For this reason, the *goszakaz* (state order) was introduced into management to replace the traditional task plan (Fortescue, 1990, p. 227). Nevertheless, a team consisting of the USSR People's Control Commission and the GKNT began an inspection in 1986 of the performance of research institutes to determine which were inefficient. Within a short period, 14 branch institutes had been examined and half of them had been closed down (Kneen, 1989, p. 74).

Simultaneously, the State Enterprise Law (SEL) and subsequent self-organization were advocated and implemented, the price-setting mechanism for R&D products ceased to be the domain of the state, and limits to the size of personal income from R&D activities were abandoned. These elements facilitated the blossoming of a nonstate R&D sector dominated by an unprecedented increase in R&D cooperatives that employed more than 320,000 persons and accounted for work and services worth more than 3 billion rubles in 1989 (*Table 3.5*). Total R&D expenditures of nonstate organizations were already more than 10% of total gross expenditure on R&D in the USSR at this time. However, R&D activity seemed to become biased toward contract work to improve the quality. Such an emphasis will not rejuvenate the R&D sector as explained in Section 7.3.

Unfortunately, real shifts in the structure and quality of R&D activities failed to keep pace with the scale of the *financial revolution*. Conditions conducive to stimulating the demand for highly efficient and science-intensive production had not been created; one of the most critical being the absence of a well-defined intellectual property rights system, which inevitably impaired the ability to capitalize on R&D achievements.

Many private firms began to resort to a type of *industrial piracy* that involved using and selling inventions and know-how developed by state organizations; its main form was the by-now legal, part-time employment of specialists fully employed by the state. Estimates show that more than half the scholars in the Soviet Union work in the nonstate R&D sector, while many continue to be employed by the state (Motorygin and Glaziev, 1991, p. 15). Many scientists were reluctant to move out of the safe framework of state-sponsored research. Thus, these firms were no more than intermediate service agents that did not carry the burden of maintaining the equipment, infrastructure, and national obligations of a state research institute.

Essentially then, knowledge and technology were consequently transferred between research institutes and from these institutes to the production sector, but did not stimulate R&D activities. Whether revenue from the sale of these intellectual products was reinvested in R&D remains doubtful. In fact, numerous nonstate R&D enterprises were consequently, indirectly subsidized by the state and may, in fact, have not been economically viable in a more competitive market without access to such resources.

The unavoidable weakening of central control over state enterprises (due to the implementation of the SEL) was accompanied by the decline of performance- and enterprise-promoted R&D. With the subsequent introduction of the new tax system, ministries lost the right to collect any portion of state enterprise profits, cutting off an important source of industrial R&D funding.

The situation worsened throughout 1990 and early 1991. Industrial R&D was plagued by financial trouble due to the abolishment of special industrial funds for science and technology development (distribution method of subsidies for R&D when regulation required all profits to be transferred to the state), the new 1991 tax system (including federal, republican, and local taxes on state enterprises' profits), decreased profit leading to reduced demand for state R&D products by industrial and agricultural enterprises,[23] collapse of the state budget,[24] and the brain drain from the state research institutes to the emerging private sector.[25] Even more simple aspects such as the obsolescence of experimental equipment and scientific instruments accompanied by the general deterioration of research premises also took their toll on R&D advances.[26]

The opening of the Soviet economy exposed previously protected areas of Soviet science and technology to levels attained in the international community, often revealing substantial gaps between the internationally publicized and the actual domestic research achievements. This is particularly true for the civilian sector. One benefit of Gorbachev's *glasnost* was the new freedom of intellectuals to exchange opinions at home and abroad. It would appear that gone are the days of Stalin's iron-fisted control of the scientific community and hassles of the Brezhnev era concerning politico-bureaucratic control of passports, visas, publications, conference travel, and postal communication. Nevertheless permission to go abroad continues to require invitations and is not as fast in coming as is deemed necessary for a flexible environment, and the formal process is still cumbersome. Today new barriers are present that may be more insurmountable than those of the past: Western attitudes and hard currency.

One aspect that has been labeled for change are the resources allocated to the defense industry. A state program for defense industry conversion until 1995 has been approved. The goal is to reorient a substantial amount of R&D resources from the MIC toward civilian purposes. Under this program 46% of the R&D resources of the defense sector should be implemented for civilian purposes by 1995, compared with only 29.6% in 1989 (Kulichkov, 1991, p. 1).

Today there is a need to change the entire R&D organization, which in the past was based on the fulfillment of state directives and nonmarket criteria for performance. Some proposals for restructuring include: integration of the processes of reorganization of research institutes and the privatization of state enterprises; dissolution of ministries and other administrative supervising bodies; restructuring of the state system of R&D finance and promotion; introduction of appropriate intellectual property rights, legislation, and state innovation policy; and reform of the education system (Glaziev, 1991, p. 3). Sufficient demand for R&D products will be necessary for R&D restructuring to be successful and to make the sector viable during and after the transition to market conditions. Thus, de-monopolization and the development of competition is a key prerequisite. There is some fear that privatization is currently taking place without de-monopolization. The transformation of state enterprises into self-managed, joint-stock companies can easily be followed by the rebirth of new organizational monopolies in the form of associations, conglomerates, and others.

Research institutes cannot be privatized like enterprises. The appropriate form should depend on the character of the research activity, whether basic, applied, developed, or any combination of the three. The reorganized institute may remain in the hands of the state, be transformed into consortiums owned by firms, firms' R&D departments (i.e., previously scientific-production unions), small high-tech firms, centers for contract R&D (mainly applied R&D), self-managed organizations leased or owned by their employees, or be transferred to universities or colleges. The transformation of research institutes must be accompanied by restructuring of the current R&D financing system. Although foundation or other private funding may be established, there will probably be a need to subsidize some R&D (particularly fundamental) during the transition to preserve accumulated R&D potential. The recipients, amount, and duration of the funding must be carefully identified.

The obstacles that hinder the realization of radical attempts to restructure include a shortage of resources (due to the distortion caused by fixed prices), lack of expertise and experience, inadequate structure of state bodies, and insufficient international exchange. A new national industrial policy is required to provide sufficient stimuli for enterprises with respect to long-term investments, innovative activities, and foreign trade. Both price and quality competition should play an essential role in determining the route that research and development managers take in the future.

Notes

[1] Economic growth is an increase in a geographic or political region's capacity to produce goods and services and the actual increase in their production. Traditionally, the accepted measure to monitor growth has been the annual rate of increase in a particular area's gross national product (or the rate of expansion of per capita national income). There is considerable awareness of the shortcomings of this measure, especially because it does not appear to always measure adequately nonmarket activities, transactions in the black economy, value of leisure or free time, and disbenefits of industrialization such as environmental damage or destruction of aesthetics. The all-encompassing term to more reliably describe actual changes in the standard of living is economic development. Essentially, development (originally from biology but also applicable to economics) refers to the progressive changes in size, shape, and function during the life of an organism (Goetz, 1988, p. 45). In this analysis, the role of the organism is taken by economic man or a regional or political economy.

[2] The original work on this topic is entitled *An Inquiry into the Nature and the Causes of the Wealth of Nations*, by Adam Smith, first published in 1776. These comments are a synthesis of the summary of some of Smith's ideas given by Chirot (1989, p. 16).

[3] In the past, the countries of Eastern Europe were classified using different expressions ranging from Iron Curtain countries and socialist countries to centrally planned economies (CPEs), administrative and command economies. The countries in this group include: Bulgaria, the former Czechoslovakia, Hungary, Poland, Romania, the former Soviet Union, and the former Yugoslavia. Today, these nations are undergoing fundamental changes in their structure and character, and are therefore often referred to as emerging market economies (EMEs).

[4] This is exemplified by the strong emphasis on importing knowledge (for long-term benefits) to Japan rather than on simply capital (for immediate, short-term benefits) during the early stages of the post–World War II buildup period.

[5] Particularly little in light of Khrushchev's vision of the USSR overtaking the USA as the leading world economic power in the second half of the twentieth century.

[6] In fact, this situation did not change much until the 1950s. At this time, GNP per capita in Japan was 17% (relatively less than the comparative figure in 1900) and in the USSR it was 34% of the corresponding US level. An interesting point regarding this indicator over the next four decades is that while the Soviet level was 118% of the Japanese in 1900, it grew to more than twice the Japanese level by 1950. In 1987 the GDP per capita in Japan was 164% of the Soviet level – a complete turnaround (*Figure 3.3*).

[7] These titles are from *New Scientist* (13 March 1986), *Science* (Vol. 238), *New Scientist* (11 March 1989), *The Economist* (24 March 1990), and *Nature* (5 April 1990) respectively.

[8] For further discussion of this material refer to Gomulka (1986, pp. 42–61). He investigates R&D and innovative activities in centrally planned economies and extracts various principles that appear to be incompatible with rapid innovation from the results of numerous empirical studies conducted in Eastern Europe.

[9] An example of this is described in a study of the machine tool industry in the Soviet Union: "The Soviet machine tool industry, developing independently of western assistance, has become the world's largest producer of machine tools. However, emphasis has been on large-scale production of relatively simple-to-produce, general-purpose machine tools at the expense of special-purpose and complex types." (Grant, 1979, p. 555).

[10] Some examples are theoretical physics, applied mathematical methodologies and other mathematics, metallurgy, advanced ceramics, nuclear fission and fusion, and lasers.

[11] Marx's words for science, R&D, and technology are translated as "practice, experimental science, and materially creative science" in Mikulinski and Richta (1983, p. 42).

[12] In the Soviet Union, calculations based on newly available data have shown that the median *one-firm* concentration ratio (that is, the share of total output by an individual enterprise in a particular sector of the economy) is as high as 61%. For comparison, the American figure for the top *four* firms is only 37% (Kahn and Peck, 1991, p. 65).

[13] GOSPLAN's involvement in the R&D policy making was due to its function in compiling production plans that would have been influenced by the realization of new products or processes.

[14] In many Western countries (i.e., United States, Germany, United Kingdom, and Canada), the universities perform the lion's share of basic research in the economy in addition to the teaching function.

[15] Total state expenditures for R&D were 37.8 billion rubles in 1988. Of this 75% was designated for use in the MIC (Yakovets, 1991, p. 2).

[16] Collected from the paper by Ageev and Kuzin (1991). The authors also thoroughly cover the Western literature on technological change as it pertains to the Soviet situation.

[17] In 1989, 15.3 billion rubles were spent on defense-oriented R&D in the USSR. This amounted to 71% of the state allocations for scientific activities.

[18] Estimates indicate that from 25% to 50% of machinery is obsolete and that annual repairs cost over 40 billion rubles in the engineering industry and employ the time of tens of millions of workers (Ageev and Kuzin, 1991, p. 9).

[19] Venture capital is an important source of R&D financing, particularly for smaller enterprises or entrepreneurs, in market economies. High capital mobility, competition between financing sources, and a sound credit and financial system contribute to the opportunities for successful advances in science and development for parties that might be excluded from the conventional type of simple, traditional financial allocation of a command system.

[20] Soviet personnel policies in the R&D field, which were based on hierarchy, secrecy, and autocracy, caused problems with respect to the stimulation of creative work, the active participation rate of skilled personnel, scientific and technological progress, and the democratization of the S&T sector.

[21] The rate of growth in the number of R&D personnel in the 1980s frequently dropped below 1% per year, whereas it ranged between 3% and 5% in the USA during the same period. The figures below indicate a much slower relative increase of R&D specialists in the USSR than in the USA throughout the 1980s (Gokhberg and Mindely, 1991, p. 5).

Number of specialists engaged only in R&D, as of January 1, in thousands.

	1981		1986		1989	
	USSR	USA[a]	USSR	USA[a]	USSR	USA[a]
Specialists	1434.2	1258.7	1599.4	1725.5	1654.6	2026.9

[a] US figures do not include consulting personnel.

[22] A statement by Gurii Marchuk in an article in the new science newspaper *Poisk* in July 1989, while he was president of the Academy of Sciences (quoted in Fortescue, 1990, p. 223).

[23] Already in 1988, the share of enterprises engaged in industrial R&D rose from 51.2% to 66.4% (Motorygin and Glaziev, 1991, p. 17). Again, the necessity to do-it-yourself has arisen.

[24] In the case of basic research the academy and the military industrial complex were largely dependent on state subsidies. In 1991, state budget revenues fell by as much as 70% (partly accentuated by the war of laws between the different levels of government). Expenditures on R&D in the MIC fell, in nominal terms, from 15.3 billion rubles in 1989 to 13.2 in 1990. With a 19% inflation rate in 1990, the real decrease is approximately 33% (ibid, p. 11).

[25] 13.5% of R&D (by value) was carried out in the nonstate sector in 1990.

[26] For example, in early 1989 the library of the Academy of Sciences subscribed to approximately 4,000 journals. The Harvard University library alone subscribes to about 160,000.

Appendix 3A

	GDP per capita[a]		Labor productivity		Total GDP[a]		Employment[b]	
	1950	1987	1950	1987	1950	1987	1950	1987
USSR	2265	5948	4784	11535	407840	1683764	85.246	145.972
France	2941	9475	6445	24806	123051	527602	19.092	21.269
Germany	2508	9964	5923	23594	125361	606404	21.164	25.702
Japan	1116	9756	2616	20484	93342	1198943	35.685	58.530
UK	4171	9178	9377	21199	210041	520270	22.400	24.542
USA	6697	13550	16540	29724	1019725	3308401	61.651	111.303
Finland	2610	9500	5342	19141	10464	47049	1.959	2.458
Sweden	3898	10328	8021	20240	27447	86403	3.422	4.269
Norway	3436	11653	7856	23351	11218	48711	1.428	2.086
Italy	2323	9023	5862	20757	108657	515158	18.536	24.819
Netherlands	3554	9197	9917	25229	35950	134420	3.625	5.328
Austria	2123	8792	4579	20610	14721	66488	3.215	3.226
Spain							10.793	11.369
Greece							2.839[c]	3.597
Portugal							3.289	4.403
Canada	4822	12702	13169	28138	66240	329525	5.030	11.711
Australia	4389	9533	10376	22007	35891	154398	3.459	7.016
Argentina	2324	3302	5844	9851	39865	104004	6.821	10.558
Brazil	1073	3417	3155	8817	55709	480752	17.657	54.524
S. Korea	564	4143	1817	11040	11584	176116	6.377	15.952
Indonesia	484	1200	1140	3286	35182	204928	30.863	62.373
Taiwan	526	4744	1443	10097	4144	92757	2.872	9.187
Thailand	653	2294	1255	4725	12704	122430	10.119	25.913
India	359	662	800	1715	129111	521772	161.386	304.227
China	338	1748	999	3697	184855	1869945	184.984	505.775
Bulgaria							4.183[d]	4.084
Czechoslovakia							5.853[e]	7.972
Hungary							4.155[f]	4.865
Poland							12.405	17.245
Romania							10.465[g]	10.586
Yugoslavia							7.411[h]	6.703

[a]GDP in million international dollars at 1980 prices (Maddison, 1989).
[b]Employment in millions (Maddison, 1989; UN, 1991; Mitchell, 1980).
[c]1951. [d]1946. [e]1947. [f]1949. [g]1956. [h]1953.

Appendix 3B

Item	Country	World rank	Quantity	Population[a]	Employment[b]	Arable land[c]	Quantity per capita	Productivity Labor (Q/emp.)	Productivity Land (Q/ha)
Agricultural goods									
Barley	USSR	1	44.50	288.74	24918.0	232570	0.1541	1.7859	0.1913
(mmt,	Germany	2	15.50	77.56	1645.2	12410	0.1998	9.4213	1.2490
1988)	Canada	3	14.40	26.31	583.0	45990	0.5473	24.6998	0.3131
	USA	4	13.30	248.23	3400.0	189915	0.0536	3.9118	0.0700
	France	5	10.10	55.99	1488.7	19459	0.1804	6.7844	0.5190
Corn	USA	1	125.00	248.23	3400.0	189915	0.5036	36.7647	0.6582
(mmt,	China	2	73.82	1112.30	8009.0	96976	0.0664	9.2171	0.7612
1988)	Brazil	3	24.70	150.75	14331.0	77500	0.1638	1.7235	0.3187
	Romania	4	18.38	23.15	3060.0	10686	0.7940	6.0065	1.7200
	USSR	5	16.03	288.74	24918.0	232570	0.0555	0.6433	0.0689
Cotton	USSR	1	8.69	288.74	24918.0	232570	0.0301	0.3487	0.0374
(mmt,	USA	2	5.49	248.23	3400.0	189915	0.0221	1.6147	0.0289
1988)	China	3	4.54	1112.30	8009.0	96976	0.0041	0.5669	0.0468
	India	4	1.36	833.42	1348.0	168990	0.0016	1.0089	0.0080
	Pakistan	5	1.24	110.41	14054.0	20760	0.0112	0.0882	0.0597
Eggs	China	1	4.53	1112.30	8009.0	96976	0.0041	0.5656	0.0467
(mmt,	USSR	2	4.42	288.74	24918.0	232570	0.0153	0.1774	0.0190
1988)	USA	3	4.06	248.23	3400.0	189915	0.0164	1.1941	0.0214
	Japan	4	2.41	123.22	4890.0	4708	0.0196	0.4928	0.5119
	Germany	5	1.11	77.56	1645.2	12410	0.0143	0.6747	0.0894
Meat	China	1	19.54	1112.30	8009.0	96976	0.0176	2.4398	0.2015
(mmt,	USSR	2	19.30	288.74	24918.0	232570	0.0668	0.7745	0.0830
1988)	USA	3	17.83	248.23	3400.0	189915	0.0718	5.2441	0.0939
	Germany	4	6.69	77.56	1645.2	19459	0.0863	4.0664	0.3438
	France	5	3.91	55.99	1488.7	12410	0.0698	2.6265	0.3151
Milk	USSR	1	100.65	288.74	24918.0	232570	0.3486	4.0392	0.4328
(mmt,	USA	2	66.01	248.23	3400.0	189915	0.2659	19.4147	0.3476
1988)	Germany	3	35.48	77.56	1645.2	19459	0.4575	21.5658	1.8233
	France	4	33.70	55.99	1488.7	12410	0.6019	22.6372	2.7156
	India	5	20.10	833.42	1348.0	168990	0.0241	14.9110	0.1189
Oats	USSR	1	15.29	288.74	24918.0	232570	0.0530	0.6136	0.0657
(mmt,	Germany	2	3.32	77.56	1645.2	19459	0.0428	2.0180	0.1706
1988)	USA	3	3.18	248.23	3400.0	189915	0.0128	0.9353	0.0167
	Canada	4	3.00	26.31	583.0	45990	0.1140	5.1458	0.0652
	Poland	5	2.30	38.17	5006.9	14739	0.0603	0.4594	0.1560
Potatoes	USSR	1	62.71	288.74	24918.0	232570	0.2172	2.5167	0.2696
(mmt,	Poland	2	39.00	38.17	5006.9	14739	1.0217	7.7893	2.6460
1988)	China	3	29.55	1112.30	8009.0	96976	0.0266	3.6896	0.3047
	Germany	4	20.93	77.56	1645.2	19459	0.2699	12.7219	1.0756
	USA	5	15.88	248.23	3400.0	189915	0.0640	4.6706	0.0836
Sugar	USSR	1	8.60	288.74	24918.0	232570	0.0298	0.3451	0.0370
(mmt,	Brazil	2	8.45	150.75	14331.0	77500	0.0561	0.5896	0.1090
1988)	Cuba	3	7.89	10.45	579.0	3320	0.7550	13.6269	2.3765
	India	4	7.02	833.42	1348.0	168990	0.0084	5.2077	0.0415
	USA	5	5.42	248.23	3400.0	189915	0.0218	1.5941	0.0285
Tea	Turkey	1	0.756	55.36	49.8	27927	0.0137	15.1807	0.0271
(mmt,	India	2	0.625	833.42	1348.0	168990	0.0007	0.4636	0.0037
1988)	China	3	0.566	1112.30	8009.0	96976	0.0005	0.0707	0.0058
	Sri Lanka	4	0.225	16.88	363.7	1887	0.0133	0.6186	0.1192
	Kenya	5	0.160	24.35	257.0	2420	0.0066	0.6226	0.0661
	USSR	6	0.148	288.74	24918.0	232570	0.0005	0.0059	0.0006

Item	Country	World rank	Quantity	Population[a]	Employment[b]	Arable land[c]	Quantity per capita	Productivity Labor (Q/emp.)	Productivity Land (Q/ha)
Tobacco	China	1	2.350	1112.30	8009.0	96976	0.0021	0.2934	0.0242
(mmt,	USA	2	0.612	248.23	3400.0	189915	0.0025	0.1800	0.0032
1988)	USSR	3	0.490	288.74	24918.0	232570	0.0017	0.0197	0.0021
	India	4	0.439	833.42	1348.0	168990	0.0005	0.3257	0.0026
	Brazil	5	0.386	150.75	14331.0	77500	0.0026	0.0269	0.0050
Wheat	China	1	88	1112.30	8009.0	96976	0.0787	10.9265	0.9024
(mmt,	USSR	2	84	288.74	24918.0	232570	0.2925	3.3891	0.3631
1988)	USA	3	49	248.23	3400.0	189915	0.1986	14.4971	0.2595
	India	4	47	833.42	1348.0	168990	0.0563	34.7849	0.2775
	France	5	30	55.99	1488.7	12410	0.5301	19.9369	2.3916
Manufactured Goods									
Beer	USA	1	228.96	248.23	20935.0		0.9224	10.9367	
(mln.hl,	Germany	2	112.20	77.56	11654.9		1.4466	9.6269	
1986)	UK	3	60.10	57.03	5398.0		1.0538	11.1338	
	USSR	4	51.20	288.74	38225.0		0.1773	1.3394	
	Japan	5	48.50	123.22	14250.0		0.3936	3.4035	
Butter	USSR	1	1.670	288.74	38225.0		0.0058	0.0437	
(mmt,	Germany	2	0.890	77.56	11654.9		0.0115	0.0764	
1986)	India	3	0.720	833.42	6263.0		0.0009	0.1150	
	France	4	0.640	55.99	4636.8		0.0114	0.1380	
	USA	5	0.548	248.23	20935.0		0.0022	0.0262	
Cement	China	1	203.00	1112.30	32092.0		0.1825	6.3256	
(mmt,	USSR	2	139.00	288.74	38225.0		0.4814	3.6364	
1988)	Japan	3	71.60	123.22	14250.0		0.5811	5.0246	
	USA	4	71.50	248.23	20935.0		0.2880	3.4153	
	Italy	5	38.20	57.56	4639.0		0.6637	8.2345	
Cheese	USA	1	2.51	248.23	20935.0		0.0101	0.1199	
(mmt,	USSR	2	1.75	288.74	38225.0		0.0061	0.0458	
1986)	France	3	1.28	55.99	4636.8		0.0229	0.2761	
	Germany	4	1.20	77.56	11654.9		0.0155	0.1030	
	Italy	5	0.67	57.56	4639.0		0.0116	0.1444	
Cigarettes	USA	1	655300	248.23	20935.0		2639.89	31301.65	
(mln.,	USSR	2	381300	288.74	38225.0		1320.57	9975.15	
1985)	Japan	3	303000	123.22	14250.0		2459.02	21263.16	
	Germany	4	190200	77.56	11654.9		2452.29	16319.32	
	Brazil	5	146300	150.75	8986.0		970.48	16280.88	
Newsprint	Canada	1	9.97	26.31	2044.0		0.3789	4.8777	
(mmt,	USA	2	5.43	248.23	20935.0		0.0219	0.2594	
1988)	Japan	3	2.64	123.22	14250.0		0.0214	0.1853	
	Sweden	4	1.73	8.40	960.0		0.2060	1.8021	
	Finland	5	1.65	4.96	534.0		0.3327	3.0899	
	USSR	6	1.60	288.74	38225.0		0.0055	0.0419	
Paper &	USA	1	76.40	248.23	20935.0		0.3078	3.6494	
paper-	Japan	2	18.40	123.22	14250.0		0.1493	1.2912	
board	China	3	12.10	1112.30	32092.0		0.0109	0.3770	
(mmt,	Germany	4	9.86	77.56	11654.9		0.1271	0.8460	
1988)	USSR	5	6.30	288.74	38225.0		0.0218	0.1648	
	Canada	6	6.00	26.31	2044.0		0.2281	2.9354	
Passenger	Japan	1	9.05	123.22	14250.0		0.0734	0.6351	
cars	USA	2	6.82	248.23	20935.0		0.0275	0.3258	
(mln.,	Germany	3	4.79	77.56	11654.9		0.0618	0.4110	
1989)	France	4	3.41	55.99	4636.8		0.0609	0.7354	
	Italy	5	1.97	57.56	4639.0		0.0342	0.4247	
	USSR	8	1.22	288.74	38225.0		0.0042	0.0319	

Item	Country	World rank	Quantity	Population[a]	Employment[b]	Arable land[c]	Quantity per capita	Productivity	
								Labor (Q/emp.)	Land (Q/ha)
Radios	Hong Kong	1	43.40	5.71	918.6		7.6007	47.2458	
(mln.,	USA	2	23.62	248.23	20935.0		0.0952	1.1283	
1986)	China	3	16.00	1112.30	32092.0		0.0144	0.4986	
	Japan	4	13.00	123.22	14250.0		0.1055	0.9123	
	Singapore	5	12.82	2.67	318.9		4.8015	40.2007	
	USSR	6	8.03	288.74	38225.0		0.0278	0.2101	
TVs	China	1	24.90	1112.30	32092.0		0.0224	0.7759	
(mln.,	USA	2	20.17	248.23	20935.0		0.0813	0.9635	
1986)	Bangladesh	3	14.99	114.72	n.a.		0.1307	n.a.	
	S. Korea	4	14.67	43.35	4416.0		0.3384	3.3220	
	Japan	5	14.27	123.22	14250.0		0.1158	1.0014	
	USSR	6	9.63	288.74	38225.0		0.0334	0.2519	
Wine	Italy	1	76.99	57.56	4639.0		1.3376	16.5962	
(mln.hl.,	France	2	73.50	55.99	4636.8		1.3127	15.8514	
1987)	Spain	3	36.70	39.42	2588.9		0.9310	14.1759	
	USSR	4	30.00	288.74	38225.0		0.1039	0.7848	
	Argentina	5	20.50	31.91	962.2		0.6424	21.3053	
Wool	Australia	1	0.822	16.45	1151.4		0.0500	0.7139	
(mmt,	USSR	2	0.463	288.74	38225.0		0.0016	0.0121	
1986)	N. Zealand	3	0.358	3.37	301.0		0.1062	1.1894	
	China	4	0.177	1112.30	32092.0		0.0002	0.0055	
	Argentina	5	0.155	31.91	962.2		0.0049	0.1611	
Energy consumption									
Electricity	USA	1	2727500	248.23			10987.79		
(mln.kWh,	USSR	2	1630200	288.74			5645.91		
1987)	Japan	3	699000	123.22			5672.78		
	Germany	4	537600	77.56			6931.41		
	China	5	497300	1112.30			447.09		
Coal	China	1	916.4	1112.30			0.82		
(mmt,	USA	2	751.8	248.23			3.03		
1987)	USSR	3	695.0	288.74			2.41		
	Germany	4	506.1	77.56			6.53		
	Poland	5	236.7	38.17			6.20		
Natural	USA	1	650686	248.23			2621.30		
gas	USSR	2	498847	288.74			1727.67		
(mln.m^3,	Germany	3	71180	77.56			917.74		
1988)	UK	4	65233	57.03			1143.84		
	Canada	5	57558	26.31			2187.69		
Crude	USA	1	4680	248.23			18.85		
petroleum	USSR	2	3692	288.74			12.79		
(mln.	Japan	3	1147	123.22			9.31		
barrels,	China	4	786	1112.30			0.71		
1988)	Germany	5	644	77.56			8.30		

[a]Population data (in million) 1989.

[b]All employment figures (in tousands) are from 1987 except: Brazil, Cuba, India, Sri Lanka, and USSR, 1986; Pakistan, Romania, and Turkey, 1985; and Argentina, 1984. Agricultural employment includes agriculture, fishing, forestry, and hunting. Employment for manufactured goods is only manufacturing employment.

[c]Arable land (in thousand ha) refers to land under temporary crops, temporary meadows for mowing or pasture, land under market of private gardens, land temporarily fallow or lying idle, and land cultivated with crops that occupy the land for long periods and need not be replanted after each harvest (1987).

Data sources for calculations in *Table 3.1*, FAO, and UN.

Appendix 3C

	GDP per capita[a]				Annual growth rates (in %)[b]			
	1900	1929	1950	1987	1900–1929	1929–1950	1950–1987	1900–1987
Austria	1615	2118	2123	8792	0.94	0.01	3.92	1.97
Canada	1808	3286	4822	12702	2.08	1.84	2.65	2.27
Germany	1558	2153	2508	9964	1.12	0.73	3.80	2.16
Japan	677	1162	1116	9756	1.88	−0.19	6.03	3.11
Netherlands	2146	3373	3554	9197	1.57	0.25	2.60	1.69
Sweden	1482	2242	3898	10328	1.44	2.67	2.67	2.26
UK	2798	3200	4171	9178	0.46	1.27	2.15	1.37
USA	2911	4909	6697	13550	1.82	1.49	1.92	1.78
China	401	444	338	1748	0.35	−1.29	4.54	1.71
India	378	403	359	662	0.22	−0.55	1.67	0.65
S. Korea	549	749	564	4143	1.08	−1.34	5.54	2.35
Taiwan	434	631	526	4744	1.30	−0.86	6.12	2.79
Argentina	1284	2036	2324	3302	1.60	0.63	0.95	1.09
Brazil	436	654	1073	3417	1.41	2.39	3.18	2.39
USSR	797	1044	2265	5948	0.94	3.76	2.64	2.34

[a]GDP per capita in international dollars at 1980 prices.
[b]Data for growth rate calculations compiled from Maddison (1989, p. 19).

Chapter 4

Inputs to the Soviet R&D Sector

The three main factors crucial to the strength of a national R&D sector are:

1. Education.
2. R&D personnel.
3. R&D financing.

All three are usually dependent on one another. Generally, the quantitative and qualitative niveau of one will affect that of one or both of the others. So, it follows that if the education system produces graduates with suitable knowledge and skills, then the stock of R&D personnel will be of respectable quality. Qualified and competent staff will attract more R&D financing through interesting and applicable project proposals and results. The expectations of respectable remuneration will attract more students to these fields to prepare them for a career in research and development, and so on.

This chapter deals with these three inputs in the Soviet R&D sector. In order to best demonstrate the size and extent of scientific resources in the former Soviet Union comparisons with Western and Eastern nations are made.

4.1 Education

Education is the process of acquiring knowledge by instruction of specific technical skills. These skills become an individual's human capital that can be sold in the market. The cumulative total of the individual human capital within the borders of a country represent that nation's stock of knowledge – a valuable national resource.

On the whole, education policies that sustain R&D should provide the higher levels of education that fulfill certain criteria.[1] These include the requirements to:

1. Respond to new needs at the national, local, and community levels.
2. Contribute to revitalizing the economy by producing suitable types of highly qualified manpower and to further training of the labor force in the context of rapidly changing technologies and economic conditions.
3. Sustain adequate levels of technological innovation through scientific research progress.

In a study on national innovation systems, Richard Nelson (1992) comes to the important conclusion (among others) that a distinguishing feature of the countries in his sample, which were sustaining competitive and innovative firms, was the presence of education and training systems that provide the firms with a flow of people with the requisite knowledge and skills.[2] Indeed, universities consciously train their students with an eye to industries' needs.

Consequently, education becomes the cornerstone of technical progress which is fundamental to economic growth and development. Technological advance demands from both consumers and producers require evermore information, training, and skills. Of course, *producers* include everyone from enterprise managers to workers on the shop floor, to research and development scientists, engineers, and technicians, to university scholars and assistants, and many, many more. Increased awareness on the part of producers and consumers of innovation and technology stimulates competition, raising the general standard of living and increasing the social benefit to all.

4.1.1 General education and literacy: The foundation for a scientific culture

The sheer size of the Soviet Union and before that the Russian Empire has throughout history diverted attention from the economic and technological situation of the nation. This becomes more clear when data are viewed on a per inhabitant basis. Estimates made in the past have revealed that Russian per capita national income in 1913 was only 15% of the United States, 22% of British, 33% of German, 50% of Italian and Austro–Hungarian levels, and was roughly equal to that of Bulgaria and Romania (Falkus, 1972, p. 12). These rankings appear to reasonably correspond to those based on GDP per capita from *Table 3.1*.

Numerous authors on this topic have alluded to a deleterious economic situation (as illustrated by the low per capita income) and a growing inferiority of military force as indicative of Russian relative technological backwardness with respect to Western Europe and the United States already in the late 1800s (for a comprehensive account, see Chirot, 1989). In fact, after early, impressive successes (such as the repulsion of the Napoleonic invasion in 1812) the Russian military faced humiliating losses to smaller but technologically superior foes in the Crimean War (1855) and the Russo–Japanese War (1904–1905); at these times Russia was experiencing economic stagnation (Gregory, 1982, p. 5).

Recognizing their country's increasing economic and technological backwardness, Russian policy makers of these early times reacted in a very similar fashion to that of their Soviet counterparts during the twentieth century who were responding to the growing technological gap between the USSR and the West. Compelled by all the disadvantages that accompany growing technological inferiority, a situation that had begun to cost many lives, the Russians reverted to a deliberate program of forced industrialization. The state, previously disinterested in industrialization and the factors that would have accompanied it, finally recognized the importance of a strong manufacturing sector built on solid technology (both domestic and imported), and a radical improvement in the level of general education and specialized training.[3]

The strong educational base in the former Soviet Union has already been referred to several times in this study. Statistics indicate that the general *educationalization* of the Soviet Union took place within a fairly limited period of time. In fact, in less than 50 years (by the late 1950s) the Soviet population went from being just over 20% literate to being 99% literate. A figure that still holds true today. This dramatic change is especially impressive considering that the various peoples spread across the great expanse of the Russian Empire were, by and large, illiterate before the Bolshevik Revolution.[4] By the end of the nineteenth century, the average literacy rate for the total population was 24% – 52.3% in the cities and only 19.6% in the countryside (Lane, 1985, p. 265). In spite of the high percentage for the towns the average percentage was low because Russia was a predominantly rural society at the time (see *Figure 4.1*). Regarding the difference between the sexes, a 1897 census revealed that in European Russia 35.8% of the men and only 12.4% of women were literate (Nove, 1989, p. 16).

Yet despite the striking increase in the average educational level (the completion of four years of formal, basic elementary education) of the population, there is little to indicate an increase in the attainment of higher

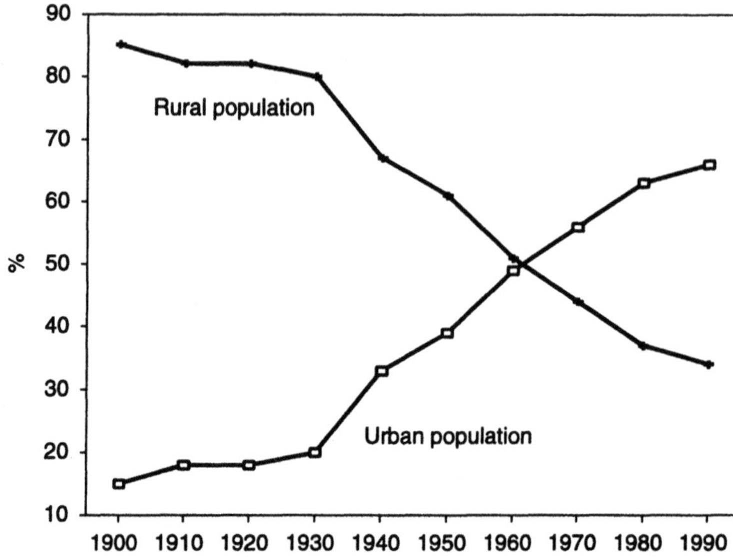

Figure 4.1. Soviet demographic change, 1900–1990.

education. The overall figures also do not reflect the past and current regional unevenness or the impact of urbanization. The schools in rural areas were often equipped with inferior physical and human capital to that in the urban educational institutions.[5] Therefore, the transition of the population from 85% rural in 1900 to 50% urban in 1960 and 66% urban in 1990 greatly contributed to the increase in the Soviet literacy rate during the twentieth century (see *Figure 4.1*). The figure shows a sudden and rapid increase in the rate of urbanization in the 1930s that coincides with Stalin's forced industrialization and mass education programs.[6]

As to the regional differences, data reveal gaping variations between the levels of literacy in the individual republics of the USSR. While the literacy rate had already attained a respectable 57% as the Union average in 1926, republics like Tadjikistan at 3.8%, Uzbekistan at 11.6%, Turkmenia at 14%, and Kirghizia at 16.5% were far below the average.[7] At the same time Russia, Belorussia, the Ukraine, and the Baltic republics were far ahead. By 1959, the average literacy rate for the Union was 98.5%, and the *lowest* was 95.4% in Turkmenia. The rural to urban distribution of the levels of literacy early in the century emphasizes the lack of any consistent formal education in the countryside. Even today, when rural education is better and literacy is said to be nearly 99%, the dropout rate in the first eight years of education is shockingly high, and academic studies are often disrupted by the need to help out on the farm. Although the numbers indicate a respectable improvement, they show only the widespread increase in basic abilities (up to four years of school). Therefore, the dispersion of elementary education was successful, but it did not indicate or insure an increase in the higher or specialized levels of education attained by the population at large, particularly on a regional basis. The reason for stressing these points is not to detract from the real successes of Soviet education policy, but to prevent certain misinterpretations of the data.

4.1.2 Enrollment in higher education

A comparison of the rates of enrollment in the USSR and the USA over the 90-year period from 1900 to 1990 illustrates the evolution of the extension of education in both countries (*Table 4.1*). In the United States, the numbers show a consistent level of general education with total enrollment in everything from primary to postgraduate education and training hovering around an average of 23.5% of the total population. While there are some troughs (19.9% in 1950, WWII effect) and some peaks (29.6% in 1970, baby-boom effect) in total US enrollment, the number of Soviet students in higher education as a percentage of total population or total enrollment climbed steadily throughout the decade; significant advances occurred in the 1960s and 1970s. Some 35% of the total was enrolled in part-time or correspondence education; this is a very high percentage of the total enrollment. This point is verified when looking at the difference between columns one and two for the USSR and columns one and two for the USA: 30.4% compared with 18.2%, respectively. This indicates that the USA had a much higher ratio of the population enrolled in full-time higher education than the USSR.

Perhaps some explanation is due to describe the structure of the Soviet education system. The children attended day-care and nursery schools, and then they began kindergarten. In the late 1970s, almost 80% of the children below age seven in urban areas were in some sort of preschool institution. In 1961 the figure had been as low as 10%, growing to 37% in 1974. This is an indication of the increase in families in which both parents were required to work outside the home to maintain an adequate standard of living. Children began attending primary school at age four. After four years their education may have been extended another four years to complete the first eight-year stage. Their education may then have been extended further to complete 11 years of schooling. Upon graduation from secondary school there were numerous possibilities for students, including technical trade schools (PTUs), secondary technical trade schools (SPTUs), secondary specialized schools (*technicums* or SSUZs), and general secondary school (the so-called full secondary education). Graduating from the last type of school was the direct route to enter universities (VUZs), institutes, or military academies after which there was the opportunity for a three-year postgraduate degree program under the auspices of the Academy of Sciences. It was also possible to move to technicums and technical schools after completing the general secondary school. Finally, it was possible to proceed to university education through full-time or part-time correspondence courses after completing any secondary education other than the general one. The students in the vocational schools received an education that was much closer to the demands of the market (especially industry) than those in the academic/university branch of the system.

The data for the Soviet Union substantiate the bold statements identifying astonishing growth and give evidence of the spread of education during the Stalin years. The cost of education was one of the main reasons why expenditure on "communal services" rose from 5% to approximately 10% of GNP in the 1930s (Maddison, 1969, p. 100). In 1900, only 6.3% of the population was enrolled in educational programs (compared with 22.5% in the USA); in 1930, early in Stalin's reign, only 7.0% (23.9% in the USA); by 1950 it was already 27.1% (seven percentage points more than the total in the same year in the USA); and in 1990 an impressive 35% of the Soviet population was enrolled compared with 23.2% in the USA (see *Table 4.1*). The absolute numbers for the USSR surged ahead of those in the USA in the 1930s and have stayed ahead until today (the dynamics of change are shown in *Figure 4.2*). But what was the quality of Soviet education?

Many students were in correspondence programs, and the continuing education courses for workers were also considered part of the educational program. The 1930s saw the establishment of many training schemes that were accounted for in the higher education statistics but were completely detached from the Soviet university system and would certainly not qualify for university or college ranking in the West.[8] These schemes included apprenticeship on the job, courses run by enterprises, technical colleges run by industries, the so-called FZU or factory training schools, and many others (Nove, 1989, p. 223). Problems that accompanied the rapid expansion included a severe shortage of well-trained instructors and a segregation and subsequent isolation of the various educational sectors with unclear responsibilities and coordination between them. Despite the disharmony, many programs did usually fulfill their goals.

Yet, in general, the percentage of the students in higher education in the USA as a percentage of the population has generally been above that in the USSR over the last 100 years.[9] In fact, while almost 22% of total enrollment in the USA is in higher education (though there is much discussion about the

Table 4.1. Education: USSR versus USA, 1900–1990.

	USSR			USA		
	Total enrollment as a % of population	Students in higher education as a % of population	Students in higher education as a % of total enrollment	Total enrollment as a % of population	Students in higher education as a % of population	Students in higher education as a % of total enrollment
1900	6.3	0.2	2.7	22.5	0.3	1.4
1910	6.6	0.2	2.7	21.3	0.4	1.8
1920	7.3	0.2	3.0	22.4	0.6	2.5
1930	7.0	0.3	3.9	23.9	0.9	3.7
1940	19.0	1.2	6.3	21.3	1.1	5.3
1950	27.1	1.9	7.0	19.9	1.5	7.6
1960	22.8	2.4	10.6	25.7	2.0	7.7
1970	31.9	4.6	14.5	29.6	4.2	14.2
1980	34.9	4.8	13.8	25.2	5.3	21.1
1990	35.0	4.6	13.2	23.2	5.0	21.5

Table 4.2. Scale of education in selected countries, 1989.

	USSR	USA	UK	Japan	Germany
Population (millions)	288.74	248.23	57.03	123.22	77.56
University students per 1,000 inhabitants	9.3	29.0	6.6	20.0	23.0
University teachers per 1,000 inhabitants	1.3	2.9	0.5	1.2	4.7
University students per teacher	7.0	10.0	11.0	18.0	5.0
University students per employed person	0.018	0.064	0.015	0.043	0.070
Education expenditure					
As a % of GNP	7.0	7.5	5.2	5.1	4.7
Per university student (US$1,000)	66.0	52.0	90.0	55.0	36.0
Per pupil regardless of level (US$1,000)	3.7	7.0	3.5	5.8	4.7

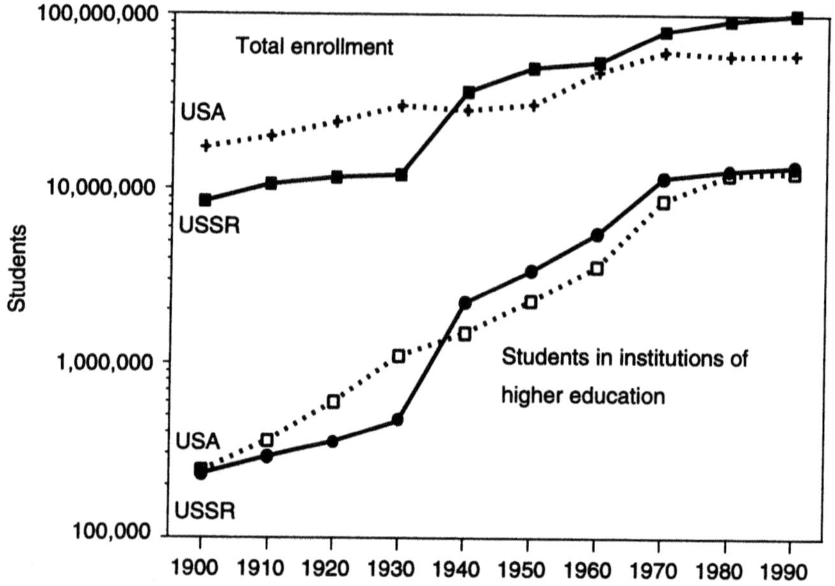

Figure 4.2. Expansion in education in the USSR and the USA, 1900–1990.

general level of the quality of this also), only 13% of total Soviet enrollment is in higher education (from *Table 4.1*).

The nemesis of Soviet higher education goes back to a Khrushchev decision in 1958 not to make full secondary education compulsory for all. Consequently, the availability of recruits for higher levels was indirectly limited in the past. Khrushchev's hope was to induce the majority of pupils to go on to technical training, either full-time or on the job, after completing a few years of compulsory education (Nove, 1989, p. 344). He felt higher education was to be part-time for most students, combined with useful work and preceded by at least 2 years of employment. Thus, the present figures representing students in higher and specialized secondary education contain approximately one-third or more who were correspondence, external, or continuing education students (many of whom do not complete their programs).

The scale of Soviet education, particularly higher education, grew to be very large indeed. By 1990, there were no fewer than 898 universities in the system, which put the USSR among the top eight countries in the world in raw numbers, with nearly 3 million university students in universities or other educational and training programs, and almost 400,000 university teachers; quite a considerable size for an organization whose role in the economy as a direct contributor to R&D output has been very minor in absolute terms and in comparison with other scientific institutions. These numbers still do not include the other institutions of tertiary education that mainly take the form of higher technical schools (called specialized secondary education) used to educate the specialized (or skilled) workers and technicians.

The 7% of GNP expenditures that went toward education in 1989, substantiate the Soviet dedication to maintaining a nearly 100% literacy rate and high general level of education (refer to *Table 4.2*). These are amazing accomplishments considering the country's cultural and regional diversities. The last two factors were surely part of the reason the Soviet Union needed to spend more on education than economically successful nations such as the UK, Japan, or Germany (as a percentage of GNP). Nevertheless, the expenditure per pupil regardless of level is among the lowest in the sample from *Table 4.2*. Unfortunately, this is the result of the costs required to maintain a large bureaucratic apparatus and directly affects the quality of educational infrastructure, especially in rural areas, as will be discussed later in this section.

Despite such substantial spending on education as a whole, the number of students enrolled in higher education per 100,000 inhabitants was clearly lower in the Soviet Union than in Western countries that actually spend less on education as a percentage of GNP. *Table 4.2* shows that only Britain had fewer students in higher education per 1,000 inhabitants than the Soviet Union; however, the UK figure does not include all the students in colleges and specialized higher educational institutions (i.e., those of finance and technology). This also explains the relatively low number of teachers per 1,000 inhabitants in the UK. The USA and Germany appear to staff their universities much more generously than the Soviets, though the German number has been inflated by the inclusion of teaching assistants and many lecturers from business and industry, usually on a part-time basis, that do not hold a steady appointment at the university. Although the USSR boasted some of the highest absolute enrollment in the world, it also had one of the lowest student to teacher ratios in university education (after adjusting the German number for the actual number of resident teachers). Normally, such a feature is very positive, but in the Soviet university system it was rather indicative of overstaffing, large bureaucracy, and inefficiency. Many professors or teachers are employed, even though the rate of growth in enrollment is, in fact, negative (see *Table 4.3*).

A final point revealed by the five-country comparison in *Table 4.2* divulges that the number of university students, and consequently graduates, per employed person was significantly lower in the USSR than in the other nations (including the UK, after an adjustment to include the students in colleges and institutes of specialized higher education). This certainly has implications for the quality of the labor force. In the United States, for

Table 4.3. Soviet graduating students by sectoral affiliation (in %) and growth in enrollment, selected years.

Sector	1970	1980	1988	1970–1980	1980–1988
	Higher education			*Annual growth rates*	
Industry & construction	34.0	37.1	34.0	3.5	–1.7
Agriculture	10.9	9.2	10.0	0.9	0.3
Transport & communication	4.5	5.0	5.1	3.7	–0.4
Economics & law	8.1	8.1	9.0	2.7	0.6
Health care, culture, & sport	6.8	7.4	8.2	3.5	0.6
Education	34.7	32.2	32.7	1.8	–0.5
Art & cinematography	1.1	1.0	1.1	2.3	0.6
Total	100.0	100.0	100.0	2.6	–0.7
	Specialized secondary education			*Annual growth rates*	
Industry & construction	40.5	37.0	33.9	1.2	–1.5
Agriculture	14.0	16.4	15.4	3.8	–1.2
Transport & communication	7.6	8.2	6.7	2.8	–2.9
Economics & law	12.9	14.7	13.9	3.5	–1.1
Health care, culture, & sport	13.1	11.9	13.1	1.1	1.6
Education	10.2	9.6	14.3	1.5	4.7
Art & cinematography	1.8	2.1	1.9	4.1	–1.5
Total	100.0	100.0	100.0	2.1	–0.4

Source: Figures for higher education and specialized secondary education adapted from Ryan (1990, p. 145); growth rates calculated by the author.

example, only 35% of scientists graduating from university are directly employed as R&D personnel, 45% are employed in related activities, and the rest (20%) are employed in completely unrelated activities (Schneider, 1991, p. 11). These university graduates contribute to the quality of the labor force and market activity by becoming involved in fields such as marketing, communication, and trade.

The USSR did portray a better picture than other Eastern European countries with respect to enrollment (see *Figure 4.3*). The number of Soviet students per capita in tertiary education in 1989 were more than double those in Hungary and Romania, and significantly above those in Czechoslovakia, Poland, and Bulgaria. But this view marks the Soviet level only as the best of the communist/socialist bloc. In truth, it was below the per capita figures of Germany, Japan, the UK, and far below those of the USA. The United States is the leader among these nations and is preparing a large, educated generation for the work force.

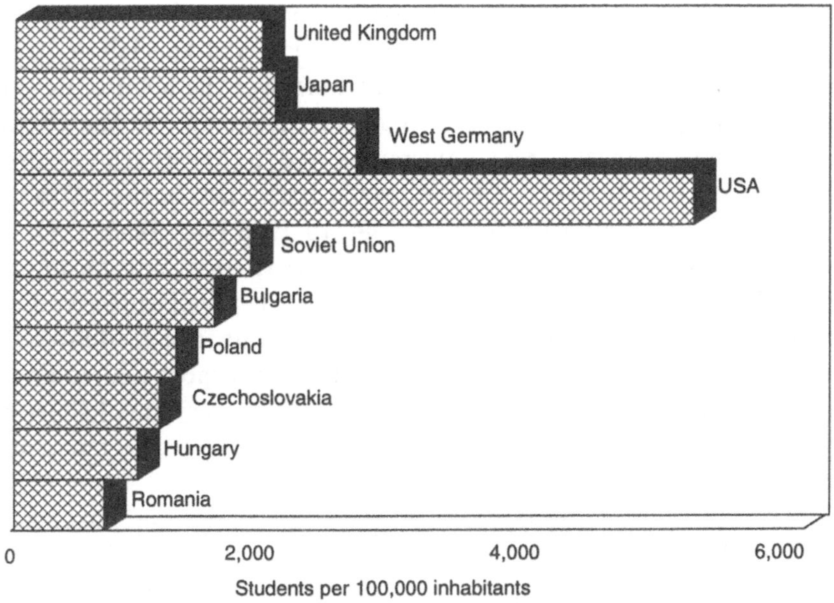

Figure 4.3. Students in tertiary education, 1989 (in selected countries).

4.1.3 Higher education and fields of study

In the past, graduates of higher educational institutions in the USSR had been directed and ensuingly biased in their areas of specialization. The fields of study, in which Soviet students have traditionally been concentrated, do not appear to be especially contiguous to the goal of establishing the intellectual basis for a reforming economy on the path of transition to a market economy. The past focus had been on particular national, or rather party, priorities. There had clearly been an emphasis (and continues to be) in the fields of industry and construction and education. Other areas that would fall under the definition of the service sector, like transportation and communication, economics and law, health care, culture, and sport, were characterized by a distinct relative lack of graduates. Part of the explanation for this trait was the Marxist and Soviet-style socialist ideology that services were unproductive and not conducive to the kind of growth targeted by central authorities. Another part of the explanation lies in the Soviet government's policy to purposely avoid developments in fields that could lead to mass, uncontrolled distribution of ideas that were not those of the state and the Communist Party.

Upon analyzing the data, some doubts seem to arise with respect to how well prepared, in terms of higher education and specialized training, the coming generations will be in order to take over the helm in developing a modern-style growth economy in a market environment. In the USSR, the growth of total graduates from universities and technical schools dropped drastically from clearly over +2% per year in both cases in the 1970s to −0.7 and −0.4% per year respectively from 1980 to 1988 (see *Table 4.3*). Studies affiliated with the sectors of the economy that constitute an important share of GNP (i.e., industry and construction and agriculture) continue to be favorite fields of study, albeit with a reduced number of graduates. Areas especially important to a modern economy (i.e., transport and communications and economics and law) must make due with a very small share of the total graduates, which have simultaneously experienced the most marked decline during the 1980s.

Some experts have charged that there has been an ensuing overproduction of engineers, many of whom end up performing tasks that would have required much less training. This may have potentially been a more serious problem than would appear at first glance. Education, like every other sector of the Soviet economy, was supply, and not demand, driven. Statistics indicate a tendency for the output of the higher levels of education to overshoot and grow faster than the demand for specialized skills. So, in spite of the declining total number of graduates in absolute terms, the rate of students completing higher education exceeded the rate at which industry was converting from manual to mechanized production. The motivation of those employed was subsequently adversely affected and the perverse pay differentials between some educated technical and manual workers implied that the private financial rate of return to education was low (IMF *et al.*, 1991, vol. 2, p. 169). In the West it is the rule that more education leads to higher monetary rewards in the market place. Lastly, the distortion arising from the older cohorts with usually inferior formal education to that of younger cohorts blocking the latter's promotion possibilities due to seniority has led to inefficiency and adverse motivational effects, as well as being a waste of educational investment.

Interestingly enough, there are two similarities in course orientation in the USSR and the USA. US graduate enrollment is also highest in the engineering field, though in the US case only narrowly ahead of the social and life sciences. Interest in engineering appears to be falling, especially over the last five years among American students, but it is a favorite of foreign students in the USA. So much so that they constitute 35% of enrollment and have prevented the level of total enrollment from declining. The second similarity to the Soviet situation is a real decline in graduates of the social sciences in the USA. On the other hand, contrary to the developments in the past decade in the USSR, the number of total graduates in all fields has been steadily increasing in the USA. If the number of degrees granted at the first level of higher education is considered the picture changes somewhat. In the 1980s, close to 40% of Soviet first degrees granted were in engineering, while it was 6.5% in the USA, 19% in Japan, 16% in the UK, and 14% in Germany (NSB, 1985, p. 192). The ratio of all other graduates with first degrees conferred (mainly humanities and social sciences) to engineers was 15 to 1 in the USA, but only 2.5 to 1 in the USSR during the same period.

4.1.4 Functions and status of higher education and its role in R&D

Essential requirements for a successful transition to and development of a sound market foundation are intellectual resources. The state of more advanced education doesn't seem to reflect this necessity. One of the main reasons for this is that a *Kultura* job has lost its past appeal. Since 1935 when Stalin ordered that the pay and privileges for the better-qualified and well-trained persons were to be enhanced, those with higher education status have enjoyed special positions in society. In the last years of the Soviet Union, graduates or "beneficiaries" of higher education such as teachers, medical personnel, offices staffs, librarians, engineers, and technologists generally received less pay and privileges than skilled workers or entrepreneurs (Nove, 1986, p. 34). "Science and scientific services" was by far the top monthly wage-earner category well into the 1970s. In 1940, the average monthly salaries for employees in this sector were 138% of those in industry, 214% of agricultural workers and employees, 156% of construction workers, and 135% of those in transportation (GOSKOMSTAT, 1988, pp. 196–199). By the late 1980s, the level of pay in science and scientific services had fallen to 97%, 108%, 84%, and 90% of the other sectors mentioned above, respectively.

Many potential or developing young academics or technicians have recognized the possible rewards from entrepreneurship or have been commissioned by new entrepreneurs and are thus a loss to the formal education system. Ever-growing numbers are not completing a formal higher education. This situation is comparable with that in the United States when professional sport organizations draft more and more college athletes before they have completed their previously compulsory four-year education. As a result, the Russians must not only worry about the "brain drain" to the West, but also about the "future-academics drain" to private enterprise at home.

Education policy in the USSR was essentially oriented toward a teaching and instructional function which, depending on the measures considered, was more or less successful. Due to various tensions and conflicts, the research element had been organized separately in specific research units in universities or in special research institutes, if it was not neglected all together. While the importance of research activity and education has given the functions of particularly higher educational institutions new proportions and strategic value in determining economic, cultural, and political features of societies in the West, the Soviet system basically served as an extension of political values of the ruling Communist Party. Pursuing research was only of minor interest.

What has been referred to with the misleadingly homogeneous term of higher education in this chapter, has actually been separated into three institutional elements in the USSR: the Academy of Sciences, the Higher Educational Institutions, and the Higher Party Schools (Lane, 1985, p. 292). The institutes of the Academy of Sciences (already described in Section 3.2) have primarily been responsible for conducting research in the various arts and sciences. This research has predominantly been of a fundamental nature and has often been criticized as being conducted detached from industry and market needs. Other than advising and/or teaching postgraduate students, members of the academy have had little active contact with universities; the former's almost exclusive preoccupation is with research.

The Higher Educational Institutions consisted of universities and institutes or polytechnics, with the former boasting a commanding theoretical component (which was largely planned by directives from above). Although both conducted some research (more in the institutes than in the universities) and taught some postgraduates, their main task was the training of undergraduates, though they have often done this independently of one another. The main problems, discrepancies, and often diverging educational objectives arose due to the differing subordination: the universities were subordinate to the Ministry of Higher and Specialized Education (see *Figure 3.5*), and the institutes were usually directly subordinate to production ministries or in some cases to the Council of Ministers. Although the practice has recently been dropped, graduates of VUZs and SSUZs were subject to administrative assignment (IMF *et al.*, 1991, p. 168). Thus there was no real competition for positions upon graduation as is characteristic of labor markets in Western societies.

The decade-long attempts to promote access to higher educational institutions by giving more prominence to part-time and correspondence study (already close to 50% of enrollment) may have improved the average levels in selected cases, but more likely it has led to a watering down of the overall quality of instruction, learning, and therefore also graduates. The education received in the correspondence and part-time programs is repeatedly stated to be of a lesser quality than that in full-time day programs. In addition, among the part-time and correspondence students dropout rates were high, so the Soviet situation compared with the situation in Western Europe, Japan, and the USA in terms of relative number and quality of graduates from higher educational programs is even worse than that portrayed by the numbers presented for student enrollment in *Table 4.2*.

In addition, there is an inherent conflict between the strict control of educational and research facilities and interactions with sectors of the economy (not to mention with one another) and with the need for independence and creativity that are prerequisites for successful research and innovation. The latter requires a certain autonomy for intellectual effort and the preservation of the institutional identity of particular interest groups – requirements which were not just frowned upon by Soviet-style socialist ideology, but also cleverly prevented.

The USA probably has the system most contrary to that which operated in the Soviet Union. The American education system is more diverse, disparate, decentralized, and dynamic than most others in the world. The various public and private institutions have offered instruction in an overwhelming number of fields for secondary students, undergraduates, postgraduates, and professionals. Beside their teaching role, the higher educational institutions, particularly the universities, play a key part in the national innovation system as providers of R&D. University science and engineering and science-based industries grew up together, explaining to a large extent the usually very close traditional links between academic science and industry science (Nelson, 1987, p. 86). In many areas, the universities have provided industry with suitably educated personnel and ideas about products and processes.

The continuous exchange between the two sectors in the US economy is enhanced by academic scientists and engineers acting as consultants to industry and industry scientists advising academic departments. More and more, industrial firms are directly funding university laboratories to gain privileged access to new scientific and research findings. Numerous academics have also been known to establish and operate private firms along side their duties as researchers and professors at universities. Often, university research is basic science oriented and somewhat theoretical, but in such a way that it points the way for industrial R&D, which produces the new technologies, processes, or products, to be productive. Thus, at times the university influence will only be indirect, but it is always present. Finally, the universities draw on their R&D activities in instructing their students and preparing them to contribute in some form to the academic, industry, or supporting sectors. This dynamic process has integrated university R&D into the national innovation system and has kept much of its work close to the needs of the market.

On the whole, higher education and research institutes were much more concentrated in the USSR (usually in large cities) than in the USA. Research centers of excellence in the USSR included Moscow, Leningrad, and Novosibirsk, with its relatively new higher educational complex, Akademgorod (Cole, 1984, p. 271). This left the potential users of academic ideas and personnel geographically very distant from the producers. A problem not easily overcome in a nation that was characterized by strict mobility and communication controls, not to mention an inadequate infrastructure. In addition, the state was solely responsible for research projects. Part of the reason for the dispersion of higher educational institutions and research centers in the United States is the active role of the private sector (often supported in part by government programs) to provide such services. Close vicinity to educational centers has had an influence on the geography and growth of some notable industrial sectors, and vice versa.

The Higher Party Schools in the USSR were, not surprisingly, subordinate to the Central Committee of the Communist Party of the Soviet Union and had only a minor quantitative bearing (Lane, 1985, p. 293). These schools focused more on social sciences, and the little research done was geared to the party's specific political programs.

Therefore, some have gone as far as to imply that higher education in the USSR was geared to knowledge and comprehension, rather than to analysis and evaluation.[10] The Soviet system of higher education, like many other state bodies, had become an administrative leviathan during the period of the planned economy. The system was also unmanageable and had almost become insensitive to policy changes due to its complex and unintelligible network of subordination. Even after attempts at a partial reform in 1984 and the presence of an elite section which equals the quality of any in the world, the education system found itself unable to cope with the demands for a flexible and technologically aware society (Sakwa, 1990, p. 292).

While conflicts between the All-Union and the republican governments added to the bureaucratic problem facing the system of higher education, ministries and departments also added to the confusion by running their own institutions for training people with special skills, as in agriculture and medicine. This led to considerable amounts of duplication and inefficiencies. Just a few years ago, 74 ministries and departments were involved in some manner, but 30 of these only ran one or two institutions (Rich, 1986, p. 716). With the advent of *perestroika*, the State Enterprise Law of 1987 and the drive toward the necessity to become self-financing made the financing of the little amount of university research that was being done more uncertain than ever before. Both universities and institutes feared that enterprises would be unwilling to invest in academically produced R&D, no matter how applied it may have been, due to the shortage of funds.

In 1986, concrete plans were being drawn up to give the universities a more prominent place in the pattern of Soviet research, currently dominated by academy and ministry institutes. Investments in equipment and physical infrastructure (such as computing facilities and more that are essential for a modern education), as well as salaries for professors, were identified as critical areas that should be improved as soon as possible.[11] The present pay structure discourages some of the best scholars and scientists from following a career in the university system. Closer links between schools and universities were a central part in the new trend. Previously, Soviet educationists had the desire to qualify as many school-leavers as possible for higher education, but this led to less-qualified students securing places in higher education at the expense of others. In order to fulfill the planned order from superior levels of the hierarchy regarding the number of graduates required, universities and other institutions of higher education tended to recruit less competent students to maintain their numbers.

As societies become more advanced and complicated, the challenges facing the education system increase. Particularly at higher levels, universities and the education and research they provide grow steadily more important. With the globalization of research, technology, industry, business, and essentially whole economies, the need arises to modify the requirements of the higher education system and its associated research function as well as to redefine the university/industry interface which has been intensified in recent years in the Western nations. This will be more closely investigated in Chapter 5.

4.2 R&D Personnel

The personnel working in research and development represent that stock of knowledge and ability in an economy which is fundamental to technological change and performance. The R&D staff contributes in countless ways to the welfare and technological progress of a nation and has an impact on society disproportionate to its numbers (NSB, 1987, p. 52). R&D personnel, usually designated to be made up of scientists and engineers, is crucial to the more or less successful functioning of an advanced industrial society.

An R&D staff's abilities largely determine the bounds to the strengths and weaknesses of homegrown technological potential.

The activities in which the scientific and technical personnel is engaged indicate the way in which the economy allocates its stock of human resources and consequently determines priority areas. The activities are measured by the number and proportion of those engaged in performing R&D, teaching, and various sorts of other related activities. The special attributes regarding R&D personnel and its functions identify it as both producing and disseminating its work. In general, these activities include product and process innovation, quality control, productivity enhancement, basic research to advance the understanding of nature, training future scientists and engineers, and contributing to the scientific and technological literacy of a nation. A technically well-trained work force is an essential contribution to scientific, technological, as well as industrial progress.

The number of R&D personnel, like the financing of R&D, is a measure of national R&D efforts. The former, as a measurement of physical units, is not complicated by changes in currency values internationally and over time (OECD, 1989, p. 22). Very precise comparisons are hampered by different definitions for units of measure, the quality of education, the nature of a particular job, the definition of a specific title, and so on. Nevertheless, the number of scientists and engineers is commonly regarded as a simple indicator for the orientation of science and technology policy, the stock of knowledge, its trend and potential.

4.2.1 Total numbers of scientists and engineers

The number of Soviet scientists and engineers (S&E) reported to have worked in research and development is astonishing. Not only did it more than triple since 1965 when it was 110% of the US level, but it was already over 1.65 million in 1987, a shade under twice the American number (see *Table 4.4*).[12] Although the numbers of Japanese S&E were half of the US S&E and only one-quarter of the Soviet S&E in absolute terms, they dominated the growth statistics, registering an unparalleled 8.06% annual growth rate for the period 1965–1975, 3.71% in the subsequent interval, and 4.7% in the 1980s, which resulted in almost a 6% yearly increase from 1965 to 1987. West Germany was probably the most consistent country, with the stock of R&D staff growing at an annual rate of 4.22% per year between 1965 and 1987. The growth was strong and never drastically different to the foregoing period. All countries, including the USSR but excluding the United Kingdom, had growth rates in the 1980s above or very near the OECD and European Communities' average rates of 3.5% for the early 1980s.[13] Yet, while most of the

OECD and EC countries were experiencing an improvement over pre-1980 years, the USSR was facing a relative decline.

Neglecting later developments for the moment, the early numbers of the Japanese leader were only approached by those in the Soviet Union, which could also boast almost 8% annual growth in the early years. On the one hand, this was the realization of the planned employment of the substantial increase in graduates of the science and engineering disciplines that were the product of the education policy during the Stalin years and afterward, and, on the other hand, the forced industrialization and the required mass (but relatively simple) technology needed to support it. In aggregate terms, the USSR employed 3.2 times more S&E in R&D in 1983 than the European Communities, and already 86% of the entire OECD total. In fact, the Soviet figure was approximately 25% of the world total by 1989. The Soviet numbers certainly also include technicians working in research and development to one extent or another.

An interesting aspect regarding the dynamics of growth of the aggregate stock of S&E personnel in the USSR is the successive reduction in the annual growth rates during the selected periods in *Table 4.4*. In the second and third time interval, 1975–1981 and 1981–1987, the growth clearly successively declined (as it did in the UK), while it increased in Japan and West Germany in the third period. In fact, the results of the growth rate analysis imply that while Japan, West Germany, and the United States were arming themselves with a pronounced increase in the stock of their total S&E personnel in R&D, the Soviets were relinquishing their previously so heralded emphasis.[14]

This drop in the growth rate of employment in the Soviet-style planned economic system has some implications for technological developments and modern economic growth in the USSR and for changes in the Russia of tomorrow. These are relatively unclear due to the questionable levels of productivity and the quality of scientists and engineers in the former Soviet-style system. Nevertheless, experts reporting on the situation in Soviet S&E employment have revealed a preponderance of older people (certainly true in the Academy of Sciences, see *Table 3.4*, and in general, see *Figure 4.5*), and too many relatively low-grade engineers and too few researchers in the developing sciences such as biology and chemistry (Sakwa, 1990, p. 291).

One reason for the slowdown may be the continuing emphasis on heavy industry. This old paradigm of economic growth and development has been based on often simple or sometimes even obsolete technological standards with respect to today's potential, has ignored the changing demands and needs of (primarily civilian) consumers, and has prevented the establishment of a service sector as we know it in the West. All these factors influence the demand for S&E personnel engaged in R&D, and the demand for their particular specializations. The relative fall in the rate of increase in employment of S&E in research and development most certainly could and will affect the number and potential of scientists and engineers who will be required as essential elements in charting the transition to a new techno-economic phase of development. Their relative decline will also affect the availability of skilled personnel as instructors at higher levels of education in efforts to secure future generations of specialists.

When drawing conclusions about the relative levels of R&D personnel in different countries the question of comparability inevitably crops up. The Soviet science and technology concept designated everyone as a scientific worker in research and development if he or she had an advanced degree in science and engineering, or was conducting research in a scientific establishment, or was teaching in a higher educational institution. Therefore, the number of almost 1.7 million Soviet scientists and engineers engaged in R&D in 1989 should rather be compared to the total number of scientists and engineers in S&E jobs in other countries.[15] For the USA, this number came to no less than over 4.6 million in 1988 (the ratio of scientists to engineers being 1 to 1.31). The numbers for other nations would also be relatively higher, making the Soviet amount look not as spectacular as it seemed at first glance. Therefore, the absolute total of S&E engaged in R&D in the USSR should not be overvalued.

Soviet scientists and engineers were known to be active in numerous positions, for many of which they were either overqualified or not adequately trained. Frequently, they also held some type of management post. Again, this would call for a comparison with the total number of scientists and engineers in S&E jobs in the other countries. In the United States in 1986, for example, only about 40% of scientists and engineers worked directly in research (basic and applied) and development, while circa 16% were in management (other than R&D), 8% in teaching, 13% in production and inspection, 10% in statistical work and computing, and 10% in other activities that included activities such as consulting, sales, and professional services (NSB, 1987, p. 218). Perhaps then, a preferable measure to use when comparing the human resources in R&D between nations would be the S&E in R&D per 10,000 workers in the labor force population.

4.2.2 Scientists and engineers as a percentage of the labor force

The percentage of the labor force employed in R&D as researchers has long been on the rise in most OECD and Eastern European countries. *Table 4.5* shows the changes for a selected group of nations including the USSR. While

Table 4.4. Total number of scientists and engineers (S&E) engaged in R&D (1965–1987) and annual growth rates (selected countries and periods).

	S&E personnel (thousands)[a]				Annual growth rates (in %)			
	1965	1975	1981	1987	1965–1975	1975–1981	1981–1987	1965–1987
USSR[b]	541.6	1,122.5	1,400.6	1,654.6	7.56	3.76	2.82	5.21
USA	494.6	527.7	683.7	832.2[c]	0.65	4.41	3.33	2.39
UK	49.9	80.5	95.7	99.5[c]	4.90	2.92	0.65	3.19
Japan	117.6	255.2	317.5	418.3	8.06	3.71	4.70	5.94
W. Germany	61.0	103.7	124.7	151.5	5.45	3.12	3.30	4.22

[a]The figures include all scientists and engineers engaged in R&D on a full-time equivalent basis (except for Japan, whose data include persons primarily employed in R&D excluding social scientists, and the UK, whose data include only the government and industry sectors).
[b]The figures for the USSR consist of the arithmetic mean of the high and low estimates from the NSB (1985, p. 186); 1984 and 1985 data are estimated; and 1987 data are taken from data from 1989.
[c]The figures for 1987 are estimated.
Sources: Data collected and adapted from NSB (1985, p. 186; 1989, pp. 260–262) and Gokhberg and Mindely (1991, p. 5).

Table 4.5. Scientists and engineers engaged in R&D per 10,000 workers in the labor force population (1965–1987) and annual growth rates (selected countries and periods).

	S&E personnel[a]				Annual growth rates (in %)			
	1965	1975	1981	1987	1965–1975	1975–1981	1981–1987	1965–1987
USSR[b]	46.5	82.7	94.8	103.9	5.92	2.31	1.84	3.90
USA	64.7	55.3	61.9	66.2[c]	–1.56	1.90	1.35	0.11
UK	19.6	31.1	35.8	35.5[c]	4.73	2.37	–0.17	2.87
Japan	24.6	47.9	55.6	67.4	6.89	2.52	3.92	4.92
W. Germany	22.6	38.6	45.5	52.3	5.50	2.78	2.82	4.08

Notes and sources: Refer to *Table 4.4*.

four of the countries experienced impressive growth before 1975, with the *lowest* annual growth rate of 4.73% in the UK and 5.5% in West Germany, and the highest in the USSR (5.92%) and Japan (6.89%), the US rate was clearly negative. During this time the American economy was employing relatively more non-R&D personnel in favor of scientists and engineers.

The trend reversed in the United States after 1975 when strong positive growth was registered and the amount of S&E engaged in R&D per 10,000 workers in the labor force population grew from 55.3 in 1975 to 66.2 in 1986. Over the same interval the other nations continued to experience an increase in the numbers of S&E per 10,000 workers in the labor force population, but at a much slower rate. So, while the USA was picking up the tempo in recruiting S&E, the other four slacked off. Japan and West Germany successfully picked up the pace again in the third period (1981–1987), but the USSR and the UK could not. The former's rate remained respectably positive at 1.84%, but the latter's dipped to –0.17%.

For the entire period of more than two decades from 1965 to 1986, the results are also quite interesting. The figures for the number of scientific workers in research and development per 10,000 workers in the labor force population in the Soviet Union stand alone; initially 46.5 (72% of the US level) in 1965, it had out-distanced all competitors by 1975 and, in 1986, reached 1.54 times the Japanese, 1.57 times the American, 1.97 times the West German, and 2.93 times the British levels. Although the Japanese had only 24.6 scientists and engineers engaged in R&D in 1965, compared with 64.7 in the USA (both per 10,000 workers in the labor force population), the Japanese had surpassed the US total in 1986 (66.2) with their own distinguishing total of 67.4 – an annual growth rate of almost 5%. West Germany and the USSR more than doubled their S&E participation in the labor force over the 21 years, with 4.08% and 3.90% annual growth respectively.

At the end of the interval, all countries (other than the UK, probably for the same reason mentioned in note 14) had more persons employed as researchers than the OECD average of about 50 of every 10,000 actual or potential workers. The favorable aggregate number for the United States is somewhat misleading because the annual growth over the whole period was a mere 0.11%. However, if the period is divided (as explained above) it becomes clear that the low growth was due to the negative developments between 1965 and 1975 (ignoring the absolute increase for the moment). The Americans were far ahead of the other nations in 1965 and maintained a very consistent and distinguished level of scientists and engineers in the work force.

A comparison of the annual growth of the total labor force indicates that except in the US case, every nation saw the percentage of the labor force employed in R&D as researchers increase significantly more rapidly than the annual growth in the labor force itself in each period. In fact, the time in which West Germany realized its most dramatic increase in R&D employment (5.5% per year between 1965 and 1975) was simultaneously the period in which the size of the labor force actually shrank by 0.06% per year. This implies that the increase of R&D workers per 10,000 actual or potential workers was also influenced by the slow general growth of the labor force (see Appendix 4A). This fact puts a damper on the impressive figures from Japan and West Germany; yet, it correspondingly improves the perspective of the low numbers for the UK between 1981 and 1986, and for all the periods for the USA. The United States has maintained a leading and very respectable balance of scientists and engineers engaged in R&D per 10,000 workers in the labor force population despite the substantial expansion, over 2% per annum between 1965 and 1986, of its already immense labor force. The Soviet Union, with the only labor force close to the American in absolute size (actually almost 30% larger), could not register successive periods of improved growth in the share of S&E employment, despite reduced rates of annual growth in the labor force (1.54% in 1965–1975, 1.42% in 1975–1981, and 0.83% in 1981–1986) for the successive periods in *Table 4.5*.

The areas of occupation of scientists and engineers are essentially a reflection of their educational specialization. Therefore, both in the former USSR and in the USA most employed scientific personnel have been concentrated in the technical fields of science. In 1986, 49.5% in the USSR and 52.7% in the USA were employed in technical fields of science, though the American share had fallen by 6.1 percentage points from 10 years earlier and the Soviet number increased by 0.8 percentage points over the same interval.[16]

This can be interpreted as an indication of the changing priorities in the USA and the largely continuing emphasis in the USSR. The US decline has been accompanied by an important shift in structure to important fields, particularly for new high-technology development, such as aeronautics, chemistry, electronics, and materials science. In Japan, the number of S&E engaged in R&D per 10,000 employees was significantly higher than in the USA in chemicals, new materials (i.e., ceramics and nonferrous metals), and electrical machinery. The overall share of Soviet specialists in the mathematical, computer, and physical sciences category declined over the period, but the number of S&E in the first two subcategories increased – still by far not like in the USA, where the general category could already boast over one-fifth of the S&E employed in 1986. Despite the decreases in the shares of life science graduates in the related fields of occupation in both countries, the absolute totals of US biologists, medical scientists, and

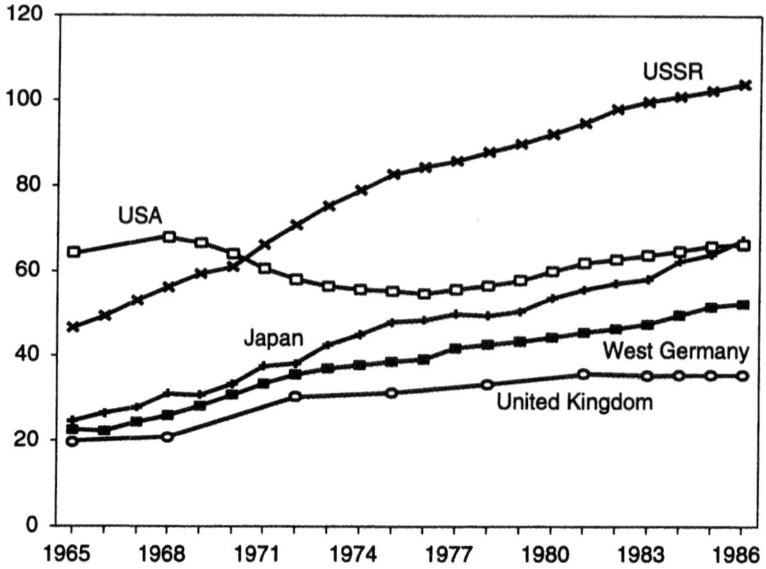

Figure 4.4. International comparison of the dynamics and growth of scientists and engineers engaged in R&D per 10,000 workers in the labor force population, 1965–1986.

agronomists almost doubled, while their growth rates had drastically slowed in the USSR.

Figure 4.4 compares the relative R&D efforts of five leading nations from 1965 to 1986, as a proportion of the labor force employed as scientists or engineers. These data allow one to draw a tentative conclusion that over the last decade or so there have been substantial increases in both absolute and relative terms in R&D efforts of the primary R&D-performing countries. All countries other than the United Kingdom, which currently appears to be in a stagnating phase, have increased the relative emphasis they place on R&D. In addition, the growing size of the R&D work force was accompanied by growth in national expenditures on R&D. This topic is discussed in Section 4.3.

4.2.3 The role, status, and activities of scientists and engineers

The importance assigned to scientists and engineers has, in most cases, been a cornerstone of technological advance and modern economic growth. The USSR was the only leading R&D-performing nation that could not convert the vast investment in human resources in R&D into a complementary improvement in the general level of technological change – there was an inherent inefficiency in their supply-driven desire to increase R&D personnel. Japan, West Germany, the USA, and the UK have all provided examples of more, effective production with less personnel. Therefore, the question arises whether such a high level of employment of scientists and engineers in R&D as that in the USSR was justifiable. Of course, this may be an indication of the massive quantity of latent capacity in the former Soviet R&D sector that could influence the global R&D market were it truly useful and actually harnessed for productive purposes.

The Soviet Union was clearly also the center of R&D activity in Eastern Europe. Almost eight times as many persons were employed in the Soviet *science research* sector than in the total of all the smaller Eastern European countries in that sector in 1988 (WIIW, 1989, p. 67); yet, the Soviet population was only three times their cumulative total. Based on employment statistics, most of the scientific activities in Eastern Europe were centralized in the USSR (part of its "big brother" politics), and within the USSR the activities were further concentrated in three locations: Moscow, Leningrad, and Novosibirsk. This was partially a function of the strictly controlled mobility, or rather immobility to more accurately describe it, that was a practice of USSR science and technology policy. Two of the larger employers of scientific personnel in Eastern Europe, Czechoslovakia and Poland, appeared to be forced or voluntarily change their policies; annual growth rates for employment of scientists and engineers had dropped practically to zero in Czechoslovakia in recent years and the Polish average annual rates were –2.34% between 1975 and 1988.[17] There are two alternative explanations for these trends:

1. The smaller Eastern European nations had realized the need to adapt to changing economic conditions and technological needs in the face of inevitable economic transformation. Their size gave them an advantage in flexibility, allowing them to put a brake on nonmarket-based growth and subsequently to reorient policy.
2. The Soviet central authorities were essentially the main source of demand for scientific and technological production – the sole market. Most of the scientific and research projects were in some way the product of Soviet-style science and technological policy or industrial policy. Thus, recognizing the overstaffing at home and based on the pride of maintaining an immense scientific community (not to mention the inability to reduce it), fewer projects were transplanted to the smaller neighbors, forcing them to rationalize earlier (though many of them may have worked more efficiently and effectively than their Soviet counterparts).

The complete answer presumably lies in a combination of these two points.

The issue of labor mobility is an important one with respect to R&D staffing. Due to strict central controls that required passports for internal travel and government permission to relocate, Soviet scientists and engineers, like the rest of their society, were very immobile. Unlike the situation in the USA and most other Western industrialized countries, Soviets got *locked* in very early in their careers to permanent assignments, with respect to location as well as field of study (Gamota, 1987, p. 233). Academy and branch ministry research institutes practically drafted skilled individuals directly from the educational system; these were the sites where higher educational degrees were completed. At many branch institutes the scientist became so specialized in a particular field, he or she was unable to use those skills anywhere else known to him or her.

In addition, the organization one worked for generally supplied housing, so to move away meant to surrender this practically free accommodation to the organization. There was no real housing market in the USSR; a remote possibility existed of obtaining quarters in the new location on the black market for housing, but the prices were usually beyond the reach of even a scientific researcher. Therefore, if there was a move in store for an individual, it was most probably an ordered one from the central authorities, but even then people were unwilling to leave centers like Moscow.[18]

This separation of fields under different hierarchies led the various ministries, academies, and state committees to have institutes of their own, many doing complementary or even overlapping work. All this required large staffs, many of whom were duplicating jobs in another organization. Each institute wanted to be self-reliant ("reinvent-the-wheel" theory) and did not want to share information,[19] because each had to negotiate with the center to obtain as large a financial allocation as possible. The idea was that big projects required big staffs and would draw big budget allocations. However, it has become clear that this type of isolation between co-workers could not lead to productive synergism in a new field and impeded technology transfer (for example, basic research results being used for developing new technology to be used for applications).

As already described in the section entitled Actors in Soviet R&D Policy (Section 3.2.4), Soviet R&D personnel was employed in the Academy of Sciences (its research and educational institutes), universities and other institutes of higher education, the institutes of GKNT, and the institutes directly subordinate to some industrial ministries. In each case the S&E were employees of the state. Until 1987, there had been no official private R&D activity at all.

Table 4.6. Employment of scientists and engineers by sector (% of total).

USSR (1989)		USA (1988)	
Institutes of higher education	10	Academic R&D	19
Academy of Sciences	13	Government and nonprofit R&D	5
Branch ministry institutes	77	Industry R&D	76
Total	100	Total	100

The Academy of Sciences, which concentrated predominantly on fundamental research, commanded 13% of the S&E work force (see *Table 4.6*). Before introducing an educational reform package in 1987, President Gorbachev noted that over 35% of the scientifically qualified personnel (incorporated technicians and specialists from PTUs, SPTUs, and SSUZs – not included in *Table 4.6*) was concentrated in higher educational institutions of the Ministry for Higher Education and the academy, including over half of those in possession of the advanced degree of doctor of sciences. However, this group carried out no more than 10% of all scientific research (Kneen, 1989, p. 74). The academy had a very nonmarket manner of dealing with employees considered to be underperforming by sporadic attestation commissions (though not unheard of in some large Western companies). These underperformers, including surprisingly many of those holding the most advanced qualifications, were customarily offered positions of reduced responsibility and salary.

Of course, new people had to be hired to fulfill the planned achievements. Consequently, employment numbers rose and the budget allocated to the "wages funds" of the R&D institutes had to be spread more thinly. This is part of the explanation for the erosion of the traditionally favorable income levels of academics engaged in scientific activity relative to the compensation for other activities in the economy. The salaries became unattractive not only relative to those in the state sector, but even more so relative to those in the budding private R&D sector after 1987. But because the latter was still very limited in scope and not accessible to all, young graduates were more and more tempted by nonacademic jobs.

Due to the academy's wide variety of activities and responsibilities an ever-larger staff had to be maintained. There was and is no truly comparable sector in the West; a combination of parts of the academic and government sectors in the USA might come close. Due to the sheer size of the Soviet R&D community, contacts between institutes and scientists were meager; poor-quality or complete absence of communication systems and computer links required each Soviet institute to carry a large stock of R&D personnel. Links to branch ministry laboratories were practically nonexistent. Only in the late 1980s did the academy succeed in linking its institutes in the scientific centers of Riga, Leningrad, and Moscow with a new communication system called *Akademset* (Sinclair, 1987, p. xii). Until this time there were no industrial ministry institutes integrated in the system and plans for possible inclusion were only just being drawn up.

The branch sector is said to have employed over 61% of R&D personnel in 1987, and as much as 76.8% of the researchers in 1989 (refer to *Table 4.6*).[20] This number is very close to the 76% of American scientists and engineers that are employed in S&E jobs in industry R&D.

Each ministry, which received its signals from the policy makers,[21] had two special management bodies: a Scientific-Technical Council (STC) and the Technical Administration (TA) (Fortescue, 1987, p. 98). The former was an advisory body that considered proposals for the initiation or continuation of research projects and the latter was responsible for staffing and coordinating the distribution of funds, but it did not have direct administrative control over individual R&D institutions – two separate bodies for activities that should always be well integrated with one another for highest efficiency and most promising results.

The organizational separation of science and production in the Soviet Union, even though industrial ministries maintained their own research institutes with a major portion of the national R&D staff, was quite different from the normal Western standards. The historical policy of centralization and of being close to the supply of resources for fear of shortages (in the R&D case, funding and educated personnel) led to the industrial research sector being traditionally based in central institutes, both organizationally and commonly geographically independent and isolated from the enterprises they were meant to serve. In the USSR, in-house research and development was consistently a negligible component of the R&D network – some estimations mark it at only 4% of both R&D personnel and funding resources (Fortescue, 1987, p. 105).[22] The separation of research and production is evident throughout the entire planning system characteristic of the Soviet-style economy. The distinction between research and production plans was maintained from the factory-floor level right up to the national five-year plan level.

The *branchdom* of Soviet production was consequently also a characteristic of the scientific sector where specialization and secrecy created monopoly power at the various levels of science or for individual institutes and is now identified as the main source of low technological progress in the Soviet national economy. Thus, a multipurpose research institution that combined all creative and administrative tasks became the most common form for organizing R&D. Each institute had in-house departments for everything, but was still considerably detached from production. Due to the internalization of activities, these institutes often became very inefficient, influencing the standard of the scientific-technological output.

The policy implemented to alleviate the problems of declining and low-quality output was to increase the number of R&D institutes. From 1960 to 1972 the number of institutes increased from 4,196 to 5,307, an annual growth rate of 1.98% (Piskunov and Saltykov, 1991, p. 9). Following this surge, strict restrictions were imposed on the process of establishing new R&D institutes due to a paranoia, on the part of the central authorities, of losing control over the network.

The result was greater employment of scientists and engineers at the existing institutes, so much so that the average size of an R&D institute between 1975 and 1985, based on personnel, grew by more than 25% (ibid, 1991, p. 9). Although estimates allocated an average of almost 300 staff members per institute, some had staff in excess of 5,000. The "better situated" institutes, particularly of the MIC and some of those in the academy, could afford to employ an enormous amount of people and attract many of the highest-quality graduates from the higher educational institutions. The remaining institutes of the academy and the other branch ministries stocked up on the rest of the available S&E (often regardless of ability), because a larger staff usually meant a greater budgetary allocation from the central government. In the 1980s, the declining number of graduates and the slower growth of S&E employment for research and development activities led to an increase in the already very well-seasoned average age of scientists and engineers employed by the institutes.

Figure 4.5 shows the age structure in the late 1980s of scientific workers with highest qualifications in the USSR and the USA, that is, the equivalent of a Ph.D. in the United States. The pie charts reveal a strong predominance of the older generation in the Soviet Union. Indeed, almost 80% of the highest level of Soviet scientists engaged in R&D were over 50 years of age in the late 1980s, while the comparable figure for the USA was 34%. The consequence was also a great disparity at the other end of the scale; only 2% of Soviets were under 40 years of age compared to 29% in the United States.

Yet, even young and potentially creative graduates were usually joining gigantic scientific organizations that were all too often only extensions of the bureaucracy and had their own traditional, entrenched scientific policy that left precious little space and incentives for academic and scientific freedom. Immobility, specialization, special benefits, and the lack of information about the activities of others provided plenty of disincentives to contemplate a move elsewhere, would it have been possible. Consequently,

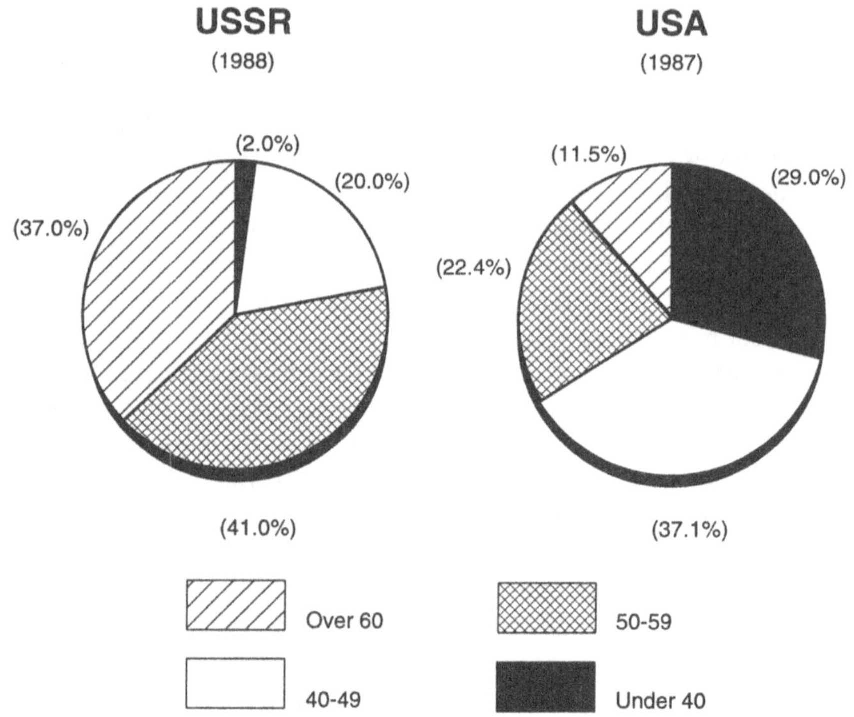

Figure 4.5. Age structure of scientific workers with highest qualifications in the USSR and the USA. Source: Compiled from NSB (1989, p. 232) and Gokhberg and Mindely (1991, p. 8).

the overall management of the R&D institutes and the large institutes' internal policy were thwarting creative developments (which are generally said to accompany growing employment of university graduates) and squandering scientific potential.

The nature of economic activity determines the need for R&D personnel. If the demand for technological innovation, the producers' desire to utilize technological superiority as the basis for competition, the consumers' demands for more selection, quality, convenience, and a higher value to price relation, and the public demand for regulation of technology continue to increase, the need for a continuous, probably increasing, supply of scientists and engineers is secured. The quantity and quality of this supply will prove to be a principal factor in the style and pace of economic growth and competitive performance, as it has been in the past.

A pool of scientifically literate workers provides the stock from which to draw much needed future scientists and engineers (Brooks, 1991, p. 134).

More and more will the need arise to integrate the world of education with the world or work.

4.3 R&D Financing

The OECD report on science and technology indicators states (1989, p. 17):

> growing demands on science and technology (S&T) by the economy and society and the increasing speed of technological progress call for some flexibility in the research system in response to evolving expectations and for sufficient continuity in the major directions of R&D and the applied resources.

The report also indicates that the level and trend of R&D resources, their allocation between sectors, and the relationship between the sectors are all factors molding the capacity and potential to produce new S&T knowledge. This is precisely the element that constitutes the *nonphysical investment* capable of and essential for generating innovations.

Persons engaged in R&D at all levels require financial support to perform their research and development activities. In Western, non–Communist countries the funding primarily comes from two sources: private firms and government. In Eastern Europe, R&D had traditionally been practically the sole responsibility of the state – the reasoning was that controlling the financing facilitated control of the activities and the ideas that were produced. The Western system relies to a large extent on competition for financing to determine which ideas are fit to be integrated into new or revised technologies or products that are used in the economy. In the past, R&D expenditures have shown considerable stability in the face of economic fluctuations. Since 1980, they have for the most part continued to grow throughout the OECD countries at a higher rate than gross domestic product.

All governments, East or West, have devised a variety of fiscal and monetary mechanisms in a continuing effort to provide an amicable climate for investment in R&D. Of course, the main difference is that Western democratic nations have very diverse and well-organized financial and capital markets, and a relatively versatile banking system that adds many possibilities for financing.

This section on R&D financing analyzes the general policy environment and funding directions in the former Soviet Union and how these compared to levels, trends, and developments in other leading R&D-performing nations. Most interesting are the sources for R&D support, shifts between the shares of the performers of R&D in an economy, and the distribution of the emphasis on basic research, applied research, and development.

4.3.1 Funding R&D activities

There is little doubt that the former USSR had made significant efforts in R&D. Although the data quoted in monetary terms have always been subject to questions with respect to its reliability (even more so than the statistics on physical units in the USSR), the figures verify a continual strong budgetary commitment to research and experimental development activities. This emphasis was partly the result of a desire to maintain a lasting tradition of promoting science as Marx had said it should be done, and partly for the more practical reason that progress in science and technology would yield solutions to economic and social problems. The latter argument is also at the foundation of market economies where the creation of new knowledge for this purpose has remained a priority, although the accent has shifted toward the need to improve the diffusion and application of technology as a contribution to modern economic development. The lack of such relevant diffusion and application was a serious cause for concern in the Soviet Union.

Early in Stalin's rule, R&D policy-making and funding activities were removed from the authority of the industrial enterprises and transferred to higher management levels (ministries, agencies, and committees). The Soviet-style central planning system extracted not only decision-making powers from enterprises, but also the resources to make decisions. Of course, what good is one without the other? For example, the state drew all the profits from the enterprises (for the most part at least) only to redistribute them to the enterprises to use for research, development, diffusion of technology, and other things determined necessary by the central plan or directives. Enterprises and their managers were essentially put under tutelage. Each year the financial allocation to R&D was a function of the budgetary process and bargaining between parties with vested interests. The main participants in the budget process were the ministries of finance at the union and republican levels and finance departments at local levels; the councils of ministers of the Union and each republic; the supreme Soviets of the Union and each republic; the local Soviets of people's deputies; GOSPLAN; GOSKOMSTAT; GOSBANK, including 200 regional offices and more than 6,000 branches; Promstroibank and Vneshekonombank (IMF *et al.*, vol. 1, 1991, p. 258).

No one from the science and technology sector, or any other sector for that matter, was directly involved in the budgetary process. In the case of science and technology, the influence was via the joint policy-making role of GOSPLAN, GKNT, and the Academy of Sciences. Until as late as July 1989, budgets were allocated according to fulfillment of the plan. Budgetary expenditures were actually undertaken by two kinds of spending units: directly by budgetary institutions, and indirectly by state enterprises, to the extent that expenditures of the latter are supported by transfers from the budget (IMF *et al.*, vol. 1, 1991, p. 259). The USSR State Committee for Science and Technology was responsible for distributing R&D monies, but enterprises also had funds for industrial R&D.

Simply allocated money through the GKNT was considered "easy money" and led to low-quality R&D and the free-rider problem. There was no natural selection of research teams or institutions in developing a particular project, since enough funds were available to carry excess staff or what has been referred to as "ballast" (Piskunov and Saltykov, 1991, p. 13). As a consequence, funds continued to be wasted on research studies that had little or no commercial value and were often antiquated but were the bargaining tools of the privileged, distinguished directors of the R&D institutes in their negotiations with the policy-making and funding bodies. Thus, despite considerable increases in R&D funding over the years, these factors unfortunately impeded essential changes in the improvement of Soviet R&D quality.

The actual pricing of R&D was only done in the applied research and development areas as these were considered to provide results that led to the introduction of new products or processes for mass production. Pricing was not used for fundamental research because it was not expected to generate a practical result that could be priced. Therefore, those institutes concentrating on basic science enjoyed stable and secure allocations from the state budget, while those R&D units focusing on applied research and development had to enter into contracts with an enterprise or respond to a work order from a branch ministry (Bornstein, 1984, p. 85). Introduced in the 1950s, this was no reason for excitement and was not accompanied by mechanisms characteristic of a "free" market. The R&D contracts, and clearly not the orders, were not usually the result of free choice and initiative on the part of the R&D performer and the client enterprise. Instead, the former and the latter negotiated a mutually acceptable agreement within the framework of plan assignments received from a superior level. Thus, competitive bidding was not a part of the contractual process.

As for other goods produced in the planned economy, the cost-based pricing mechanism was also used for R&D products. The planned costs included wages, social insurance, materials, special equipment, travel, payments to subcontractors, and general overhead expenditures including bonuses (Bornstein, 1984, p. 86). The costs of the complete R&D project were then estimated either through comparisons with previous R&D work or, in some cases, based on norms; in either incidence the estimated cost was considered the value of the project. Although the cost-based system did not consider capital investment costs (using depreciation), it often resulted in quite generous estimations primarily due to inflated wage costs. Of course, other costs increased as they were calculated on a per worker basis, leading to subsequent correction of the estimates.

In 1967, profits in R&D activities were recognized and a portion could be retained by the performer. One year later, the price of applied R&D included a profit linked to the expected or calculated economic effect.[23] The R&D performer guaranteed an economic effect to his client and could charge 1.5% of that annual effect as profit. If the effect could not be precisely calculated, as so often was the case, the profit charge took the form of a markup that was usually just an arbitrary percentage of the wage's fund. The economic effect mechanism was complex and had only a minor role in R&D pricing. There was no single official methodology for pricing applied R&D services in the USSR. So, the bulk of profits came from the excess of planned over actual costs, inducing R&D institutes not only to impute excessive costs in their accounting, but also to actually incur many of these.

In spite of the continuing budgetary rules, the R&D community was confronted with a number of organizational changes after 1987. These alterations tended to weaken the control of government agencies over the network of R&D institutions. The price-setting mechanism for R&D products was also adjusted, based less on direct central administrative influence and more on negotiations between researchers and clients. There was no method for obtaining any substantial individual reward for producing new products from successful R&D because the USSR had no patent, intellectual property, or royalty system as we know it in the West. The results of R&D were practically free, and duplication or copying was easier than initiating a breakthrough.

Official gross R&D expenditure (GERD) in the Soviet Union amounted to some 43.6 billion rubles in 1989 (see *Figure 4.6*).[24] At the going exchange rate (US$100 = 62.74 R) this came to approximately US$70 billion. While this level of Soviet budget allocated to R&D was just over half the US level, it was over eight times greater than the amount the Soviets had spent almost 30 years earlier.

The increase in GERD during the Gorbachev years was a reflection of the importance he granted to R&D, his (and the Communist Party's) recognition that the USSR was again falling further behind the Western nations with respect to technological standards, and his hope that scientific advances would spur substantial economic progress and development. In their report, Gokhberg and Mindely (1991) question the validity of the official statistics and offer their own estimates of R&D expenditures (refer to *Table 4.7*). The authors of the report claim that the official figures are based on inaccurate

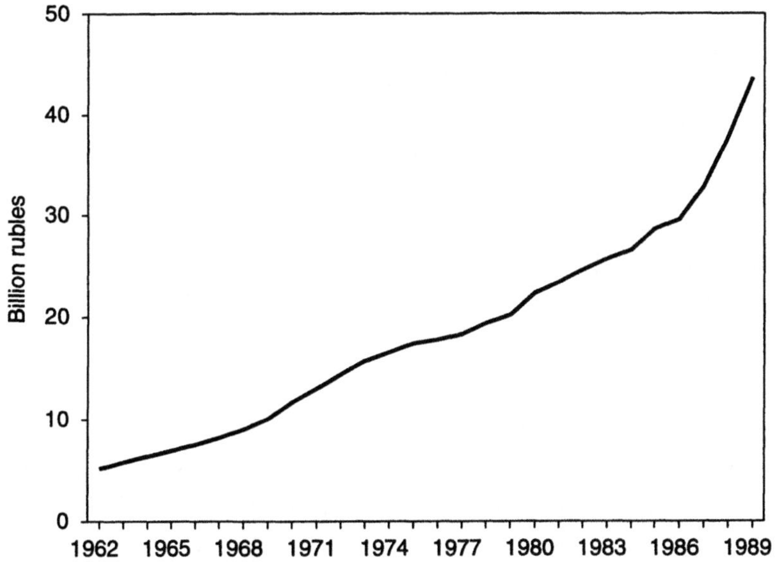

Figure 4.6. Gross R&D expenditures in the USSR.

Table 4.7. R&D expenditure in the USSR, selected years.

	GOSKOMSTAT data			Gokhberg & Mindely estimates		
	1987	1988	1989	1987	1988	1989
Billion rubles	32.8	37.8	43.6	24.0	26.0	32.0
% of GNP	4.0	4.3	4.7	2.9	3.0	3.5

Source: Adapted from Gokhberg and Mindely (1991, p. 20) and GOSKOMSTAT (1990, p. 172).

calculations and double counting.[25] Therefore, their estimates are 72.5%, 69.8%, and 74.5% of the official figures quoted for 1987, 1988, and 1989, respectively. Nevertheless, either set of data clearly indicates substantial increases in the absolute level of funding for R&D activities, securing their importance as a part of the economic strategy of the Soviet-style planned system (also refer to *Figure 4.6* which illustrates the steady progressive funding between 1962 and 1989).

The figures in *Table 4.7* do not reveal the sharp successive declines in funding for R&D after 1989. The decreasing budget revenues and the consequently increasing state budget deficit, increasing autonomy and self-financing and self-control in decision making of enterprises, and the general worsening of the economic situation meant that less funds were available for R&D. In the case of enterprises, it was difficult to convince managers to invest in innovation-enhancing activities when they were having trouble meeting salary payments. In addition to stricter budget constraints and declining availability of state subsidies, enterprises were levied with a new tax in January 1991 that abolished privileges and meant a large part of state enterprises' profits were to be collected by federal, republican, and local authorities, leaving always less to invest in R&D (Motorygin and Glaziev, 1991, p. 17). Despite the fact that R&D remained a priority area for the government, relatively and absolutely less was being spent on it after 1989, as on most other publicly financed economic activities.

4.3.2 GERD as a percentage of GNP: A comparison

The annual growth of GERD in the Soviet Union over almost three decades, 1962 to 1989, was a very respectable 8.19%. It was highest in the beginning of this period, declined in the periods 1971–1975 and 1981–1985, before recovering after 1985 (see *Figure 4.7*). Although the growth rate over the entire time appears high, it was less than the growth rate in the USA, West Germany, Japan, and periodically even the UK. While most OECD countries experienced a post-1979 recovery in R&D expenditure growth compared with previous periods, the Soviet figure really took off between 1985 and 1989, when it surpassed the OECD average which it had been below between 1981 and 1985 (for OECD figures, refer to OECD, 1989, pp. 17–37, and the relevant Appendix Tables). But aggregate numbers of GERD do not provide the best indication of national R&D effort, especially for comparative purposes.

The percentage of GDP invested in R&D is the most telling indicator of a nation's overall endeavor in R&D, despite occasional criticism, particularly popular at the science policy and political levels. *Figure 4.7* shows the evolution of GERD as a percentage of GNP for the Soviet Union from 1962 to 1989. The Soviet GERD/GNP ratio was over what the OECD calls the "magic 2%" level for the entire period;[26] in fact, it was almost 2.5 times as high in 1989. After substantial growth in the proportion of GNP spent on GERD during the first 10 years of the period (1962–1972), there was a considerable relative drop following 1972. Interestingly, the OECD countries also experienced a decline in their GERD/GNP ratios between 1975 and 1980.

An explanation for a portion of the OECD decline was the relative much greater growth in GNP with respect to the previous period (which had been burdened by the oil-price shock), and also to the reasonably stable growth of the GERD. The Soviet level clearly decreased during the 1970s; yet, most of the decline cannot be explained away with the same reason as that used for

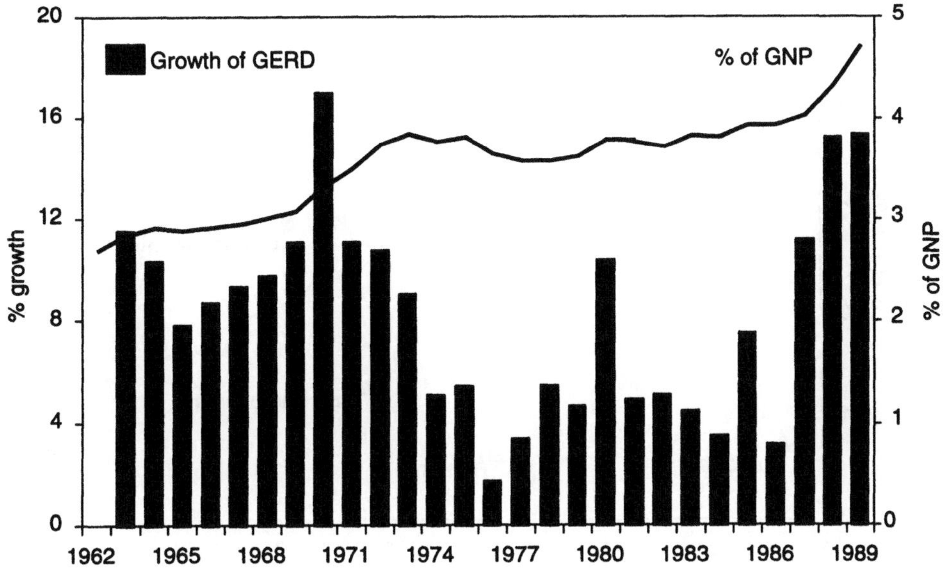

Figure 4.7. GERD growth and % of GNP in the USSR.

the OECD nations because the magnitude of their renewed economic activity was far greater than that in the USSR. This would indicate the beginning of a deteriorating position of the Soviet Union relative to the OECD countries regarding the development of R&D effort.[27]

This deteriorating status grew in the early 1980s, when a basically stable Soviet ratio was confronted by a significantly improved trend in OECD country ratios. However, after 1986 there was a temporary leveling off in GERD/GNP ratios in the OECD because GNP growth rates were rising relatively faster than the rates of increase in R&D expenditures. Simultaneous to these developments the Soviet GERD/GNP ratio ballooned according to official statistics. (Even if the markedly lower Gokhberg and Mindely estimates are taken, the increases are impressive.) Like in the OECD, R&D spending in the USSR continued an upward trend that was clearly less affected by slower economic growth than by other national activities. The resilience of the GERD/GNP ratio over a longer period in the face of economic changes and budgetary difficulties indicates the value attributed to R&D both in the OECD and in the Soviet Union. Unfortunately, the government in the USSR could not maintain this emphasis after 1989, when budgetary problems became more and more insurmountable (as suggested earlier in *Table 4.7*).

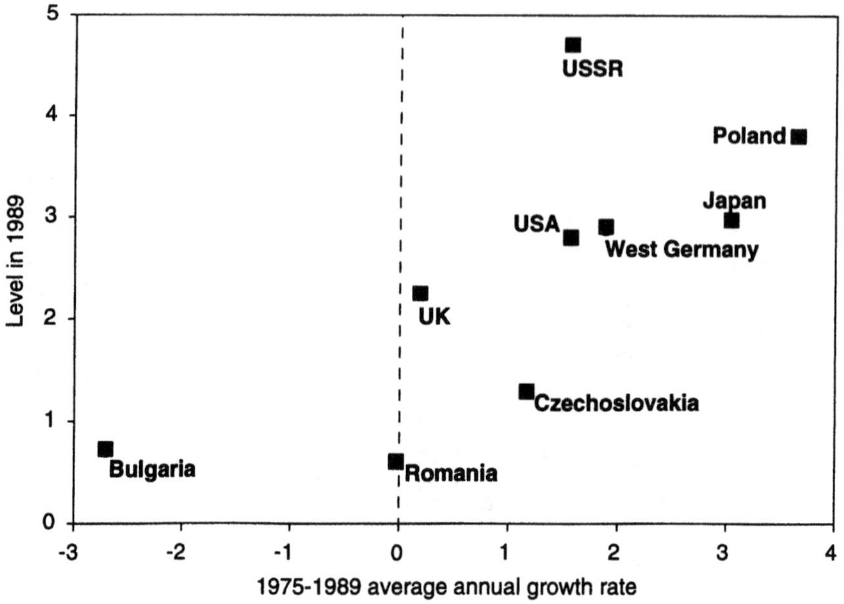

Figure 4.8. Level and growth rates of GERD/GNP, selected countries.

This discussion on the dynamics of the GERD/GNP ratio reveals a minor deficiency in using the percentage of GNP invested in R&D as an indicator for an economy's R&D effort. Namely, it is not always clear from the ratio which of the two components had the greatest influence on the final percentage trend. A comparison of GERD and GNP growth over a period can help to clarify each country's funding effort. In the five-country sample the R&D growth rates are almost always higher (for any interval) than the comparable GNP growth rates. The greater the positive difference between GERD growth and GNP growth, the greater the country's R&D effort in relation to its available resources. German, Japanese, American, and Soviet GERD growth rates between 1962 and 1989 are 3.3, 3.0, 0.2, and 2.3 percentage points above their GNP growth rates for the same period, respectively. The United Kingdom was the only country where growth in R&D expenditure was lower than growth in GNP.

Figure 4.8 shows the position of four Western countries, four Eastern European countries, and the USSR both by level of R&D spending (GERD/GNP ratio), in 1989 or the nearest year, and by average annual growth rate of R&D between 1975 and 1989. Among the Eastern Europeans, the USSR and Poland stand apart, culminating very high GERD/GNP ratios (the USSR highest and Poland second) with exceptional growth rates

(Poland highest) between 1975 and 1989. Poland's seemingly advantaged position (better than any Western country in this sample during the period) was caused by an incredible increase in the emphasis on investment in science, culture, and education during the 1980s. After practically no growth between 1970 and 1981 (0.77% average annual growth), the budget more than doubled within the next seven years (11.50% per annum). The other three Eastern European countries were unable to follow the Soviet or Polish examples and found themselves relegated to the low-growth/low-level field of the figure, far below any Western counterpart.

Japan presented the most favorable position of the Western nations, being in the high-growth/high-level field, attaining almost 3% in each category. While West Germany and the USA maintained respectable positions, Britain was slipping into the low-growth field due to an only marginally increasing GERD/GNP ratio. The Soviets may have had a higher level than the Westerners in 1989, but its growth had fallen to the US level. Warnings that official estimates tended to be inflationary (or simply overstated) lead one to believe that the situation for R&D financing had begun to deteriorate some time ago – considerably before the accelerated decay after 1989.

There is a general congruence between the level of R&D expenditures, where the high spenders devoted substantially more to R&D (as a percentage of GNP) than the low spenders, and the number of researchers employed (per 10,000 workers in the labor force population). *Figure 4.9* relates GERD/GNP ratios to the share of R&D personnel in the labor force. There is a reasonably strong correlation between countries which increase the proportion of GNP devoted to R&D over a longer period and the increases in the proportion of the labor force active in R&D. In the past, the share of labor costs in gross expenditures for R&D was often over 50%, therefore being a major determinant.

The four Western countries, the USSR, and Poland appear to be following the trend, although the last two required a significantly higher GERD/GNP ratio to support a not always correspondingly higher R&D staff. This was partly due to the always greater administrative burden that needed to be maintained, the problem of overemployment, and all the accompanying costly inefficiencies. Romania, Bulgaria, and Czechoslovakia lie far apart from the other nations in *Figure 4.9*, indicating that an enormous staff was employed even at a very low GERD/GNP ratio. Although salary costs were very low in these three countries compared with those in the West, it would appear that most of the funds were used to pay wages rather than to invest in state-of-the-art equipment. Thus, even the enlightened or industrious R&D personnel could have never been as productive as their Western

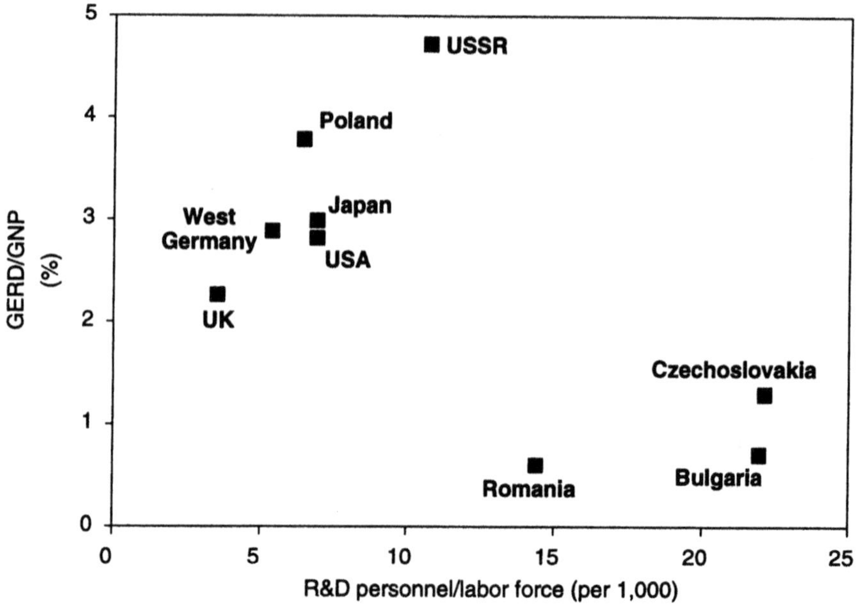

Figure 4.9. Related levels of GERD/GNP and R&D personnel/labor force, 1989.

colleagues, where there were few complaints of overstaffing, and those who were employed could rely on adequate physical infrastructure.

The relative positions of the countries presented in *Figures 4.8* and *4.9* with respect to the proportion of GNP or GDP devoted to research and development are significantly influenced by a particular nation's policy regarding expenditures for major defense research programs. The ranking of countries by the share of GDP devoted to civil R&D expenditures (see *Figure 4.10*) sheds a different light on the state and characteristics of research in the USSR, USA, UK, Japan, and West Germany.[28] When comparing only civil research rather than total, the gaps between countries are diminished, and those countries that appeared so superior in absolute terms but with a large emphasis on defense, are confronted with a relatively modest position. Among OECD countries, the USA and the UK have been known to devote considerable percentages of GERD to defense programs and consequently their contributions to civil R&D were between 20% and 37% lower than those in West Germany and Japan. The science and technology policy of the last two nations is partly the result of not being permitted to have defense sectors as they existed before World War II and partly due to different national priorities.

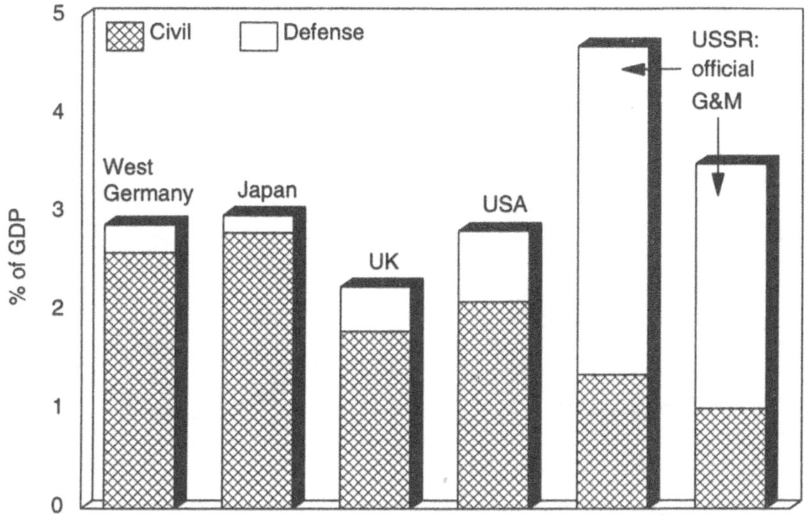

Figure 4.10. Civil, defense, and total GERD as a percentage of GDP, 1989.

In the Soviet case, whether the high (GOSKOMSTAT) or low (Gokhberg and Mindely, refer to *Table 4.7*) estimates are considered, an amazing proportion of Soviet investment in R&D went to the defense sector.[29] One reason for this is that particular areas of high-technology research and development were incorporated into the military industrial complex and funds did not carry a distinct label; so, they may have been used to develop a new radar system or to improve the state of technology in producing television sets. The spillover effect may have been somewhat higher due to this fact, but most analysts do not attribute much effect of defense R&D on production of civil goods in the West and it would be a surprise if this had been radically different in Eastern Europe. In addition (maybe partly in recognition of this), the proportions of civil R&D as a percentage of GDP has been increasing in most of the big spender OECD countries since 1970.

After analyzing the GERD, its growth, its relationship to R&D personnel, and the differential allocations between civil and defense sectors for a number of countries, the next stage is to examine the emphasis of R&D funding when it comes to the character of the work.

4.3.3 Sources and character of R&D funding

In the USSR, basic research was dominated by the academic/education sector, applied research was fairly evenly distributed among all sectors, and

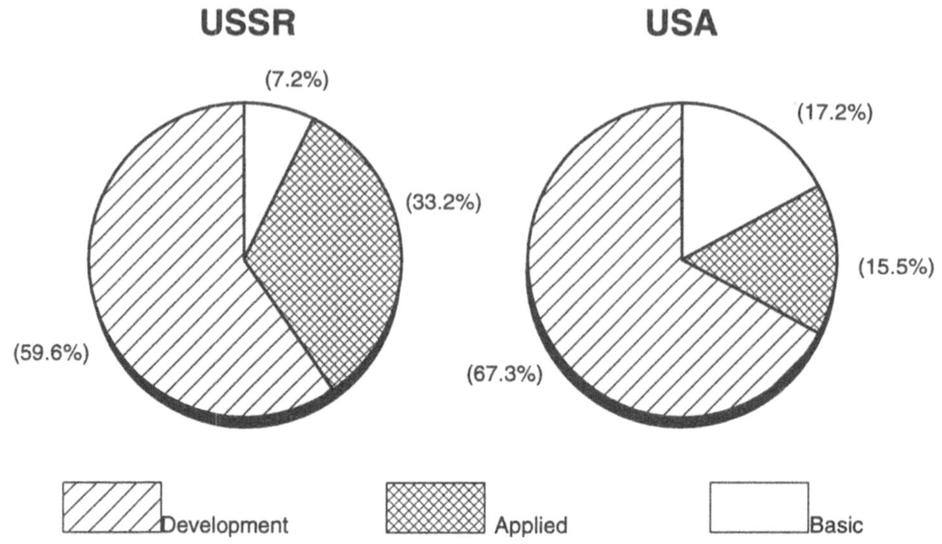

Figure 4.11. Government R&D financing by character of work, 1989. Source: Compiled from NSB (1989, pp. 5, 94, 284), and Gokhberg and Mindely (1991, p. 22).

development (as might be expected) was primarily concentrated in the factory/industrial sector. Rather unexpectedly, the statistics for the Soviet Union reveal that a relatively small share of government R&D funds was invested in basic research in 1989 – only 7.2% compared with 17.2% in the USA (see *Figure 4.11*).[30] The catalyst for this development was the beginning of reform in the Soviet R&D sector after 1987 that led to more direct R&D financing by the reasonably well-endowed enterprises. Enterprises proved to have little interest in basic science. In 1988, the basic R&D expenditures in industrial research institutes decreased by 50% although the share of enterprises investing in industrial R&D increased from 51.2% to 66.4% (Motorygin and Glaziev, 1991, p. 17). Their contribution was in the applied research area, to which government contributed only about one-third of its budget as depicted in *Figure 4.11*.

The United States government appears to have devoted 2.5 times as many financial resources to fundamental science activities. After slow years for fundamental science in market economies during the 1970s, many OECD nations registered a recovery of expenditures on basic research. US figures indicate that government left much of the responsibility for funding applied research as well as development to the private sector. The development value was high due to a distortion caused by the enormous outlays of the American government for development in the defense sector.[31]

Financial data may not be the best indicator of the allocation of funds with respect to the character of work. As stated earlier, wages form a large component of R&D spending. In the USSR the salaries of scientists and engineers in the academic/education sector had substantially declined relative to those of scientists, engineers, and technicians in the industrial branches of the economy. In addition, much of the capital and infrastructure costs in the academic/education science sector were covered by other state budget allocations. However, some Soviet policy analysts appeared concerned about what they felt was an unjustified emphasis on applied research and development when the state of fundamental science seemed so neglected, and possibly even deteriorating. In 1987, the research institutes of the branch industrial ministries were allocated as much as 82% of the funding for R&D projects from the State Committee for Science and Technology (Fortescue, 1987, p. 97).

In the United States and most other OECD countries, the R&D performers are classified according to five main groupings: the federal government, industry, universities and colleges, federally funded R&D institutions, and other nonprofit institutions. In the West, one can generalize that over the last decade or so, a new trend is becoming apparent: university and industry are increasing their roles in performing R&D, while the role of the government as a direct performer has been declining.

Although there was primarily only one funding source for Soviet R&D, there were many performers of various sizes and fields of specialization. Due to their diversity, status in the hierarchy, and the ambiguities surrounding their cumulative responsibilities, it is difficult to classify these in a similar way to those in the West. In 1989, the USSR state R&D sector consisted of approximately 4,500 research and design organizations, 528 scientific and production associations in industry, 23 intersectoral scientific and technological complexes, and 904 higher educational institutions (Gokhberg and Mindely, 1991, p. 23). Research and development activities were also being conducted by 720 enterprises and production associations, more than 1,000 design bureaus in the field of construction, and many others.

Industrial research institutes were financed by state budget sources via special funds supervised by corresponding ministries or state R&D programs, both of which were coordinated by the USSR State Committee for Science and Technology (Motorygin and Glaziev, 1991, p. 2). These institutes received additional funds directly from enterprises to conduct contract research. The importance of this last source increased in 1987 when state enterprises received the right to accumulate profits. In fact, direct financing of R&D at industrial institutes by enterprises more than doubled in 1988, the number of contractual agreements between enterprises and R&D institutes rose three to four times, and industrial R&D output increased 1.6 times (Motorygin and Glaziev, 1991, p. 13). The research institutes and organizations linked to the production ministries did by far the lion's share of R&D, with the higher educational institutions only accounting for about 10% (Kneen, 1989, p. 74). This implies that the further an organization was from production, the less scientific production it had.

In the Academy of Sciences, the same small group of elite people held multiple positions (which they were elected to by their counterparts) in top-level management, policy making, and resource allocation (Motorygin and Glaziev, 1991, p. 3). The academy was privileged in that its presidium obtained funding for the organization directly from the state budget. However, the individual institutes received research plans and the resources determined as sufficient to fulfill the plans from its relevant supervisory body. The concentration of power and control over R&D resources in the hands of small groups of academicians suppressed any real competition between scholars and institutes for resource support.

Due to such a monopolistic organizational structure, much academic R&D ended up focusing on obsolete areas that were protected by those in the academy management who were themselves usually directors of enormous institutes specializing in precisely these topics. The length of the research effort determined by institute directors meant that there was no need to constantly sell the results to obtain funding and made the swings in Soviet S&T more moderate than in the US (Gamota, 1987, p. 233). However, the question of when to discontinue work in an unproductive area was rarely addressed; possibly, only with the death of the director who had promoted it.

The fastest growing type of R&D performers were also the newest – the nonstate R&D organizations (refer to *Table 3.5*).[32] These included youth research centers, permanent research teams of the All-Union Society of Inventors and of the Union of Scientists and Engineers Society, and R&D cooperatives. By 1990, they performed 13.5% of all R&D by volume, and their share was growing rapidly. Their aggregate expenditures on R&D rose from practically zero in 1987 to already over 6 billion rubles in 1990–1991, about 14% of GERD. Their financing was chiefly secured by the value of products they brought to the growing *free market* for R&D products. Many scientists and engineers still employed in state R&D institutions had second part-time and even full-time jobs in the newly created R&D centers.[33] In this case the researchers faced little risk or responsibility since they were

Table 4.8. Distribution of government expenditures for research, 1988 (in %).

Science	USSR	USA	OECD average[a]
Natural	16.0	29.7	
Medical	2.2	10.2	}36.2[b]
Agricultural	2.4	3.9	
Technical	75.3	50.2	33.5[c]
Social and Humanitarian	4.1	6.0	6.8[d]

[a] Figures from 1987.
[b] Life sciences.
[c] Physical sciences and engineering.
[d] Social sciences and psychology.
Sources: Compiled from OECD (1992, p. 30) and Gokhberg and Mindely (1991, p. 23).

permanently employed elsewhere. The cooperatives were particularly successful due to high flexibility, rapid completion of projects, and a completely demand-oriented policy.

In order to be prepared for increasing demand on scarce budgetary resources and to operate within the bounds of existing budget constraints, governments were required to set R&D priorities. These areas received preferential treatment in the allocation of federal funds. Questions have been raised with respect to the infringement on scientific freedom and the responsiveness to market demand, but most governments have withstood the criticisms and have established, and subsequently authorized, high-level advisory bodies in one form or another to set national R&D priorities.

The USSR is no exception; however, the whole collection of bodies involved is very large – the greater the priority, the higher the funding. This policy was followed to the extreme with respect to military-related areas; these areas could not help but perform respectable R&D as they obtained the best financial, human, and physical resources. Low priority areas were barely able to survive on the resources they were given; this could not have been conducive to productive, progressive research anywhere. From this perspective, some of the achievements by Soviet scientists were even more amazing.

In 1988, the Soviet priorities differed significantly from those in the nonsocialist countries of the Western industrialized world. An overwhelming emphasis was given to technical sciences, 75.3% of government R&D expenditures (see *Table 4.8*). These sciences were primarily physics, mathematics, and engineering. The OECD average for this category was as low as 33.5%. Even the USA, 50.2% in this general field, and Japan, tops in the OECD with 21.6% in engineering, had lower budget allocations than the USSR, although they have been widely considered proponents of this field. The life sciences, which include such important timely topics as biotechnology, environment, and health, were clearly neglected in setting priorities in the Soviet Union – less than 21% of the budget. In the USA, the proportion of R&D expenditures allocated to the life sciences was almost 45%; the OECD average was 36.2%. Finally, the support granted to the social and humanitarian sciences in the USSR lags 32% and 40% behind the US and OECD levels respectively.

Notes

[1] Education policy is the single most important factor with which a nation can influence the potential abilities of its population. Under socialism, the educational system is responsible for the formal socialization of the "correct" attitudes in a socialist society and, according to David Lane, for the creation of a "communist man" (Lane, 1985, p. 262). The operation of a national system of education molds the intellectual basis, the knowledge, and impressions of the population at an age when information and ideology is most readily absorbed and will to a large extent orient the aptitude and capability of individuals for the rest of their lives. In this way, education is the most crucial input for human development – the resource that facilitates individuals to engage in economic activity, more or less successfully, more or less creatively.

[2] This recent comparative study of national innovation systems included 15 nations in 3 groups: large high-income countries, France, Germany, Italy, Japan, the USA, and the UK; small high-income countries with a strong agricultural resource base, Australia, Canada, Denmark, and Sweden; and lower-income countries, Argentina, Brazil, Israel, South Korea, and Taiwan. Nelson suggests that the comparison between the USA and Germany, on the one hand, and France and the UK, on the other, supports his conclusion. He summarizes that a principal reason why the former two countries surged ahead of the latter two, around the turn of the century, in science-based industries, is that their university systems were much more responsive to the training needs of industry (refer to Nelson, 1992, p. 23).

[3] Until late in the nineteenth century, such all-encompassing programs as mass education and railroad construction were viewed as possible threats to the established political order and were even discouraged. The developments in Russia, remarkably similar to those in Japan at the time, are depicted as a model where the state launched a deliberate and consistent program to accelerate industrialization and to reduce the technology gap between it and its more advanced and steadily advancing neighbors (Gregory, 1982, p. 7).

[4] About 250 years ago, Peter the Great brought in numerous foreign technicians and initiated the vestiges of intellectual life (Maddison, 1969, p. 83). As a result, universities and libraries were built and the Academy of Sciences established. These facilities were primarily reserved for the elite, so some of the aristocracy had a cosmopolitan education and there were a few distinguished

Russian scientists. In spite of this, the masses remained illiterate and the national technological level was low.

[5] It has been reported that roughly half of the schools in the Soviet Union lacked central heating and running water or sewage, a quarter of all students attended school in split shifts, and 53% of all school children were not in good health (Sakwa, 1990, p. 22). Additionally, the absence of appropriately enticing benefits for instructors in isolated areas had an impact on the quality of those hired to teach.

[6] These figures for growing urbanization thus coincide with the increases in total enrollment in education and enrollment in higher educational institutions as shown in *Table 4.1* and *Figure 4.2* during the same period.

[7] An additional reason for these low numbers in the republics was the presence of their own culture and language that was often very distinct from Russian. The Soviet Union consisted of 15 republics (Russia the largest in area and with consistently almost 50% of the population), 12 main ethnic groups (and more minor ones), and over 15 different languages. To become literate meant to learn Russian – a foreign language for many.

[8] All improvements are to be seen positively considering the low level which had been inherited from the Czarist period and the emigration of many educated people and technicians shortly before and during the 1917 Revolution.

[9] This was not always true. Under the leadership of Joseph Stalin, forced industrialization beginning with the first five-year plan in 1928 resulted in a severe shortage of well-trained technical labor. Many millions were recruited from the numbers that fled from the countryside. Unskilled peasant labor caused many breakdowns, was exceedingly inefficient and unpunctual, and resulted in a high labor turnover. The planned extension of the labor force called for great efforts to teach new skills, to increase the inadequate number of engineers and technologists, and to expand educational establishments (Nove, 1989, p. 188). The annual growth rates for graduating engineers and technicians ballooned to an amazing 15% between 1928 and 1941. Particularly in the 1930s and still for an extended period thereafter, the result was the establishment of many new schools called *technicums* and a very hasty production of semi-qualified personnel.

[10] This is an interpretation of the work of J.I. Zajda (*Education in the USSR*, 1980, p. 105) by Lane (1985, p. 296).

[11] In order to secure computer literacy among students in higher education a course on the "Basics of Informatics and Computer Techniques" has been introduced (98% of the students have enrolled). The problem is that only 14% of the full-time, day higher educational institutions have computer facilities (GOSKOMSTAT, 1988, p. 254).

[12] The numbers in *Table 4.4* do not reveal the impressive advances the USSR made in increasing its stock of qualified personnel in the economy during the 1950s and early 1960s. At this time, the number of engineers and agronomists already tripled, greatly outpacing the rate of growth in Western Europe (Maddison, 1969, p. 128).

[13] Refer to Table 2 (p. 97) in the *Technical Annex* of OECD, 1989.

[14] The decline in the British numbers may be a result of an exclusion from the data of sectors other than government and industry. In the transition to a tertiary economy, more and more S&E are self-employed or becoming employed in services and nonindustrial, private branches of the economy. These, as stated, are not included in the UK calculations.

[15] Gokhberg and Mindely (1991, p. 3) report that official figures for Soviet R&D personnel did not always include *all* scientists and engineers from some research, design, and experimental divisions of industrial enterprises (the so-called *factory science* sector), and from some higher educational institutions and other organizations. They estimate that the total number of all types of S&E employed in scientific organizations could have been as high as 3.3 million in 1989, 2.1 million of which were engaged in R&D. This is almost double the official estimate and should itself be treated with caution as the definitions for S&E are unclear. The amount, however, is still considerably below the 4.6 million scientists and engineers in S&E jobs in the United States.

[16] Refer to Table 5 in Gokhberg and Mindely (1991, p. 9).

[17] Part of the explanation of the rapid decline of S&E employment in Poland was the increasing lack of supply since 1980. From 1980 to 1987, an estimated 8,000 Polish academics immigrated to the West – the greatly feared "brain drain" phenomena (*The Wall Street Journal*, April 3, 1992). These immigrants constituted over 24% of the total drop in employment of 33,000 S&E between 1980 and 1987.

[18] Soviet policy on migration and demographics was said to be generally motivated by the task of economic development. The key concept was to distribute the population (usually selected for particular skills) in those places where it could do the most to improve productivity (see Zwick, 1980, pp. 142–171). The great concentration of untapped resources in eastern Russia was one of the reasons for the relocation of the population to that area and the establishment of the scientific center in Novosibirsk.

[19] Thus, personnel transfers were uncommon and even prevented by direct and indirect measures such as the dependency on special benefits and the like. The unfortunate result was that these institutes added internal isolation to the already existing and impeding international isolation, but both were grounds for increasing the number of domestic R&D personnel.

[20] The data have been compiled from Fortescue (1987, p. 97), Gokhberg and Mindely (1991, pp. 3-5), and NSB (1989, Appendix Tables, p. 179).

[21] Recall, from Chapter 3, that the main bureaucratic institutions contributing to R&D policy making were the Academy of Sciences, the State Committee for Science and Technology (GKNT), and GOSPLAN.

[22] In comparison, the journal *Science & Engineering Indicators* (1989), published by the National Science Board, reports that approximately 72% of R&D was performed in-house in the American industrial sector.

[23] In 1967 the resolution of the USSR Council of Ministers was "On Changes in the Method of Planning Expenses on Scientific Research Work and on Expanding the Rights of Directors of Scientific Research Institutions"; and in 1968 the party government resolution was "On Measures to Increase the Effectiveness

of Scientific Organizations and Speed Utilization in the National Economy of Achievements of Science and Technology" (Bornstein, 1984, p. 91).

[24] This amount represents the sum of current expenditure (on work performed by *independent* scientific organizations as well as by divisions of enterprises, scientific-production and production associations, higher educational institutions and other business entities), and capital investments in construction and installations connected with the development of science (scientific organizations, their experimental and production bases, independent laboratories, meteorological service installations, botanical and experimental garden, wildlife preserves, etc.) (Gokhberg and Mindely, 1991, p. 18).

[25] The double counting was the result of work that had been fulfilled on a contractual basis by enterprises and research organizations and consequently credited to both the executing agencies (which place the orders) and the contractors.

[26] The OECD (1992, p. 111) has designated 2% as the "apparently most desirable target figure."

[27] The gap widened primarily with respect to the main R&D spenders in the OECD. Seven countries (United States, Japan, Germany, France Italy, United Kingdom, and Canada) accounted for 91% of the OECD total in 1985 (OECD, 1989, p. 20). In addition to these countries (except Canada and Italy), Sweden, Switzerland, and the Netherlands spent nearly 3% of GNP on R&D in 1987 (OECD, 1992, p. 111).

[28] The OECD divides GERD into *civil and defense*, while the National Science Board (of the USA) makes the distinction between *nondefense and defense*, yet they both refer to the same sectors.

[29] The Soviet figures are as a percentage of GNP.

[30] Under the Soviet-style central planning system, it made no sense to make a distinction between government and other sources of financing because the state was sole financier. State-sponsored R&D may have been carried out by various parties (as will be described later), obtaining monies through a number of channels, but the origin was always the state budget.

[31] The ratio of US federal obligations for development of defense to nondefense industries was almost six to one in 1989.

[32] In operation since the enactment of the State Enterprise Law and the adoption of the government decree "on transformation of research organizations on the basis of complete self-accounting and self-financing" in 1987 (Motorygin and Glaziev, 1991, p. 12).

[33] Very often these employees sold or distributed the results of work that had actually been done in the state R&D institutes. These were, in part, like clearinghouses for new scientific and technological advances. The state was therefore generously subsidizing this private sector or more correctly *quasi-private* R&D activity. This is not always considered negative, since in Western nations the government directly or indirectly sponsors and supports substantial portions of R&D performed in private industry. In 1987, 33% of American industrial R&D was federally financed.

Appendix 4A

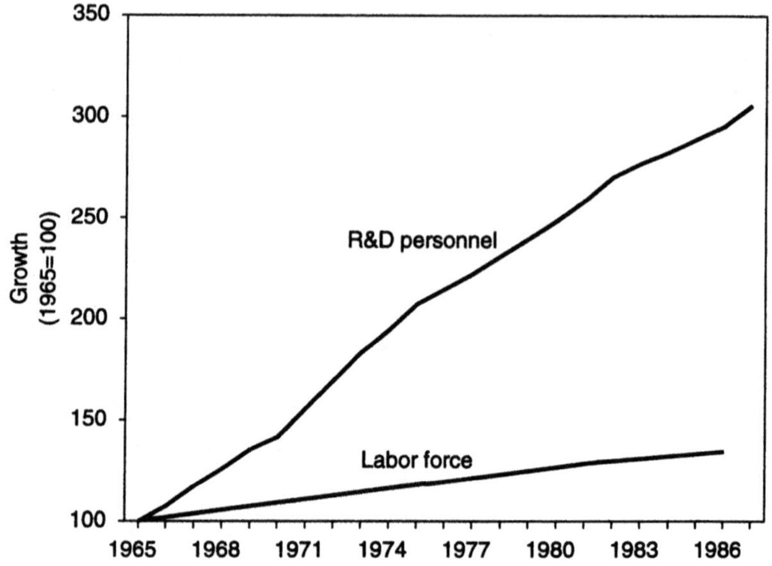

Figure 4A.1. Soviet Union – dynamics of growth: total R&D personnel versus total labor force, 1965–1987. The year 1965 equals 100.

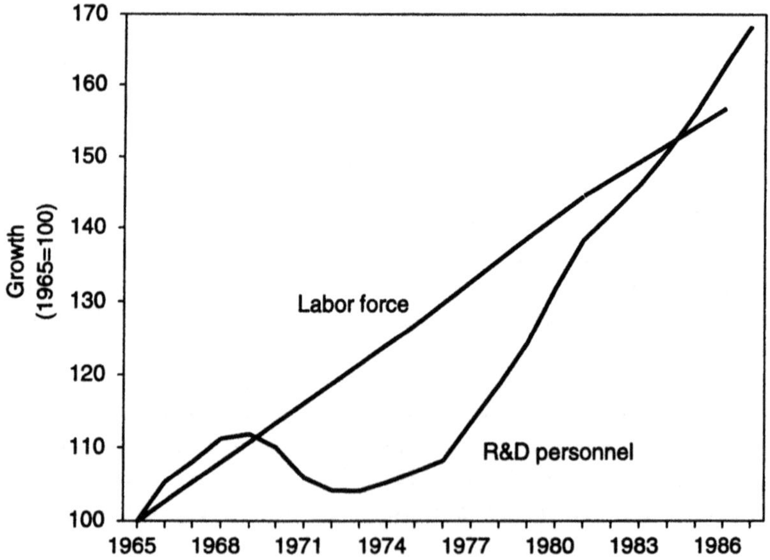

Figure 4A.2. United States – dynamics of growth: total R&D personnel versus total labor force, 1965–1987. The year 1965 equals 100.

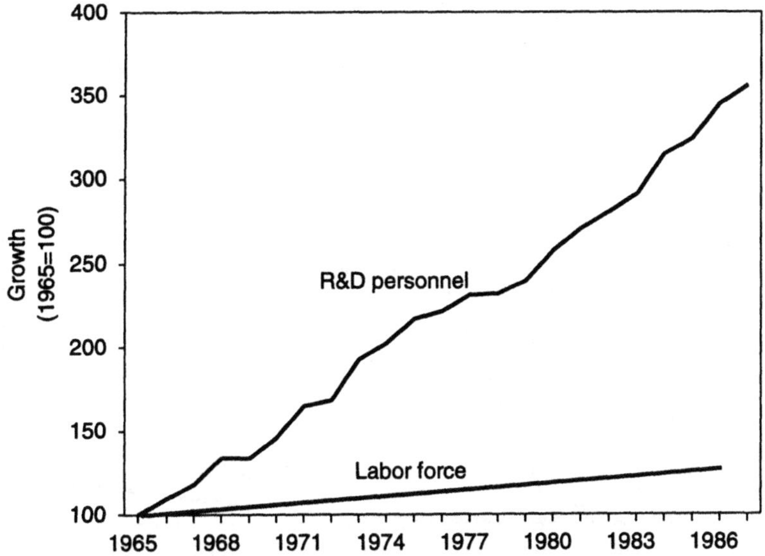

Figure 4A.3. Japan – dynamics of growth: total R&D personnel versus total labor force, 1965–1987. The year 1965 equals 100.

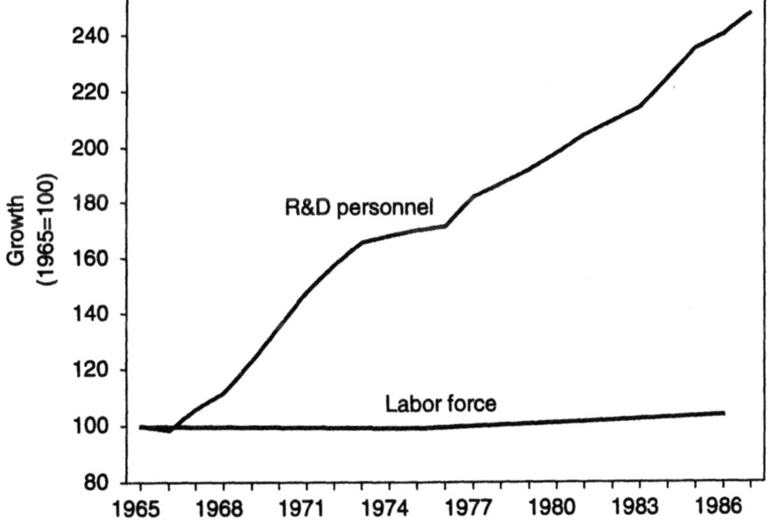

Figure 4A.4. West Germany – dynamics of growth: total R&D personnel versus total labor force, 1965–1987. The year 1965 equals 100.

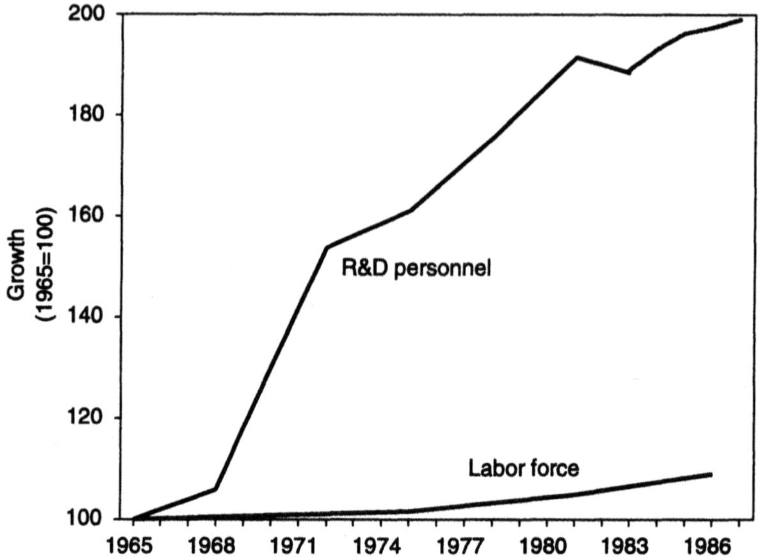

Figure 4A.5. United Kingdom – dynamics of growth: total R&D personnel versus total labor force, 1965–1987. The year 1965 equals 100.

Chapter 5

Internationalization of Research and Technology

Internationalization and globalization are two relatively new words in the vocabulary of scholars and scientific analysts in research and development. While the actual meaning and acceptance of these terms have developed slowly in science and technology policy, the activities they describe have stimulated scientific advance and technological transformation for centuries, but particularly in recent decades with the increasing speed of change. Especially since the 1950s, the relaxation of strict national boundaries in favor of a more integrated global economic system has changed the nature of the world economy. Increasing internationalization of production and trade has generated new demands on domestic R&D, while facilitating diffusion of ideas and technologies. The weakening of geographical and political protection of markets has forced more and more industries and firms to measure their competitive success not only on local, regional, and national scales, but also on the international scale.

National innovation systems tend to concentrate more and more on topics where there is a competitive advantage to be had. New materials and information technologies, telecommunications, electronics, health and the environment, and biotechnology have become generally recurring priority topics in the plans of Western governments. Yet each nation has developed special emphasis in selected fields: the USA has covered almost all aspects of materials research; Japan has been more selective and has given priority to fine ceramics, carbon fibers, technical plastics, amorphous alloys, and superconductors; Germany has focused on high-temperature metallic materials, new polymers, ceramics, and new conductors; Switzerland has specialized in alloys and materials for electronics; Norway has stressed the study of materials for offshore techniques; Denmark has developed materials for instrumentation and catalysis; and so on (OECD, 1992, p. 31). Countries in the West have highlighted particular topics within a large array of R&D endeavors, which have been carried out in the international community. Therefore, the combination of specialization and international cooperation has secured advancement in existing scientific fields and induced headway in expanding new areas.

Specialization in a few areas should not lead to the complete disregard of other topics of interest in science and technology. The growth of global R&D activities provides more incentive for developing solid overall national innovation systems based on strong research and development activities than for solely relying on the successes of specialization. A certain amount of domestic research is essential in order to be receptive to scientific progress and technological advances made in foreign countries.

Indeed, one may question why it is important for a nation to be active in the internationalization of R&D, on both the producing end and the receiving end. The scientific and technological levels of the United States and the Soviet Union provide the answer by displaying two contrary scenarios. Even if one is a major R&D producer, such as the USA or the USSR, the rest of the world may still be inventing something of interest for them with respect to production, policy, or improvement in the standard of living. The USSR essentially cut itself off from this world stock of knowledge, leaving many potentially advantageous innovations beyond their reach. Now scientists in the former USSR find themselves far behind the technological levels of nations that are substantially inferior to them in domestic R&D output. In addition, the absence of internationalization has eliminated the possibilities for the republics of the former USSR to accrue economic returns on a given invention domestically and abroad, reducing the general ability to secure economic benefits.

Different nations possess different capabilities to innovate and imitate, which determine their domestic flows of product and process innovations. The descriptive evidence would appear to indicate the presence of a strong correlation between active participation in the international market place and internal technological and economic development. Isolation and inbreeding have not exhibited the ability to generate the same successes as open market policies with respect to achieving technological advance, particularly not at similar levels of efficiency.

After 1945, postwar rebuilding began and a new world economic system emerged that reflected the sharp division between political, economic, and consequently social policies of different groups. The primary division in the world after 1945 was essentially that between the West (led by the United States) and the East (the Soviet-dominated nations of Eastern Europe). In effect, the Soviet bloc defined clear boundaries around itself and its Eastern European satellites and created its own political and economic systems (Dicken, 1986, p. 16). The practically impermeable border was known as the *Iron Curtain* and the policies were a Soviet style of socialism referred to as Communism. And it was behind this Iron Curtain that the nations formed the Council of Mutual Economic Assistance (CMEA), more commonly known as COMECON, that determined their economic organization, strategies, and practices.

Particularly since the end of the World War II, but intensified with the beginning of the Cold War, repercussions of intergovernmental policies and East–West political tensions have severely been inhibited and have frequently specifically forbidden East–West scientific cooperation and exchange. However, science, like other sociocultural aspects, could have provided a means for more rapidly easing the tensions. Especially the trend toward internationalization, characterized by improved global access to science and technology, provided the opportunity in the past and continues to do so today for countries to break free from the vicious circle of lack of technological and scientific capabilities.[1]

The true extent of the ramifications of partially self-imposed and partially inflicted isolation of the Soviet science and technology community from the industrialized Western world became clearer with the opening of the USSR in the late 1980s. Without *perestroika* and *glasnost* the great Communist superpower of the century may have been able to go on deceiving the rest of the world and itself with respect to the quality of its S&T establishment, among other things, for some time to come. Yet, this was not to be. The crumbling of political barriers and the opening of the Soviet economy have exposed all sectors to international scrutiny, including research and development management and the entire S&T system. A comparison with the international standard has revealed large gaps in the apparently solidly founded R&D in the USSR. The civilian sectors were particularly lacking; neither the currently available results nor the quality of scientific potential could ensure the output of new products, innovations, or technologies to be competitive on the world market.

This chapter first addresses the issues associated with the building blocks of technology, namely, research and development, in a global perspective. Comparisons are drawn whenever possible to the Soviet system, where the presence or lack of particular international aspects directly influenced the techno-economic growth and development. Closely linked to this topic have been the increasingly significant effects of a globalization of transnational corporations' strategies as they pertained to numerous factors of operation including foreign R&D laboratories and other such activities. The second part of the chapter then deals with the subsequent issues regarding the international development of technology, which include technology agreements, transfer of technology, and the role of private business in these two areas.

5.1 International Research and Development

In recent decades, the gradually increasing internationalization or globalization of production and trade processes has extended far beyond simply manufactured goods to include the key resources of production such as capital, labor, skills, technology, and know-how. The 1980s have already provided evidence of an accelerating, more complex, and geographically wider pattern of international exchange and cooperation, with access to and diffusion of technology and its components playing a major role (OECD, 1991b, p. 113). In order to be successful in securing continued growth and rising welfare, it was becoming essential to be adequately integrated in these global processes in response to the new economic forces.

Therefore, one of the most important occurrences that dramatically escalated in significance over the years was the internationalization of R&D planning and outlays. Initially, the institutionalization of science caused S&T policy to be mainly conceived within the framework of national interest and R&D effort was consequently restricted by national boundaries in both East and West. However, the West soon recognized the need for international communication and collaboration, while the East remained self-contained.[2] Particularly the Western European nations, which in numerous cases were characterized by a lack of critical mass of competencies and funds, were assiduous in establishing joint R&D programs and facilities.

5.1.1 Foreign direct investment as a measure of R&D internationalization

Foreign direct investment (FDI) as a percentage of gross fixed capital formation (GFCF) is a measure of the interest one or more economies have in another, and vice versa. In the last decades, FDI has become an increasingly influential component in promoting economic growth according to analysis based on Western nations. Moreover, trends in FDI constitute an important channel for the internationalization of technology, including the development of both scientific collaboration and industrial R&D cooperation, and opportunities for technology transfer. Direct investment has been recognized as

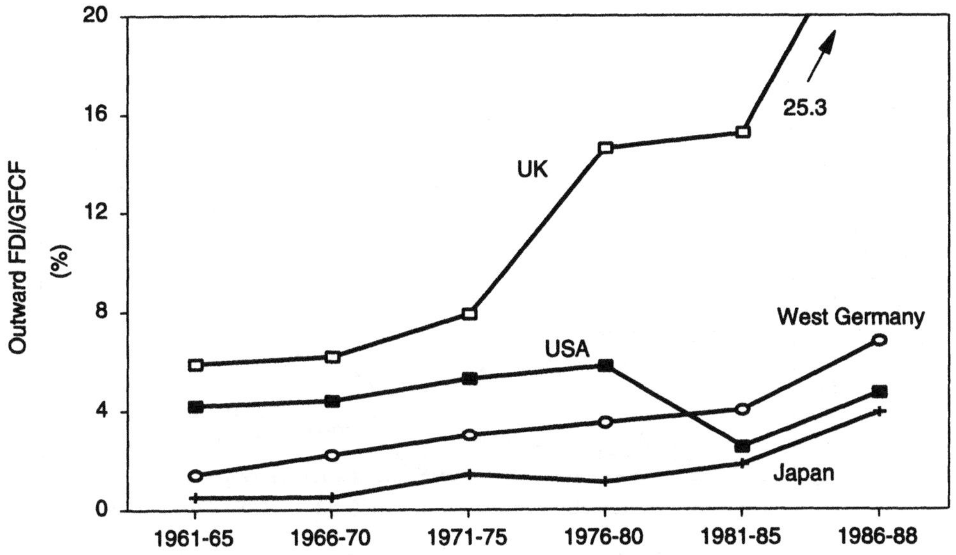

Figure 5.1. Outward FDI as a percentage of GFCF, annual averages per period.

the main vehicle for access to, and diffusion of, technical knowledge and innovation and has often been accompanied by R&D activities and facilities.

In general, FDI as a percentage of gross fixed capital formation has been increasing fairly steadily over the past 30 years in the top R&D investor countries of the West. The rising absolute totals reveal that activities and collaboration with partners abroad and the operations of foreigners domestically became a progressively crucial element of national strategy. Nevertheless, national governments and firms from the same parent nations followed individual strategies for investing abroad that have resulted in significant differences regarding the nature of outward and inward FDI.

Outward FDI as a percentage of GFCF has grown continually in the four countries as shown in *Figure 5.1*, except for short-term dips in Japan during the late 1970s and in the USA in the early 1980s. National governments had realized the increases in benefits and the reductions in risk of investments if they went beyond their own borders and collaborated with others. Enterprises also utilized the internationalization of production and the improvements in information technologies to achieve higher returns from their foreign investments, which in the case of R&D increasingly included cooperation with domestic research organizations in other countries.

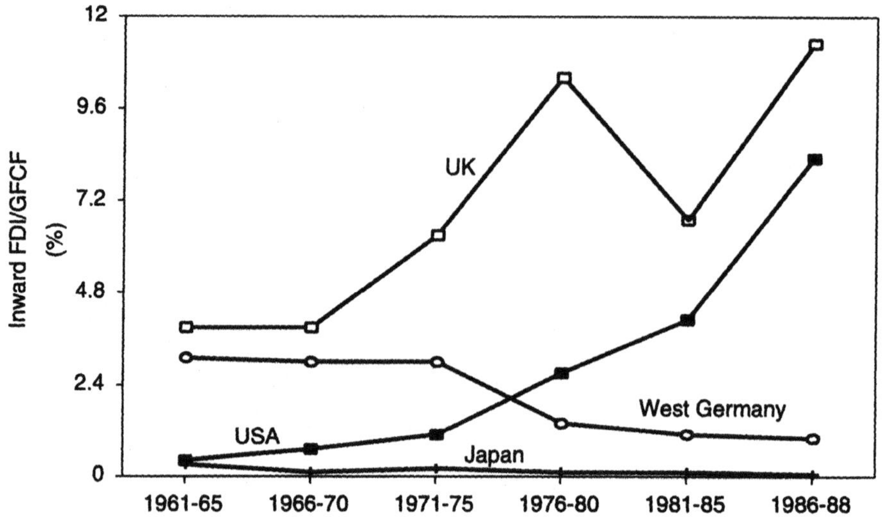

Figure 5.2. Inward FDI as a percentage of GFCF, annual averages per period.

The low and declining levels of inward FDI as a percentage of GFCF in Japan and West Germany over the period shown in *Figure 5.2* gives evidence of the extremely high levels and rapidly growing rates of national investment, making the importance of foreign interests relatively less important. It also indicates that these two countries had greater interests abroad than others had in them, whereas the opposite was true for the USA and the UK, especially after the early 1970s. However, these figures omit evidence of the crucial historical relevance of inward FDI for these nations early in the rebuilding period after World War II, despite the rigid controls. In fact, when direct investment into Japan was gradually liberalized in the late 1960s and early 1970s, it was becoming less important as a means for transferring international technological development.

The USSR and the Eastern European countries provided a completely different picture. There is no appropriate official statistical data available regarding FDI in Eastern Europe, primarily because it was practically insignificant. For all intents and purposes, inward and outward FDI in the Soviet Union and its neighbors was essentially zero, at least until the early 1980s. In the latest official GOSKOMSTAT statistical publication (1990), there were still no figures on FDI.[3] The rigidity and isolation of the Soviet Union and Eastern Europe prevented their sharing any such benefits of international economic activities, of which foreign direct investment was only one aspect that contributed to competitive advantages in the world markets.

So, while the West was generating widespread economic progress based on considerable technological progress, the Eastern bloc (led by the USSR) believed it could achieve not just comparable but superior levels left to its own devices.

5.1.2 Involvement in international scientific activities

Scientists and officials in East and West were often concerned, albeit not always for the same reasons, with both official and informal exchanges with the Soviet Union. International scientific contacts to interesting parties were conventionally promoted, directed, coordinated, and controlled by the government rather than simply arranged by the individual scientist, institute, or organization. The program of the NATO Science Committee in supporting civil science in the alliance has been a positive example in proving that science develops best in conditions of the true uninhibited circulation of ideas (Sinclair, 1987, p. xiii). In contrast, the Soviet-style R&D system was typified by an isolation of R&D workers from their peers both domestically and internationally.

International scientific cooperation has taken a wide variety of forms. Many of these were unknown to or out of the reach of scholars and scientists in Eastern Europe and the Soviet Union, while they were often taken for granted in the West. These types of collaborative activities in R&D include international meetings of experts, exchange of students and scientists, peer review of research proposals and publishable results, open competition for funding of scientific work from both government and private sources (i.e., venture capital), and direct collaboration leading to joint projects and coauthored research publications.

Scientific Meetings and Academic Exchanges

With respect to the Soviet Union, it was extremely difficult to obtain reliable data (if any at all) on most of the factors mentioned above. Countless political motives and simply the Soviet socialist ideology in general made travel all but impossible internationally (though some restrictions were eased in the late 1980s). Although the number of Soviets traveling abroad for scientific exchange was said to have increased 2.5 times between 1960 and 1980, the number of 3,200 nominated for travel by the academy in 1981 was very small by international standards. *Table 5.1* gives some indication of the level of Soviet participation in informal international communication. Clearly, the figures for the USSR are far below those of the Western nations leading in technology (in most cases by an order of magnitude), and are

Table 5.1. Participation of the Soviet Union and selected Western nations in international S&T activities, late 1970s.

	USSR	Japan	GER[a]	UK	USA
International meetings in the country	5	27	48	67	137
Presentations by country's citizens at meetings in the country	113	538	436	988	4,026
Presentations by foreign citizens at meetings in the country	479	1,006	1,597	1,847	2,593
Presentations by country's citizens at foreign meetings	118	842	1,250	1,504	4,251

[a]Refers only to West Germany.
Source: Adapted from Parrott (1987, p. 140).

incredibly small considering the enormous population of R&D experts in the USSR. If the calculations had been based on per capita terms, the Soviet figures would portray a much worse picture, particularly with respect to the much smaller Western European nations.

The number of international meetings in the Soviet Union was practically nonexistent, only five, in the late 1970s, and consequently the number of presentations by foreigners and residents was comparatively low on an aggregate scale. The Soviets did follow the trends of most other Westerners, in that more foreign presentations were entertained at the meetings than domestic ones. Only the USA had a ratio favoring presentations by domestic citizens to those of foreigners, but this is just evidence of the large number of US scholars. The Soviet meetings would not have been considered very conducive to valuable exchange between experts due to the incredible size – more than 118 presentations per meeting. The comparable figures for USA, UK, West Germany, and Japan were 48.3, 42.3, 42.4, and 57.2 respectively. Perhaps it is unjust to compare the international participation of the Soviets, who speak a relatively uncommon international language and do not always easily communicate in English, with that of the Americans, British, and even Germans. Yet, even in comparison to Japanese international S&T interaction, a nation with a unique language, the Soviets were far behind.

Therefore, Soviet researchers undoubtedly suffered from not being able to exchange ideas with accomplished foreign researchers. Even worse than the low amount of international activities domestically, was the Soviet participation in scientific and technological meetings abroad. The number of Soviet scholars traveling to foreign countries to participate in meetings was already seven times smaller than the number of Japanese in the late 1970s and over 36 times smaller than the number of Americans. The potential for Soviets to be introduced to possible foreign collaborators was unfortunately extremely minimized and constituted a serious barrier to better progress of Soviet science and technology. The resources seemed to be laying in wait, underutilized, and losing their potential.

The number of academic exchange (AE) visas granted to scientists to travel to the USA gives another indication of how many Soviets traveled abroad for scientific exchange relative to recipients from other countries.[4] The number of AE visas issued to Soviets was always low (0.26% of the total in the 1970s), but fell steadily and dropped to only 0.1% of the total issued in 1984. Not only the share, but also the absolute number fell. Almost twice as many AE visas were issued to Iranian, and 10 times as many to Polish scholars. Only the Iranian figure had dipped in the wake of the hostage crisis but was recovering in absolute terms in the 1980s; all other nations registered absolute increases between 1978 and 1984 (NSB, 1985, p. 211). In 1984, the UK, France, West Germany, Japan, Taiwan, and other Eastern European countries accounted for 9%, 5.1%, 7.6%, 7.8%, 1.3%, and 1.7% of the total respectively.

Ideas and work not required by central directives were either disallowed or developed in secrecy, so the results were inaccessible. Negotiations for funding were based on the political status of research institutes' directors rather than on scientific merit. The R&D specialists in the industrial R&D institutes did not publish any of their work – monopolization of knowledge provided power and facilitated new ways to deceive the central authorities in a plant's ability to fulfill the plans. At research institutes there was actually a disincentive to publish because it was the director whose name was placed on each publication, often with no recognition to the actual author.[5] An additional problem has always been the language factor; Soviet scholars were not known for their fluency of foreign languages, and therefore could not have productive collaboration with colleagues from the West.

Scientific Literature and International Collaboration

In the West, numerous methods are utilized to measure international scientific collaboration. One of those most preferred is the number of coauthored research publications. The simple reason is that, as opposed to the situation in Eastern Europe and the USSR, the West possesses extensive systematic data on this topic. Open scientific literature has been the primary channel for the diffusion of R&D information both within countries and between countries. Publication not only draws attention to a researcher's results, but opens the work to suggestions and criticisms from colleagues, allowing for potentially incremental improvements.

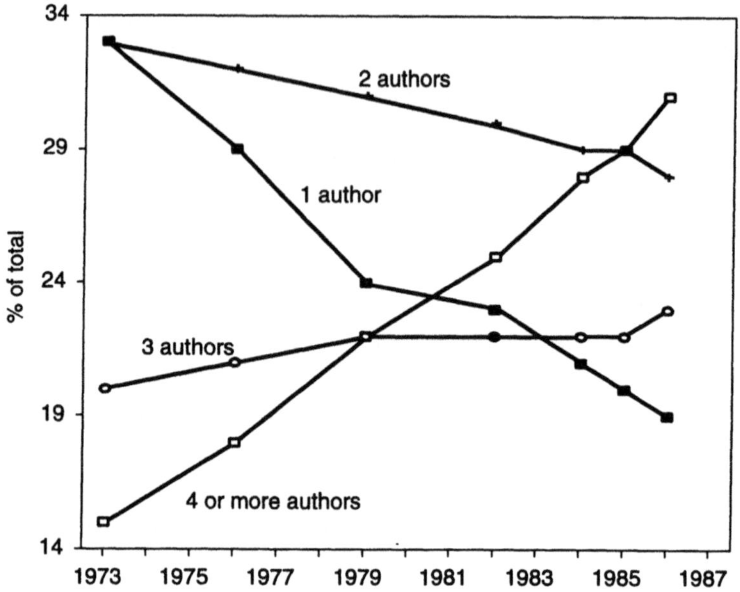

Figure 5.3. World publications by number of authors, 1973–1986.

An analysis of the trend regarding the number of authors per research paper that is considered a contribution to the stock of world scientific literature reveals an increasing tendency toward multiple coauthors. *Figure 5.3* shows that especially since 1973, scientists and engineers throughout the world have increasingly been coauthoring papers with researchers from other countries. In 1973 almost 35% of world S&E publications were still produced by only one author; however, by 1986 less than 20% of the papers had only one author. This number has declined irrespective of the particular field of research. It was most pronounced in clinical medicine and biomedical research, and least in mathematics and chemistry. The number of papers completed by two authors has also declined slightly over the same period corroborating the trend of the multiple author international research paper.

The most dramatic increase was found in a continuation of the trend that began in the 1960s but received little attention until it made impressive gains in the 1970s – research papers by four or more authors. With the exception of mathematics (a Soviet specialty), this category practically doubled in each research field, from 15% to 31% (on average in each field), between 1973 and 1986. By 1986, this category had attained the largest proportion of internationally coauthored scientific publications.[6] It seemed, that due to their involuntary isolation, Soviet researchers and scientists were in a

Table 5.2. Growth rates of the participation of selected regions and nations in international research, 1981–1986.

Regions	Growth rate (%)	Nations	Growth rate (%)
OECD	–0.02	United States	–0.17
USSR, Eastern &		United Kingdom	–0.24
Central Europe	–1.47	West Germany	–1.64
Asia	5.15	France	–0.40
South America	–1.42	USSR	–1.02
Africa	–2.09	Japan	2.52
Rest of the world	–0.65	Canada	1.97

Source: Growth rates calculated based on data on percentages of all international publications in world literature compiled from OECD (1992, p. 70) and NSB (1989, p. 331).

way forced to focus on fields like mathematics and chemistry where single authorship was still common.

How has each nation taken advantage of the opportunities for international cooperation within the global scientific community based on the share of international publications? These data reveal the predominant position of the OECD countries with respect to scientific collaboration, where almost 82% of the coauthored work in the world took place. Six countries, led by the United States and followed by the UK, Japan, West Germany, France, and Canada, commanded approximately four-fifths of the OECD total. The OECD's share of international research was quite stable in the 1980s (refer to *Table 5.2*). The relatively minor declines or negative growth, other than in West Germany, of the international level of participation of four out of the top six were compensated by strong positive growth in the remaining two nations, Japan and Canada. Primarily Japanese collaborative activities, but also those of China, South Korea, Taiwan, and India, were responsible for the striking growth of Asian international cooperation; the only region to experience growth between 1981 and 1986, and that at 5.15% per annum.

The Soviet contribution to world scientific literature was measured at 7.6% in 1986, less than one-quarter of the US contribution but just slightly lower than the British at 8.2% and the Japanese at 7.7%, and above the West German, French, and Canadian contributions. Despite this seemingly positive aggregate number, the data indicate a relatively rapid decline in the Soviet share of scientific cooperation in recent decades. The statistics reveal negative growth of 1.02% per year of Soviet participation in international research (see *Table 5.2*). Statistics indicate that this trend began in the early 1970s, if not before. The USSR was the main motor of scientific activity in Eastern Europe, and its declining share of international scientific output was the main reason for the high negative growth rate of the entire region. Only Africa portrayed a more deleterious situation in the late 1970s and 1980s.

The number of internationally coauthored science and engineering articles as a share of the Soviet Union's total publications grew by 65% from 1976 to 1986. This appeared quite paltry compared with a 97% average for the big five R&D nations, West Germany, Japan, France, the UK, and the USA, where the individual increases were as high as 116%, 114%, 107%, 82%, and 66% respectively (based on data collected from NSB, 1989, pp. 331–335). These figures also give an indication of the high emphasis on scientific collaboration in countries of the European Communities.

In addition, international coauthored publications constituted only a meager 3.3% of all Soviet scientific publications in 1986 after being as low as 2% a decade earlier. The average of the big five R&D nations named above was 17.6%, with Japan the lowest at 9.5% due to the language barrier. Perhaps a comparison between the Soviet Union and the best of the West seems unfair, but the Soviet 3.3% is even inferior to the levels in countries further from the technological frontier. The number of internationally coauthored publications as a percentage of total national publications was, on average (OECD, 1992, p. 71):

- 31.5% for the group of four small Western European countries that included Switzerland, Austria, Belgium, and Denmark.
- 20.9% for Canada and Australia, two large, resource-rich countries, yet not as wealthy as the big five.
- 26.8% for a group of less well-off European countries that included Ireland, Yugoslavia, Greece, and Spain.

International R&D Networking

The comparisons in the previous section reveal that regardless of the potential or capacity of R&D resources or other economic criteria, most nations (and certainly all those from the industrialized world) were much more active in international research cooperation than the USSR. The trends also indicate that the Soviet presence in the international R&D community has been shrinking steadily during at least the past 20 years (if not more), while Western nations have made great efforts to participate in multinational scientific and technological exchange for mutual benefit.

The smaller Eastern European nations were also trying to improve international scientific collaboration in the 1980s, and were a step ahead of their Soviet neighbors in bids at Western cooperation. While during the years under Communism they had been their own best partners with most cooperations with the Soviet Union, the 1980s saw these countries intensify their scientific relations with the West until the amount of collaborative scientific work was more equally balanced between Eastern and Western partners. Hungary had been the boldest; the United States was its number one scientific collaborator (by number of cooperations), ahead of the USSR. Poland and Czechoslovakia began adjusting in the same fashion – a process in which the USSR was actually becoming even more isolated and left to its own resources.

The international character of research fields was influenced by the focus of particular nations. The USSR, for example, and most Eastern European countries focused international collaboration more on chemistry and physics and less on mathematics. In the United Kingdom there has been a rather even distribution across fields, perhaps with a slight emphasis in clinical medicine and biology and less stress on physics and chemistry. This structure was fairly representative for most of the international scientific collaboration of OECD countries. A few exceptions to the rule were the significant effort of Japan in engineering/technology and chemistry, and that of West Germany in mathematics.

Big science, that is, research organized around expensive facilities, has traditionally influenced the characteristic distribution across fields due to a concentration in physics and earth and space sciences. The motivations for international cooperation in these areas have been a consequence of the desire and often need to share the high cost of constructing and operating sophisticated facilities and conducting associated research (OECD, 1992, p. 77). Coordinated planning and activity should ensure the best complement of highest-quality facilities and personnel at least overall cost and optimal opportunity for appropriate diffusion of results.

Efforts in R&D networking and collaboration are important for two essential reasons: firstly, resources for supporting research and development can be optimally and most efficiently utilized because each partner's contribution is usually based on his particular speciality; secondly, the results are most rapidly diffused among the participating nations in an uncomplicated manner. These R&D policy directions have been the critical influence on the scientific and technological landscape in Western countries, just as their absence typified the R&D management in Eastern Europe and the USSR.

An OECD survey (1992) has revealed that almost all member countries were contributing substantial human and financial resources to international R&D collaborative efforts and new initiatives for cooperation at bilateral and multilateral levels. Under these conditions, Germany has lately spent an average of almost 10% of its science and technology budget in international cooperation, and Spain more than 12%.

Approaching this argument from the opposite perspective requires an examination of how much foreign R&D is done domestically as a percentage of national R&D expenditure. The data from the OECD publications substantiate the preceding statements of the significance of international R&D. Most OECD countries have been characterized by the presence of some foreign-controlled R&D. In fact, the high-level/low-growth (of GERD) nations already described in Chapter 4, such as Canada, the United Kingdom, France, and Italy, exhibited foreign R&D to be as much as 26.3%, 16.9%, 10.3%, and 9.6% of national R&D expenditure in 1988 respectively. In contrast, foreign R&D proved to be relatively less important in expenditure terms for those nations in the high-level/high-growth category. They were spending disproportionately more on domestic R&D themselves. Thus, in Sweden, Germany, and Japan foreign R&D was only 2.1%, 1.5%, and 0.1% of national R&D expenditure in 1988 respectively.

A search through the official statistics reveals no evidence of any foreign-controlled R&D activities in the Soviet Union. This is not really surprising because typical Soviet-style ideology would not have permitted the existence of such operations. The statistics also lack any sign of Soviet budgetary expenditures for scientific cooperation with the West. Scholars from the USSR have said that this was because there was none. Therefore, the Soviet scientific community could not directly benefit from the significant amount of international R&D activities. At times there were some indirect benefits from the results of arduous reverse engineering procedures (primarily conducted by the KGB), but these were mainly for the defense sector and reached the scientific community with a significant time lag.

Considerable discussion has surrounded the precise origin of domestically spent R&D. The issues have arisen due to the questionable reliability and the inadequate systematic data collected within the framework elaborated by the Frascati manual. However, experts have acknowledged the increasingly important role of large international companies as one of the main sources of foreign-controlled domestic R&D and technology.[7] These key institutions in the global system of production and trade were traditionally referred to as the multinationals, until the United Nations recently officially adopted the term transnational corporations.[8]

5.1.3 Transnational corporations and R&D

The amount of R&D performed throughout the world has been dramatically enhanced by the international activities of firms. The OECD terms the growing transnational character of (mainly industrial) R&D and innovation as *techno-globalization.* As shown in Chapter 4, industrial R&D traditionally accounted for a major and over time increasingly dominant share of national R&D in both market economies and the Soviet Union. With the momentum of the changing post–World War II global economy a new structural trend was being nurtured. This trend became an especially awesome phenomenon during the 1980s when it took on imposing dimensions.

Research, development, and technological innovation increasingly became critical factors in competition as costs and risks of product development were rising and the length of product life cycles was declining. Domestic markets became too small for the expanding transnational corporations and international competition increased, causing firms to relocate various aspects of their operations – including those involving R&D and technology – closer to target markets. These large vast enterprises intensified their R&D activities in foreign countries, strengthened linkages to domestic research organizations in host countries, escalated interfirm collaboration in R&D at the transnational level, and expanded exchange and sharing of technology by companies of different countries (OECD, 1992, p. 83). The motivation behind the formulation of a more global firm strategy over the years was the desire to use resources (especially R&D) more effectively and the need to be demand responsive in the particular target market.[9] Consequently, extensive networks of firms cooperating in R&D and technology at the international level was created in the world without Soviet-style central planning.

Not only did transborder collaboration increase between firms, but the large transnationals actually transplanted or erected their own facilities in foreign countries. Political borders, at least in the West, had less and less influence on the operations of the large enterprises operating on a global scale. Transnational corporations had a major advantage over nations in economic competition; that is, they were essentially not restricted to bilateral trade or arms-length influences. These firms exhibited a high degree of locational flexibility insofar as their production and distributional networks, as well as the location of their R&D laboratories, have transcended the borders of individual nations. Transnationalization implies that the target area, spurred by a firm's foreign investment, undergoes development that moves it from being a net consumer to a net producer of the particular product of interest.

The transnational corporation (TNC) has been given an increasing amount of credit as playing a major role in shaping the new global economy. The trends toward decentralization in these often enormous international companies have also led to a dispersion of their technological research and development efforts. The operations of transnationals have influenced the state of whole economic sectors in host countries. The extent of the effects of TNC activities on a national economic system are still somewhat of a controversial issue; nevertheless, there is no doubt that some influences have resulted.

The consistent operations of foreign subsidiary R&D laboratories have been identified as providing a long list of benefits to the host country. The interactions between transnational R&D activities and the local, regional, or national scientific community and other social and economic as well as political components have generally depended on the type of R&D undertaken. Locally integrated R&D laboratories, which were responsible for local product innovation and development and transfer of technology, were the most beneficial units for interactions. The simple support laboratory (of a TNC's production operation) and the internationally independent R&D laboratory proved advantageous for host areas in selected fields of activity. Interactions between the TNC's R&D and the host country included:[10]

- Contract jobs from the R&D unit to local scientific institutions.
- Supply of consultants or contract work by R&D subsidiaries to local organizations.
- Exchange programs of scientists with local research institutions.
- Support and assistance by subsidiary R&D units to local suppliers.
- Use of seminars by subsidiary R&D units.
- Publication of research findings of subsidiary R&D units.
- Copying of R&D units' output by local firms.
- Local personnel in total employment.
- Turnover rate of local personnel in subsidiary R&D laboratories.
- Movement of host country personnel within the TNC.

In their bid to remain competitive and profitable in the global market, TNCs have traditionally spent more than other firms on R&D. In fact, the R&D function is highly significant for both the TNC itself and the countries in which it operates, particularly because these firms tended to be disproportionately involved in the more technologically intensive sectors of industry (Dicken, 1986, p. 197).

Discussion in the previous section alluded to the increasing absolute and relative importance of foreign-controlled R&D as a percentage of R&D conducted nationally in the 1980s, yet this trend began much earlier. This should come as no surprise considering the R&D budgets of some TNCs and their devotion to international operations. *Table 5.3* provides an opportunity for comparing the research and development budgets of government agencies and private companies from the same countries in 1985. The outcome of the comparison is very illuminating.

In the United States, the Department of Defense had an unparalleled budget in comparison to any other firm or state agency in the West.[11]

Table 5.3. R&D budgets of selected countries, agencies, and firms[a], 1985.

Country	Government agencies		Private firms		Total GERD
USA					116,026.0
	Defense[c]	30,332.4	General Motors	3,625.2	
	Energy[c]	5,834.4	IBM	3,457.0	
	Health and Human Serv.[c]	5,493.6	AT&T Bell	2,209.7	
	NASA	3,561.5	Ford	2,018.0	
	NSF	1,419.1	Du Pont	1,144.0	
	Agriculture	983.6	IT&T	1,085.0	
	Transportation	410.6	General Electric	1,069.0	
	Commerce	403.0	Eastman Kodak	976.0	
	Interior	395.9	United Technologies	916.2	
	Environmental Protection	320.4	Digital Equipment	717.3	
Japan					40,064.4
	Science & Technology	1,894.7	Matsushita Electr.	1,171.7	
	MITI	980.4	Toyota	1,126.6	
	Agri., Forestry, & Fish.	299.6	Hitachi	1,090.6	
	Defense	298.4	Nippon Electric	1,036.5	
	Education	260.2	Nissan	766.1	
			Toshiba	747.2	
			Fujitsu	670.1	
			Honda	549.8	
			Mitsubishi Electr.	473.2	
			Sony	454.3	
W. Ger.[b]				19,983.6	
	Research & Technology[b]	2,804.0			
	Defense[b]	1,006.3			
	Economic Affairs[b]	473.7			
	Education & Science[b]	389.9			
France					14,571.1
	Research & Technology	3,294.4	Thomson	949.1	
	Defense	2,902.3	CGE	660.3	
	Post & Telecomm.	860.4	Renault	467.7	
	Transport	286.1	Rhône-Poulenc	392.9	
			Soc. Nat. Elf Aqu.	371.4	
UK					14,443.5
	Defense[b]	4,106.8			
	Education & Science[c]	952.5			
	Trade & Industry[c]	656.8			
	Energy[c]	389.3			
	Agri., Fish., & Food[b]	213.2			
Australia[d]					2,583.6
Austria					1,035.1
Belgium					1,788.7
Denmark					785.3
Finland					879.1
Greece					201.7
Ireland					202.9
Netherl.					3,437.3
N. Zeal.[e]					355.6
Norway					940.2
Portugal[d]					254.4
Spain					1,629.3
Sweden					3,067.5
Switzerl.[d]					2,857.6

[a]In million $ ppp. [b]Ministry. [c]Department. [d]1986. [e]1989.
Sources: Compiled from OECD (1989, p. 29) and OECD (1991a, p. 16).

From *Table 5.3* it becomes apparent that the General Motors Company spent not only more on R&D than any other private firm with the USA as the parent nation, but more than NASA in the USA; approximately the same as the top five Japanese government agencies together (based on their R&D budgets); only slightly less than the top four West German ministries; and significantly more than such relatively big-spending R&D nations as the Netherlands, Sweden, Switzerland, and Australia.

The average R&D expenditure of the 10 leading private multinational firms in the USA was 121.3% of the budget of the US National Science Foundation, and greater than the average GERD of the Nordic nations. As a result, the R&D allocations of American TNCs to foreign destinations grew three times faster than the R&D allocations by domestic firms in the United States (OECD, 1992, p. 84).

Many other countries were and are parents to TNCs with impressive R&D budgets. So too, in Japan the average amount of R&D funds handled by the top five private international corporations was 139.1% of the average among the top five government agencies including MITI and the Science and Technology Agency. This amount was also greater than the total GERD of numerous smaller well-off nations such as Austria and Denmark.

Therefore, transnational corporations command substantial S&T resources that influence R&D activities in nations depending on the size and character of their own expenditures on research and development and the particular government's priority areas. *Table 5.3* also reveals that with respect to the budgetary allocation of R&D funds, the USA and the UK inherently made all other federal interests clearly subordinate to the military or defense objectives. In contrast, the governments of Japan, West Germany, and even France emphasized science, research, and technology development in favor of military product procurement.

The USSR was known to be the home of very large firms, yet they were all state owned and did not engage in the international R&D market actively themselves. In addition, during the 55-year period between 1931 and 1986 no foreign firms were permitted to control operations within the borders of the Soviet Union. These conditions were not only detrimental to the state of science and technology and consequently to the level of product development in the USSR, but also resulted in a loss for the global S&T sector. Soviet priorities were like those in the USA only much more oriented toward the military sector.

Renowned TNCs, such as Hoechst of Germany, IBM of the USA, and Philips of the Netherlands, have long been in the business of establishing R&D facilities abroad. Other firms did not take long to recognize the advantages of such actions and began to follow the leading TNCs' examples in global strategies with perpetually increasing intensity. In order to gain the best access and to optimally service new markets, TNCs were required to be in touch with and if possible have rights to R&D and technology developments in numerous countries.[12] Such global tactics solidified a company's domestic stance back home by providing a much wider base upon which to draw ideas for innovation and adaptability. So, simply stated, benefits from international operations of TNCs actually increased the level of social welfare in the home country. This is a key aspect of techno-economic development which the Soviets cut themselves off from for more than half a century.

Characteristics of the regional environment provide the conditions that induce TNCs to establish R&D facilities in a foreign place. During the course of its activities, the TNC draws upon the available resources that initially influence its locational choice and subsequently contribute to the long-term growth and development of the region by returning positive externalities to the area. These often scarce and at times geographically relatively immobile factors include availability of human resources and their corresponding skills, access to knowledge, and local suppliers' know-how and networks (OECD, 1991b, p. 124). Precisely such features are required to attain long-term growth and development.

An additional explanation for the growth in amount and importance of international R&D activities by transnational corporations was due to the increasing complexity of the research process. This process consists of three phases, each tending to have different locational requirements (Dicken, 1986, p. 198):

1. Scanning the scientific and business environment: requires access to the basic sources of science and marketing information (research institutes, universities,[13] trade associations, and so on).
2. Product design and development: requires large-scale team work and access to a sufficient supply of highly qualified scientists, engineers, and technicians.
3. Debugging and adaptation to local circumstances: requires uncomplicated and direct two-way, *feedback* contact with the users of the innovations.

TNCs have usually only been interested in national R&D policies of the host countries in as much as these can be exploited to the firms' benefit. Many host countries have outdone themselves in providing incentives to attract certain large corporations, trying best to integrate the activities of the corporation into their national policy objectives. The most current examples of this phenomenon are the measures taken by the smaller Eastern

European countries to entice large TNCs like Dow Chemical, General Electric, and General Motors of the USA; Siemens, Mercedes, and Volkswagen of Germany; Hitachi of Japan; and Samsung of Korea. In fact, host nations have in the past been, and must in the future be, wary not to compromise national policies too much just to suit the global strategy of TNCs.

R&D activities of transnational corporations tended to be strongly concentrated in developed market economies with a substantial proportion being located in the firm's parent or home country (Dicken, 1986, p. 201). The other parts of the world had not provided attractive enough conditions: in Eastern Europe and the USSR the Iron Curtain was the political barrier to an area where the resources would have been attractive; in the less developed countries (LDCs) politics was less of a problem if the size of investment was high enough, but the existence and quality of the intellectual infrastructure was often the limiting factor.

Even within countries, key factors influenced the location, type, and size of the R&D investment. While R&D-support laboratories are relatively widely dispersed, large-scale R&D activities tend to be confined to areas that can provide appropriate resources for well-functioning operation. Particularly the need for qualified human resources and proximity to other facilities (such as universities, research institutions, suppliers, collaborating competitors) have confined R&D centers to established urban complexes. The Soviet example of building cities around R&D institutes in isolated places is obviously the product of a planned economy.

International research, and particularly the dependence on TNCs to conduct it, should be viewed as a complement to rather than a substitute for domestic research and S&T policy. Tapping into the globalization of research activities and benefiting from the results thereof have been and will continue to be a crucial element of national economic growth. However, a number of issues are mentioned in the following sections of this chapter indicating that reliance on foreign research and technology has not been proved to be the *save-all* measure for domestic technological development.

5.2 International Development of Technology[14]

Historically, there have been numerous clear examples of the importance of access to technology, whether domestic or foreign, for economic growth and development. This participation in the production, diffusion, and implementation of technology has been a relatively well-recognized factor in the industrialization of the United States and many Western European countries in the nineteenth century, and more strikingly of Japan in the twentieth century. Today, the most current examples of the importance of foreign technology and its international diffusion are the newly industrialized countries (NICs) in Southeast Asia, whose GNP growth rates are more than just comparable to those of the industrial world leaders.

Research and development is an embodied element of innovation and has spread as a part of the global transfer and development of technology. Gaining access to technological products or processes inherently facilitated the access to R&D incorporated in those products, though not necessarily with a clear definition of the components. Domestic R&D facilities and specialists were responsible for ensuring the assimilation of the technology and its potential further development – as in the case of Japan over the past four decades.

Technology-gap trade has become a determining factor in the global development of technology. The basic assumption of modern technology-gap trade accounts is that technology is not a freely, and universally, available good, but there are substantial advantages to being first (Dosi and Soete, 1991, p. 103). As a consequence, other nations are motivated to accrue some benefits to themselves through imitation. If these nations are successful in utilizing the acquired R&D or technology products and develop them further, more benefits will amass. These gains can take a number of forms: very high social returns and erosion of the monopoly position of the initial innovator. In addition, if the new product is sufficiently different from the one that was imitated, then the imitator becomes an innovator with a short-term monopoly position. While postwar Japan has provided an excellent example of such a progressive nation, the USSR's extremely limited interaction with international trade in scientific and technological goods has prevented it from acquiring such characteristics. If the Soviets did procure some type of foreign technology, it was generally not developed further and was left to die the death of prolonged obsolescence. Only goods of special military interest came under closer scrutiny.

The internationalization of technology is partially a consequence of the post–WWII trend (that has dramatically accelerated in recent decades) toward industrial and economic globalization. This process, which includes cross-country investment, production, marketing, and trade, has significantly influenced the international pattern of technological development (OECD, 1992, p. 83).

It is interesting to note that the countries suffering most economically and technologically after WWII, Japan and West Germany, registered technology balance of payments ratios considerably less than one during the rebuilding period – an indication of higher payments than receipts. Even today, these powerful and solidly growing economies still have ratios below

Table 5.4. Technology balance of payments ratio (receipts/payments) for selected countries and the USSR, 1985–1990.

	1985	1986	1987	1988	1989	1990
Austria	0.23	0.21	0.21	0.25	0.30	n.a.
West Germany	0.51	0.83	0.82	0.84	0.84	n.a.
Italy	0.26	0.31	0.38	0.54	0.50	0.58
Japan	0.80	0.86	0.76	0.79	0.99	n.a.
Spain	0.25	0.24	0.18	0.13	0.18	0.18
UK	1.13	0.95	0.92	0.92	n.a.	n.a.
USA	6.73	6.83	6.65	5.29	5.26	5.78
USSR	0.99[a]	1.01	1.37	1.14	1.10	2.40

[a]Average for 1981–1985.
Sources: Compiled from OECD (1991a, p. 58) and Kiselev and Voskoboy (1991, p. 2).

one (refer to *Table 5.4*). Newly growing economies like Austria and Spain also register far greater technology payments than technology receipts. Italy, considered a very successful but late starter nation, has recorded ratios substantially below one as well. The United States, which has seen its technological superiority significantly eroding since WWII and its growth notably slowing, possessed and continues to maintain one of the highest positive technology balance of payments ratios. Prior to 1985, the UK ratio had also traditionally been substantially over one. The high ratios for the USSR may be an indication that the Soviets were neglecting the development of domestic technology in favor of technology for export to procure hard currency.

However, despite the relatively high-technology balance of payments ratio, the absolute revenue from sale of licenses was fairly low in the USSR – between one-third and one-half of most of the larger Western nations listed in *Table 5.4*, and as much as 25 times less than in the USA (Kiselev and Voskoboy, 1991, p. 3). Although the trade in technology was done at world market prices within the CMEA, the sales of Soviet licenses to this area (which made up 60% of total sales) brought little income indicating that the absolute number of licenses sold was also not overly high. Only 20% of the licenses were sold to developing market economies. The denominator of the ratio, the payments for foreign licenses by the Soviet Union, was traditionally small and sharply decreased in the 1980s. Even early in the decade the giant USSR was spending about one-quarter of that spent by the larger market economies and seven times less than Japan.

Until the 1980s, when foreign policies became somewhat more lax on both sides of the then still existing Iron Curtain, Eastern Europe and the Soviet Union had not substantially participated in the international science or technology community to an extent that would have reflected this region's potential. In fact, some experts argue that Western policies on technology and trade controls have frequently been based more on national political and economic considerations than on scientific assessments of the importance of technology transfer in the East–West economic, technological, and military balance (Bertsch, 1986, p. 115). The potential deleterious effects on the global development of technology and the associated potential improvements in living standards have also generally fallen on deaf ears.

Since the advent of changing policies in these nations dominated by Soviet-style socialism, questions have been raised with respect to the ultimate impacts on the technology development and associated economic growth of the countries involved, their S&T relationships with the advanced industrial nations in the West, and the effects on the global scientific, technological, and economic processes. One might expect a sudden boost in the internationalization of S&T, on the whole, and in the level and quality, in particular.

5.2.1 Technology agreements

Intergovernmental agreements on scientific and technical cooperation have always been an important official form of technology transfer, even between the West and the Soviet Union. With the ending of World War II came also the end of the troubled wartime alliance between the West (mainly the United States) and the USSR and, unfortunately, the beginning of the prolonged Cold War period which was to last more than four decades.

During this 40-year period, the industrialized Western countries (led by a determined US government, followed by more reluctant Western European allies) forged restrictive policies to deny the Soviet Union and the Eastern European states the benefits of trade and technological relations with the West (Bertsch 1986, p. 128). The limitations imposed by the Coordinating Committee on Multilateral Export Controls (COCOM), established in 1949 and 1950, were to place an embargo on exports, including technology, that might have contributed to either military or civilian economic performance. The limitations took the form of exceptionally high tariffs, discouragement of credits, and restriction of trade and technology transfer facilities and mechanisms. The notion was to foil the root of the S&T system as well as the products. In many ways COCOM achieved its goals; for example, scientific cooperation like countless other activities in the USSR were, until recently, frequently paralyzed by the continued reliance on antiquated communications networks.

Table 5.5. Soviet scientific and technical cooperative agreements with selected Western nations, in the 1970s.

With the United States	Year	With other nations	Year
Science and technology	1972	France	1966, 1973
Environmental protection	1972	United Kingdom	1974
Medical science and public health	1972	West Germany	1973, 1978
Space	1972	Italy	1974
Agriculture	1973	Sweden	1970
World oceans	1973	Japan	1973
Transportation	1973	Canada	1971
Atomic energy	1973	Australia	1975
Artificial heart R&D	1974	Finland	1974, 1975, 1977
Energy	1974		
Housing and other construction	1974		

Source: Derived from Bertsch (1986, p. 120).

Trade and exchange in research, science, and technology became a component of Western strategic policy. Led by the United States, Western democratic nations thought they would be able to influence (or rather make more acceptable to them) Soviet foreign policy by following a more positive linkage approach. These policies began in the Kennedy administration, expanded during the Nixon years, and were very prevalent during President Carter's term in office (Bertsch, 1986, p. 129). In fact, during his term, President Nixon actually terminated the White House science and technology advisory structure and transferred its responsibilities to the director of the National Science Foundation (Beckler, 1988, p. 31). Before the US congress reinstated the S&T advisory function in the executive office of the president in 1976, a surge of US/Soviet technology transfer agreements were made under the auspices of the NSB (refer to *Table 5.5*). A total of eleven intergovernmental agreements in less than three years. This gave evidence of the void that had been left by years of isolation from the international S&T community and the backed-up demand or global *thirst* for S&T exchange from both sides of the Iron Curtain.

Unfortunately, the Soviets were not always keen to utilize Western technology advances. Strong anti-import lobbies in the Soviet Union, particularly from the scientific community, impeded potentially more rapid progress, especially in times when and in fields where scientific innovation and technological change were accelerating the fastest.[15] During the Brezhnev decades, scientific research, mostly in computers, scientific equipment and instruments, telecommunications, and robotics, was seriously neglected (Glenny, 1986, p. 21). This proved to be a crucial error in policy because it occurred during a time when the Soviet Union still had relatively free access to buy technology from the West. The combination of this ignorance and the subsequent wide-ranging controls on technology transfer as a result of the COCOM agreement between the United States and its allies severed Soviet possibilities of keeping up with global technological leadership (at least in the civilian sector).

In spite of the limitations of COCOM on the high-technology goods, more simple products such as industrial technology, machines, and supplies were relatively free of limitations. In part, this may to some extent explain the Soviet strong expansion in these areas in the postwar period. Thus, it becomes clear that the COCOM directly or indirectly influenced the development of Soviet high-technology products and processes. An additional explanation lies in the inability of the Soviet Union and its Eastern neighbors to progress along the path of *technology transfer evolution* due to COCOM. The Soviets could not reach the optimal level of traditional trade in which technology is supplied entirely from the innovator and given directly to the recipient and, thus, could not move to the subsequent level of technology transfer: namely, jointly developed and pooled technology.

However, the power of COCOM pressure was inconsistent for two reasons: first, the more lenient Western European attitudes; and second, the results of Soviet/American foreign policy. The Europeans were very hesitant with respect to most of the US initiatives. *Table 5.5* reveals that the Western European nations were active early in establishing scientific and technical cooperation based on intergovernmental agreements. These nations were also eager to renew existing agreements and saw the level of their S&T collaborative efforts only sporadically complicated or influenced by US insistence.

American initiatives based on the Soviet invasion of Afghanistan (1980), Soviet complicity in the imposition of martial law in Poland (1982), and the Soviet shooting down of the KAL airliner (1983) severely harmed S&T ties between the two nations specifically and with the West as a whole. Yet, this was precisely the time when the industrialized world was witnessing unprecedented rates of technological advance which were the cornerstones for improved economic growth and development. In response to the Polish incident, three crucial areas of S&T cooperation were terminated between the two superpowers; the agreements in space, energy, and science and technology were allowed to lapse. These had been active for 10, 10, and 8 years respectively (see *Table 5.5*). The KAL incident led to the US cancellation of renewal of the 1973 transport agreement. The resulting effects of continual revisions of the COCOM restricted products list had many Soviet–Western

Table 5.6. Scientific and technical coordinating centers in the Soviet Union and Eastern Europe, 1971–1982.

	1971	1975	1982
Bulgaria	n.a.	2	2
Czechoslovakia	4	6	5
Hungary	n.a.	2	5
Poland	2	5	5
Romania	n.a.	3	5
USSR	11	25	37

Source: Adapted from Sobell (1986, p. 152).

collaborations running into trouble when Western scientists were forbidden to take scientific instruments to the USSR.

After discussing the difficulties faced by the Soviet Union and other Eastern European countries in their attempts to establish cooperative relationships in S&T with the industrialized West, the question arises with whom they did have links with respect to international research and technology. The answer is not difficult or unexpected: these nations were their own best partners. Soviet-style research and development management and technology transfer spread with their economic dominance in the Eastern bloc. The extension of intra-CMEA S&T cooperation became a necessity and was in effect in response to the exclusion of these nations from much of the Western advancement in many important fields.

The central coordination mechanism of many CMEA research and development activities was initiated quite early by the USSR. By 1966, so-called coordination plans for research had been instituted. Subsequently, between 1966 and 1970, 246 coordination plans were recorded, covering 3,000 projects of special importance, and representing 40% or the total budget for research (Poznanski, 1987, p. 13).

Table 5.6 illustrates two important aspects of intra-CMEA S&T cooperation. The Soviet Union completely dominated not only the activities themselves, but also the actual coordination. Although the degree of dispersion throughout the Eastern European countries increased during the 1970s and 1980s, the USSR was home to 65%, 58%, and 63% of the S&T coordinating centers in 1971, 1975, and 1982 respectively (not including East Germany). In addition, the figures give evidence of a perceived and tangible increase in Western S&T embargoes to the USSR during and after the period shown in the table. This growth in West–East *techno-economic hostility* and the generally accelerating trends in the level of global technological development were catalysts for the intensification of intra-CMEA S&T relationships, agreements, and establishment of coordinating facilities. Of course, it was based on the same ill-fated, biased, anti-competitive, and noninternational centrally planned mechanisms as the economies in these nations.

The extension of the Soviet management style representative of the planned economy to CMEA S&T collaboration resulted in the development of more tedious and awkward national and international bureaucratic control. The S&T cooperation within the CMEA framework was based on negotiations and agreements at four levels: coordination of the five-year and annual plans at the national state-planning commission level, cooperation of national branch ministries arranged by CMEA standing commissions, coordination of S&T activities by a special subcommittee of the executive committee, and bilateral and multilateral agreements and payment settlements (Chiang, 1990, p. 23). The underlying principles of the intra-CMEA, Soviet-dominated S&T cooperation essentially eliminated the market for research and technology. The unique identities and characteristics of the smaller, and historically very productive, Eastern European S&T systems were giving way to a uniform, uninspired, and unimaginative international but isolated one. Not surprisingly, some of the smaller CMEA members began to resent the pro-Soviet bias, which may affect future cooperation.

The CMEA science and technology community and its output was directed as a single centrally planned unit, only with even more bureaucracy. The consequence was a further reduction of diversity in national R&D programs, and the elimination of any remaining hints of comparative advantages and competition. Most of the required elements for economic growth and development based on improving performance criteria had been eliminated. Therefore, numerous specialists referred to the process of S&T cooperation within the CMEA not as transfer of technology, but as transfer of inefficiency.

The globalization of R&D activities and S&T relationships have revealed certain aspects of national systems that were previously concealed. In some cases, nations protested that government interests caused some segments of scientific and industrial communities to be unbalanced to the benefit of one nation or another. The same internationalization that facilitated such disclosures in the West, simultaneously provided a means for solving the dissatisfaction associated with them. A case in point was the friction regarding fairness and balance in S&T relationships between the American and Japanese scientific and industrial communities. An agreement established areas of national importance in which both countries had complementary capacities; it called for both governments to provide comparable access to their government-sponsored or government-supported research facilities and scientific infrastructure, and set forth provisions for adequate protection of intellectual property and the distribution of related rights arising from collaborative activities (OECD, 1992, p. 36).

In addition, many cooperative agreements were the consequence of collaboration between firms that were both dominant domestically and active in the international market. Evidence from recent studies has revealed that the majority of collaborative activities has taken place between companies at home in Western developed market economies – that is, the United States, Japan, and Western Europe (Chesnais, 1988; Mytelka, 1990; and Hagedoorn and Schakenraad, 1991). These interfirm agreements and alliances have in many instances already led to more concentrated world market structures and tended to increase global market dependence. The result has been the collective establishment of entry barriers and other attempts to limit access to key technologies for potential newcomers. This again emphasizes the need to be a participant in the global economy and supports the crucial argument against isolation. After so many years of self-reliance, the Eastern bloc countries including their dominant force, the Soviet Union, were faced with increasing exogenous difficulties impeding participation in various sectors of the global economy and influencing their ability to be internationally competitive.

5.2.2 Transfer of technology

Technology transfer has been defined as "the process whereby the productivity of resources of one country can be increased by the transmission from other countries of information or of products and processes embodying that information" (Hanson, 1981, p. 14).

The items of transfers include products, information, processes, research, and know-how. The means of transfer between Western nations have conventionally been the trade of goods embodying technologies, communication, exchange of experts, student exchange, and other bilateral or multilateral activities. Due to the restrictions on transfers to the USSR and other Communist countries, additional methods of transfer such as reverse engineering, technological and industrial espionage, and others became more popular for the Easterners.

Western industrialized countries have often made substantial concealed and visible efforts in the past to control and restrict such transfer to the Soviet Union.[16] Usually as a result of American pressure based on either military or economic reasons, several technologically leading Western nations erected trade and exchange embargoes on R&D and scientifically or technologically advanced products to the Soviets. However, the USSR overcame multiple international barriers in order to gain access to a very minimal amount of technology originating in the West since the 1940s, particularly given the size of the Soviet economy. In addition, the impact of these technologies was limited due to Soviet difficulties in assimilating and diffusing advanced technologies that essentially inhibited the realization of expected benefits. As a consequence, Soviet scientific and technological advance and industrial growth were largely achieved independently of Western technologies.

Over the years, West–East technology transfers have taken on a multitude of forms, ranging from overt to covert. While the former type included commercial, official, and legal transfers that were largely part of the international trade function, the latter form was usually much more difficult to identify and measure. It is impossible to review in complete detail all the West–East technology transfer relationships, but an examination of a number of selected factors gives a view of the situation which existed in this sector.

International trade in engineering goods provides a good example of the level of integration of the Soviet Union and Eastern Europe in the global transfer of technology. Not only have the engineering industries occupied a major place in the manufacturing sectors of the industrialized nations of both West and East, but the share of engineering goods in total trade of manufactured products has increased rather steadily over the last two decades in these regions. The rate of growth has been higher only for the newly industrializing countries. Products of the engineering industries ranged from the most simple to the most technologically advanced – acting as an ideal medium to transfer all sorts of scientific and technological innovations. Indeed, all investment goods, which have been carriers of technical progress, originated in the engineering industries, as did consumer goods such as washing machines, refrigerators, color television sets, watches, and countless others (ECE, 1989, pp. 7–12).

The statistics in *Table 5.7* reveal that the directives of the Soviet-style planned economy caused the bulk of Soviet and Eastern European trade to take place within the boundaries of the CMEA. In this protected market, the Soviet-style planned economic system determined the trade linkages for supply-oriented production irrespective of true consumer demand and void of any competitive aspirations. The Soviet Union stood out as the single most important trading partner of all of Eastern Europe distributing almost 50% of its exports in engineering products there in 1987. Eastern Europe sent a grand total of no less than 53.2% of its engineering goods exports to the competition-free world of the secure Soviet market. The USSR exported only 6.7% of their engineering goods to developed market economies in 1987; in the same year all of Eastern Europe exported only 7.6% of these goods to developed economies. This was not a special year, just an example of a situation that had already existed for decades.

Table 5.7. Origin and destination of engineering goods exports, 1987 (percentage shares of world total).

Exporter	Destination: EC	Western Europe	United States	Japan	Eastern Europe	Soviet Union	Asian NICs
EC	47.4	66.2	10.9	1.4	1.2	0.9	2.1
Western Europe	47.4	65.9	10.6	1.4	1.5	1.5	2.2
United States	23.1	28.1	n.a.	6.8	0.1	0.1	8.0
Japan	16.7	21.7	40.8	n.a.	0.3	0.5	14.0
Eastern Europe	3.9	7.0	0.4	n.a.	29.6	53.2	0.1
Soviet Union	3.0	6.5	0.1	0.1	49.3	n.a.	0.1
Asian NICs	14.8	18.1	45.4	5.6	0.1	n.a.	8.5

Source: Derived from ECE (1989, pp. 7–9).

Not only were Soviet and Eastern European *technologically advanced* goods not going abroad to challenge the products of market economies in their markets, but the Western engineering exports could hardly transfer technology to Eastern Europe or stimulate high-quality production there because they barely penetrated the Iron Curtain.[17] Only 1.5% of Western Europe's engineering goods exports went to the Soviet Union in 1987 (the same amount went to Eastern Europe). Although Soviet trade with the somewhat closer EFTA members was at 3.3% of all their exports, it was merely 0.1% and 0.5% of US and Japanese engineering goods exports respectively, and but 1% of all those from developed market economies. The trade intensity for engineering goods trade was generally an order of magnitude higher between the USSR and the Eastern European countries than between any two developed market economies (ECE, 1989, pp. 7–12).

This illustrates conclusively that the Soviet Union and the rest of Eastern Europe were essentially completely isolated from the benefits of the rapid advances in scientific and technological development that had been achieved under competitive conditions characteristic of open market economies. Particularly, as the pace of technological change was picking up in the 1970s, and even more dramatically in the 1980s, improved technology transfer via trade in technologically advanced goods would have contributed much required impetus to Soviet R&D and subsequent technological progress, a driving factor of economic growth and development. Another negative aspect of this trade imbalance was the limitations to the international diffusion of Soviet innovations, depriving the global S&T community as well as all possible consumers.

The results of a US Department of Commerce study of the volume of Western high-technology goods imported into the Soviet Union and Eastern

Europe in the 1970s and early 1980s corroborate the ECE findings and confirm the conclusions drawn above.[18] Both the share and absolute amount of Western high-technology exports destined for Communist countries were extremely low and actually falling at an annual rate of –1.23% during the period. In fact, one outcome of the study indicates that the amount of technology transferred to the Soviet Union and other Communist countries through commercial sales have been minor, even when compared with the shares of the industrialized West's high-technology exports to the rest of the world.

In addition to the inadequate international technology transfer, the USSR suffered for decades from insufficient internal technology transfer. The Soviet-style planned economic system lacked the fundamental mechanisms to convert countless potentially useful innovations into actual products. Administrative management and an anti-innovation incentive structure led to a separation of science and production, simultaneously acting as a barrier to diffusion. Technology transfer was thought of less in the sense of importing goods embodying various technological standards, but more as a function to transfer research, development, innovation, and technical advance from where it was produced, in the R&D sector, to where it should have been utilized, the production sector. Ministries and their research institutes used the system to basically balk the acceptance of technology from other ministries. Given the increasingly interdisciplinary nature of so much of the R&D and the narrow specialized nature of the Soviet ministerial structure, the question of interministerial technology transfer took on a whole new meaning.[19]

This predicament was recognized by the Soviet leadership from time to time; typically when an event called attention to a technological lag behind the leading capitalist countries. Thus, considerable emphasis was placed on better integrating the R&D sector and industry by Soviet planners. A perceived remedy was seen in the establishment of science and production associations (about 500 in 1987), scientific and industrial amalgamations in industry (387 in 1987, almost four times more than in 1973), and intersectoral scientific and technical complexes (23 in 1987).[20] In light of the existing Soviet technological development, these unions usually did little more than increase an already overly burdensome bureaucracy.

So, the lack of both upstream and downstream international and internal links to the Soviet R&D sector, in particular, and to the S&T community, on the whole, influenced the technical level of production and consequently the quality of output. *Table 5.8* draws a comparison of the technological production levels in six selected product groups between the Soviet Union and other selected industrialized countries. In each case, the Soviet Union lagged considerably behind the market economies with respect to the rate and period of diffusion of either the more advanced product or process technologies.

The statistics also reveal that the Soviet-style of planning economic growth and development hindered the country from catching up in various fields of production where it was necessary to assimilate modern technologies in favor of those tending toward obsolescence. Most market economies have proved this ability, though to differing degrees. Even something as controversial as nuclear power, where expansion in Western nations was often substantially limited due to public outcries, provided a far greater share of electricity output in the market economies than in the Soviet Union.[21]

Examples of other technologies used in industry shown in *Table 5.8* reveal that market economies can be technological laggards also (mainly due to adjustments on the supply and demand side, and in the institutional setup), but not for long. Thus, while France and Britain were behind other Western industrialized nations in the method of steel production, turning out only 40% and 52% using the electric and basic oxygen process in 1970, Britain had converted completely to this method by 1980, and France by 1985. The USSR was not very far behind the British and the French in 1970, but as late as 1989 it was still only producing 47% of their steel using the new technology.

A study of the speed of diffusion of 23 selected technologies in the Soviet Union between 1971 and 1987 indicates a drastic slowdown in the dissemination of these technologies. The speed of diffusion fell rapidly from 1.8% per year between 1971 and 1975 to 1.4% between 1976 and 1980, 0.8% between 1981 and 1985, and finally to as low as a mere 0.3% between 1986 and 1987 (Kontorovich, 1992, p. 217).

The economic and administrative ties were just not facilitating the necessary technology transfer between institutions and economic sectors within the USSR. At times, foreigners who had gained access to Soviet innovations developed them faster and better than was the case back in the USSR, the country of origin. The following examples have frequently been cited in the literature:

- Abel Aganbegyan, a renowned Soviet economist and adviser to President Gorbachev, toured a Japanese steel plant in 1987 and discovered that they were using 26 Soviet patents under license. These technologies, he indicated, were not in use in the USSR (Crawford, 1986, p. 1,644).
- Another example is directly associated with research and development rather than the use of resulting technologies. Plasma experimentations have been conducted at Princeton, USA, using the TOKOMAK; this is

Table 5.8. Development of the technological level of various products in the USSR and selected industrialized nations, 1970–1989.

	1970	1980	1985	1986	1987	1988	1989
Percentage of total electricity produced by nuclear power plants							
USSR	0.5	5.6	10.8	10.1	11.2	12.6	12.3
USA	1.3	10.8	15.1	16.1	17	19	n.a.
UK	10.4	13.1	20.5	19.5	17	22	n.a.
Japan	1.3	14.3	22.8	24.9	26	24	n.a.
Germany[a]	2.5	12.2	31.5	29.9	32	35	n.a.
France	3.9	23.7	65.3	70.1	70	70	n.a.
Percentage of steel produced by electric and basic oxygen processes in total steel output							
USSR	26	39	44	46	47	47	47
USA	63	88	93	96	97	95	95
UK	52	100	100	100	100	100	100
Japan	96	100	100	100	100	100	100
Italy	72	98	100	100	100	100	100
Germany[a]	66	93	100	100	100	100	100
France	40	98	100	100	100	100	100
Percentage of steel produced by machines for continuous billet forging in total steel output							
USSR	n.a.	11	14	15	16	17	17
USA	n.a.	20	44	54	59	60	61
UK	n.a.	27	55	61	65	70	n.a.
Japan	n.a.	59	91	93	93	93	n.a.
Italy	n.a.	50	79	84	90	94	n.a.
Germany[a]	n.a.	46	80	85	88	89	89
France	n.a.	41	81	90	93	94	n.a.
Percentage of finished rolled steel in total steel output							
USSR	70	70	70	70	70	71	72
USA	67	73	81	85	85	83	84
UK	78	89	82	91	90	89	n.a.
Japan	81	91	95	95	95	95	95
Italy	85	74	74	75	77	79	n.a.
Germany[a]	80	85	89	91	92	92	n.a.
France	79	91	92	93	95	89	87
Percentage of thermoplastic output in total output of synthetic resins and plastics							
USSR	n.a.	47	55	55	56	55	56
USA	70	70	70	72	70	71	70
UK	73	72	72	70	70	70	70
Japan	77	78	82	82	82	83	84
Italy	79	86	85	86	85	85	83
Germany[a]	65	65	65	65	65	65	64
France	71	80	86	85	85	85	85
Percentage of cement clinker produced by dry method in total cement output							
USSR	14	14	14	15	16	17	17
USA	40	42	56	56	58	56	59
Japan	72	78	78	78	78	78	78
Germany[a]	87	90	90	90	90	90	90

[a]Germany refers only to West Germany.
n.a. = not available.
Source: Compiled from GOSKOMSTAT (1989 and 1990).

a Soviet concept, but the American work using the machine is ahead of Soviet research conducted with the machine (Sinclair, 1987, p. xiv).

Deficient intranational and international transfer of Soviet research and technology on both the input and output (product) sides was a partial cause of increasingly deteriorating quality aspects in the 1970s and even more in the 1980s. In the 1988 GOSKOMSTAT statistical review of the Soviet economy this is substantiated by data and the following statement (p. 51): "technological standards and the quality of output of many articles remain low." The evidence indicates that a large and increasing number of consumer goods were subject to repairs before the expiration of the guaranteed service period in the 1980s. The sums of money required to eradicate the defects became exorbitant, reaching almost 30% of the original production costs for some goods.

Access to foreign scientific and technological literature has, in the past, been another very common means for technology transfer, though predominantly in the West. As described earlier in this chapter, Soviet integration in the international publication market for S&T articles, books, and journals was far too inadequate to substantially influence and aid technology transfer. Additionally, the Soviet R&D and industrial sectors did not enjoy free access to Western publications for political and economic reasons.

The Soviet scientific apparatus developed its own methods for tapping information concerning the advances in research and development published in Western literature. The review of Western scientific and engineering publications was an important means of research and technology transfer. The main actor specifically designated with the responsibility for managing flows of scientific and technical documents was the All-Union Institute of Science and Technical Information (VINITI), also referred to as the All-Union Data Institute. In the late 1980s, this organization employed over 26,000 people, including 2,300 senior science writers and 2,000 translators. Its handling capacity was impressive; over 1.2 million articles and 38,000 scientific journals were fed into the reference system each year (Semeria, 1987, p. 145).

Yet, in the 1970s, the USSR S&T community received only about half of the scientific and technical books and journals published in foreign countries with substantial R&D establishments, a trend that did not change well into the 1980s (Parrott, 1987, p. 133). Limited availability and freedom to use hard currency impeded the acquisition of foreign publications, so much so that the academy had to reduce the total number of subscriptions by 5% in the 1970s. Indeed, until the late 1980s, members of the Soviet Academy of Sciences were obliged to obtain permission from its president to subscribe to a foreign journal whose hard currency cost exceeded an established limit.

As of 1974, the USSR was to adhere to the International Copyright Convention, officially disallowing VINITI to simply copy and distribute foreign publications as had become standard practice in the past. As a result, only about 1,750 foreign journals were subsequently available on microfiche to researchers, scientists, engineers, and other scholars (Parrott, 1987, p. 134). The delays in administering and completing the conversion of foreign documents caused the citations of foreign sources in Soviet research journals often to be many years older than the domestic sources in a wide variety of fields.

Two final notes on the transfer of technology to and in the Soviet Union refer to the hard currency bottleneck which plagued the S&T sector for decades and the apparently positive increase in non-state R&D activities.

Under the conditions imposed by Soviet politics, enterprises were traditionally dependent on the state to acquire foreign technology for them. A major barrier was the extremely strict control over foreign exchange; Soviet enterprises essentially had no hard currency at their disposal to buy high technology from the West until 1985. The inefficiency and slow demise of the system was a product of the system itself, of its irrational segregation of decision makers from producers. In addition, those responsible for central payments for imported technology, really had no responsibilities for how and if the imports were used. The planning agency formulated directives on, often purposely distorted, information biased in favor of the enterprises provided by the enterprises. However, this backfired on the enterprises when the central agency bought technology which appeared to fulfill the plan on paper, but was of little or no use to the enterprise. The central agency bought foreign technology because it had control over the hard currency allocated for this purpose. The entire process finally backfired on the whole Soviet-style planned economy in the sense that the international technology transfer which was centrally managed did not significantly reduce the Soviet technological lag, and frequently actually made the existing system and infrastructure malfunction.

Since the enactment of the 1987 State Enterprise Law, the growth of R&D cooperatives and other organizations outside the state sector has looked like a promising boost to the sagging R&D output.[22] However, the great majority of these institutions seems to be engaged primarily in consulting or performing transfer of technology rather than in the creation of new knowledge (Kontorovich, 1992, p. 232).

5.2.3 Joint ventures and TNCs in technology transfer

Joint ventures (JVs), as a form of business operation, have become a common method of interfirm cooperation to facilitate various activities, including the transfer of technology, for the most part in Western industrialized nations. Until the late 1980s, this type of commercial enterprise had little if any influence on economic activity involving advances in know-how and diffusion of R&D results. However, though their absolute impact remained small, it increased dramatically throughout Eastern Europe and the Soviet Union as *perestroika* progressed in the late 1980s (refer to *Figure 5.4*). Combined with the increasing importance of the internationalization of R&D, the globalization of technological development, and the expanding influences of transnational corporations, it can be anticipated that JVs will play an increasingly important role in the techno-economic evolution of the USSR and Eastern Europe. Therefore, it is worthwhile to mention a few words about East–West JVs as a medium for technology transfer.

Over the last 30 years, joint ventures in Western countries incorporating R&D operations have been identified as an indicator for the growing trend toward strategic alliances by companies on the international scale. Beginning in the 1970s, there was notably rapid growth in joint ventures involving R&D activities (OECD, 1991b, p. 119).

Joint ventures with the participation of foreign companies became a new institutional form, instrument, and source of funds for research and development in general in the USSR, and for the evolution, production, and diffusion of specific advanced forms of equipment and technologies. In the late 1980s when new laws increased the possibilities of joint ventures with Western partners, the establishment of this category of international cooperation on a large scale was novel in the Soviet Union.[23] The past had seen isolated instances of cooperation with Western countries and companies before, but these were the exception rather than the rule. In actual fact, the operation of mutual business activities between Soviet and Western (non-Communist) partners was not permitted for more than half a century before 1986.

The rapid growth in the number of JVs depicted by *Figure 5.4* revealed that the latent potential in this previously absent institutional niche was very voluminous. While the beginning was quite meager with only 19 JVs established in 1987, the subsequent explosion saw an excess of 3,000 established by June 1991 – an annual growth rate of almost 255%. Since January 1987, JVs have been the main form of inward foreign direct investment.

A major motive behind the increasing number of joint ventures was their ability to facilitate the acquisition or transfer of sophisticated technologies

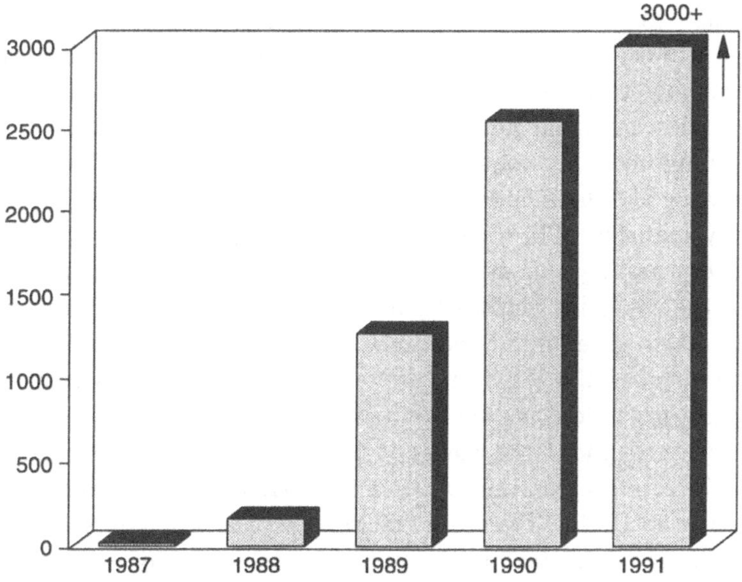

Figure 5.4. Number of joint ventures in the Soviet Union, 1987–1991.

and subsequent implementation into products and processes. Additional advantages included the utilization of management experience and material and financial resources for the development of quality science-intensive production in the USSR. However, out of the 1,274 joint ventures registered in the Soviet Union as of 1 January 1990, only 307 were actually operational (Gokhberg and Mindely, 1991, p. 26). By mid-1990, 1,754 had been registered, of which 541 were active (IMF *et al.*, 1991, p. 76). While the vast majority of JVs was set up with partners based in OECD countries (72%), CMEA countries were the home of 11% of the partners, and 7% of the partners were from developing countries.

Less than 2% of the total number, but over 7% of those that were operational, engaged in R&D. Uncertainty regarding long-term economic stability and appropriability of returns caused many foreign investors to shy away from long-term investments. R&D has typically been in areas in which it is very difficult, if not impossible, to achieve an immediate return on the initial investment. Germany, Finland, and the USA have led in the absolute number of partnerships, and Germany and Italy have had top ranking with respect to the size of total initial capital investment. The average size of initial contribution per investment by a foreign partner has decreased from 2.4 million rubles in 1987 to less than 1 million rubles in 1989 (Gokhberg and Mindely, 1991, p. 26).

By 1990 joint ventures were already making an impact on the Soviet economy. Almost 67,000 persons were employed in JVs, of which more than 98% were Soviet citizens (IMF *et al.*, 1991, p. 78). The JVs began attracting highly qualified personnel because they were paying at least 300% of the average monthly wage at the time. Finally, the new business unions were following the theories regarding their activities influencing international technology transfer. The vast majority of JV imports (86%) was made up of machinery and equipment, in particular computer technology.

Nevertheless, joint ventures have not achieved the extent of impact reflected by their sheer numbers due to an inbred ideological misconception about the purpose of a joint venture in Eastern European socialist thinking. This misinterpretation has led to the lowly ratio of JVs active in R&D and is pervasive throughout the Soviet-style planned management characteristic of economic activities carried out in the CMEA for generations. In Eastern Europe and the USSR, JVs were first seen as a secure and less bureaucratic trading link, in which technical equipment delivered by a Western partner was exchanged for Eastern goods, generating some very scarce hard currency in the process (Hentze and Wiechers, 1991, p. 227). The Western partner is usually lured by the possibility of gaining access to large new markets particularly to government-controlled markets in the short or long term.

The absence of many goods which are taken for granted in the West have made JVs in Eastern European countries attractive because they can prolong the life of a product or technology that has reached saturation (maximum potential diffusion) in Western markets. Such ventures will do more than supply the new foreign market. Eventually, after mastering the production process and satisfying domestic needs, the excess products could be exported to earn much needed hard currencies. The Japanese system of relocating aging but still important production of high-technology goods to economic satellites has given the increasing role of JVs in the Soviet Union and Eastern Europe new relevance. In addition, high initial costs of R&D were usually carried by the foreign partner, leaving the domestic partner the opportunity for further modifications with relatively low incremental R&D costs. The main costs of the Eastern European partner would be in engaging in R&D that would facilitate assimilation of R&D and technology from the foreign partner.

Until 1988, Soviet central government agencies, primarily the USSR State Committee for Science and Technology, were in charge of obtaining or selling licenses for technologies utilized or produced domestically. Previously, no enterprise could directly sign an agreement with a foreign partner regarding technology transfer. Each agreement was negotiated, organized, and finally allocated to enterprises by state bureaucrats, not scientists or managers. After 1988 enterprises were permitted to make such agreements, but only with the approval of the State Committee. The majority was approved, notwithstanding a long administrative application process.

With the increasing freedom of enterprises after 1987, a more stabilized general economic and political environment have made technology transfer at the firm level play a more significant role in the future for the region. Joint ventures have been only one such form. As the previous political and ideological borders and barriers break down, large foreign corporations could begin to have an impact on the transfer of technology and R&D facilities to the emerging market economies of Eastern Europe.

The great advantage of a transnational corporation is that simply by locating some particular operation abroad it becomes capable of transferring technology. However, the mere existence of a foreign-controlled activity may not be enough to generate active transfer of R&D, know-how, techniques, skills, or other elements. With respect to the benefits to the host economy, the critical factor is the extent to which the technology is made available to potential users outside the firm either directly, through linkages with indigenous firms, or indirectly via the "demonstration effect" (Dicken, 1986, p. 362). Caution with respect to the magnitude of the spillover of TNC operations should be maintained.

On the one hand, a TNC can be very beneficial to the domestic S&T community if it possesses assimilation potential and the TNC engages the intellectual resources of the host country. However, TNCs have been known to be protective in very new markets, keeping their knowledge and technology for themselves and only distributing finished products. In some cases, the TNC is sufficiently powerful to force the host nation to make considerable concessions, further impeding the transfer of technology from the foreign-controlled operation to the domestic market. Such concessions also prevent the natural evolution of an economy and the market mechanism. Recent examples of this have been the large international Western car manufacturers investing in the newly opening Eastern European economies. In the Third World, TNCs have been commended for transferring the best in production technology but simultaneously criticized for generally not transferring the capability to generate new technologies to the affiliates. The big internationals have been depicted as transferring *know-how* (production engineering) and not *know-why*, that is, basic design and research and development (Lall, 1984, p. 10).

The Soviet Union presents a different case than most less developed countries due to its enormous stock of scientists and engineers, elaborate S&T organization, and strong tradition in developing domestic R&D. Therefore, TNCs could benefit at least as much from tapping the host country's intellectual resources as the USSR could benefit from the establishment of foreign R&D laboratories within its borders. Foreign companies would bring with them the crucial elements of a market system, especially those most needed in the USSR such as competition, global perspectives, and requirements for high quality and efficiency.

Notes

[1] Of course, those nations that cannot generate or attract enough investment to make technological leaps forward may in effect fall further behind due to the same internationalization process, subsequently increasing the gap between rich and poor countries.

[2] Although the exchanges between Eastern European countries including the Soviet Union were quite extensive, the similarities of their adopted Soviet-style system, which was common to all, resulted in little variety and no real need for any competition.

[3] The latest figures found for FDI (only inward) in the Soviet Union are only for the Russian Federation after the collapse of the Union. In the last quarter of 1991 it was only about US$1 billion (*The Economist*, April 11, 1992, p. 69).

[4] There were also restrictions placed by the Americans on various foreigners to enter the USA depending on their countries' specific political relation to the USA at a point in time. US restrictions would intensify or ease depending on the perceived threat.

[5] Dr. Yury Struchkov, for example, a Russian chemist from the Institute of Organoelemental Compounds in Moscow, was named as the author of a total of 948 scientific papers between 1981 and 1990 (*The Economist*, 1992, p. 87). On average he was producing 1 every 3.9 days. Interestingly, half of his papers have not been referred to once, not even by himself. His nearest competitor for most publications in the same period was a Western scientist with 773 papers, cited on average 21 times each.

[6] A study of the importance of contributions to world scientific literature conducted in EC countries found that the largest number of citations were to publications by researchers from two or more countries (for more details refer to the study by Narin and Whitlow, 1990).

[7] Porter (1990) addresses this issue at length. He states that, by far, the most important influence on innovation has come from the R&D efforts of firms (p. 634). Firms themselves must apply technology to the needs of their industry, putting the principal emphasis on research in commercially relevant technologies. Firms are typically also interested in speeding up the rate of innovation rather than slowing diffusion.

[8] A transnational corporation is a firm which controls operations in more than one country.

[9] The logic was simple: if company A did not challenge its competitors in, say, the European market, then competitors would use profits in that market to

finance their attacks on company A in its home market or the market where it was strongest.

[10] For a very detailed discussion (based on survey and interview results) of issues relating to both parent company perspectives on dispersed R&D and the viewpoints of their foreign subsidiary laboratories performing this work refer to Pearce and Singh (1992). Chapter 7 reviews the interactions between R&D subsidiaries and host countries.

[11] Though not extensively involved in financing foreign R&D, some universities in the USA were also renown for having very high R&D budgets; for example, the research fund administered by the top-spending university (Johns Hopkins) exceeded the total GERD of New Zealand, was 1.5 times greater than that of Portugal, and almost twice that of Greece or Ireland.

[12] One direct method to achieve this was the acquisition of foreign firms which had R&D laboratories (OECD, 1992, p. 84).

[13] A review of OECD and national statistics (i.e., from the NSB) indicates that international industrial–academic R&D has recently been expanding more rapidly. This trend had been present for some time, but became increasingly common during the 1980s. A TNC's motives behind the establishment of R&D facilities abroad in collaboration with resident academic institutions have gone beyond the desire to have first rights to discoveries of new products, processes, and trends of demand. The global strategy of these international firms requires them to unite resident expertise in fields like basic research or others with the TNC's particular style for technological development. Simultaneously, host countries have traditionally had great interests in such international industry–academic alliances in the hope for multiplicity of new growth sites or the establishment of science parks or *technopoli* or both.

[14] This section reviews the practical issues relating to the importance of foreign technology and its application in the appropriate measure, particularly focusing on the Soviet Union and the East–West relationships. It is not the intention of this section to review the voluminous literature on this subject. For a critical examination of the role of technology in current theories of international trade and competitiveness refer to Dosi and Soete, 1991, pp. 91–118.

[15] The anti-import lobbies seem to have become a part of Soviet-style ideology. It can be traced to all the leadership cliques throughout this century, whether by free choice (personal conviction) or by necessity (due to isolation from and restrictions by the West). Even under Gorbachev in the late 1980s, at the 27th Soviet Communist Party Congress, then Prime Minister Ryzhkov criticized branch industry and science for excessive keenness to purchase products from abroad that could have been manufactured at home and referred to an "unrestrained chase after imported technology" (Kneen, 1989, p. 71).

[16] The Soviet Union did a great deal to combat this forced isolation and gain access to or adapt foreign technology. There were no legal constraints such as royalty, copyright, patent, or licensing arrangements to inhibit copying from the West (Maddison, 1969, p. 130). However, the absence of these very measures may have also acted as a major disincentive for greater domestic S&T productivity and progress.

[17] Until the late 1980s, all exporting and importing of the Soviet Union was under the joint direction of the State Committee for Foreign Economic Relations, which oversaw 12 specialized All-Union Foreign Trade Organizations (FTOs), and the Ministry of Foreign Trade, which oversaw 30 FTOs, while GOSPLAN was responsible for the foreign trade plan (IMF *et al.*, 1991, p. 435). All administrative bodies based their plans on supply-side objectives, with little or very *filtered* input from the actual producers.

[18] This study is cited and described in detail in Bertsch (1986, pp. 117–120). A few key points are reiterated here.

[19] The behavior of state enterprises contributed to the deterioration of the situation. Besides acting on ministerial directives, the enterprises were always hedging against changes. So, in the 1980s, as the economic conditions became ever more precarious, the enterprises were not implementing their cherished new equipment (whether domestic or a rare foreign import) but stockpiling them. Official statistics reveal stunning increases in enterprises' inventories of technologically advanced engineering goods including automated manufacturing systems, electrical equipment, machinery and equipment for the chemical and food industries and power generation, etc. In addition, uncertainty regarding the replacement of foreign capital assets caused them to be overutilized far beyond their productive and efficient life, leading to a waste of valuable resources, and way beyond the period these high-technology products are operated in non-Communist countries (Goldman, 1987, p. 131).

[20] Official statistics from the State Committee of the USSR on Statistics (GOSKOMSTAT, 1989).

[21] The Soviet-style command system was impervious to public opinion; that is, if the public had sufficient accurate facts at its disposal to form an opinion, which was rarely the case, it was generally not permitted to voice an opinion contrary to the central directives.

[22] The growth of these institutions, their financing and performance of research and development, and their employment of scientists and engineers are discussed in Chapters 3 and 4.

[23] The growth of JVs in European countries of the former CMEA including the USSR has been tremendous. In the four months between June and October 1989 the number shot from 1,375 to 2,090 such operations (OECD, 1992, p. 101). This is clear evidence of an extensive backed-up and unsatisfied demand.

Chapter 6

The Burdens of Abundance: R&D, Technological Change, Resource Allocation, and Productivity

This chapter attempts to reveal the extent of the ample supply of natural and human resources at the disposal of Soviet planners. Upon reviewing the evidence, it becomes plausible to visualize that these immense reserves of inputs together with the stranglehold of the central planning system (CPS) on the economy have influenced the technological requirements determined by Communist policy to achieve economic growth. The management of R&D was influenced in the same process, as it was intrinsic to the level of technology demanded from above.

However, only minor improvements in the efficiency of resource utilization could turn the entire situation around and secure enormous advances in techno-economic growth and development in the former Soviet Union. Developed market economies have been saturated with much higher levels of *technologization* and growth has slowed as gains from increases in efficiency have become more difficult to realize. Significantly smaller efforts toward advance could bring the regions in the former Soviet Union incrementally much greater rewards than the same efforts would in the West. The potential is there.

The issues discussed in this chapter are not solely relevant to the R&D issue, though the purpose is to determine linkages and relationships. The reader interested only in R&D may wish to skip this chapter. It addresses the bearing of the central planning system and the bargaining, which was characteristic of the Soviet-style system, on R&D. The exposition also concentrates on how the organization influenced the management of R&D, the incentives, motivation, and consequent productivity of researchers and scientists. Basically, the chapter attempts to reveal the extent of the ample supply of natural and human resources at the disposal of Soviet planners and how these may actually have been ***burdens of abundance*** to a more productive R&D sector.

Understanding the nature and logic of the policies characteristic of Soviet-style central planning that governed the R&D sector of the USSR, requires a perception of one of the greatest man-made paradoxes of this century and perhaps beyond: namely, the *crisis amid plenty* in the Soviet Union. In spite of being bequeathed with an abundant supply of mineral and human resources, Communist Party politics successfully cultivated an economic system in which shortages of outputs were common, and those products produced were typically of low quality. Yet, probably, it was precisely the abundance that was the actual origin of the dilemma. Therefore, the Soviet Union's good fortune may, in fact, have been the nation's major misfortune, at least in the past. With today's experience, knowledge, and rapidly democratizing political environment, measures could be introduced to promote socioeconomic growth and development beyond that in the saturating economies of the West.

Extensive-style economic growth in the USSR was frequently identified as a natural product of the great size and endowments of the Soviet nation. A typical postwar five-year plan prescribed basic application of funds and capital investment to increase 1.5 times, fuel and raw materials extraction to expand by 25% to 30%, and an additional 10 million to 11 million persons to be recruited into the national economy (Aganbegyan, 1988, p. 7). Therefore, the generous availability of relatively educated labor and valuable mineral and energy resources largely determined the manner of economic growth and development under the long years of Communist rule, particularly with respect to industrial policy. Due to the thorough use of the supply-driven planning mechanism, this policy subsequently influenced the policies and plans for the upstream and downstream sectors of the economy.

The entire central planning system determined everything in the economy from the priorities of and the resources for research and development of innovations, the needs for and objectives of scientific activities, and the technologies used for production, to the prices and quantity of output of all products produced and how and to whom these would be distributed. Theoretically, Soviet-style central planning was really an incredible system. The coordination and planning by a single central agency, GOSPLAN in the USSR, could have facilitated the optimal allocation of resources and the maximum benefits to society as a whole. However, it did not. In effect, the opposite took place – and society became poorer for it.

Misallocation of resources and static inefficiencies arose. The levels of technology required to fulfill the quantity-oriented plans were not modified and did not mature due to the absence of the need to be profit-making in a market sense; costs and revenues were based on artificial prices. The enormous supply of labor in the full-employment economy and the access to an undervalued and seemingly bottomless pit of raw material resources negated the demand for more advanced, efficiency-enhancing, and input-saving technologies. Numerous accounts of Soviet industrial production refer to the negative aspects of the Soviet-style incentive mechanisms that essentially stifled innovation. Thus, the demand for new products and processes and other advances in knowledge and know-how came primarily from the top down (the planning agency only subordinate to the USSR Council of Ministers), and not from the bottom up (the managers of production facilities). Soviet economic policy caused the nation to become stuck in second gear of industrial evolution.

As a result of total state ownership and the CPS, Soviet producers did not face the limitations on inputs or the rising costs of production that forced producers in market economies to invest in R&D. In the more or less democratic West, both governments and enterprises were interested in methods to reduce costs and increase gains. Research and development were crucial in providing new techniques and products that improved a nation's or firm's competitive position, accumulating benefits which raised the standard of living.

The CPS prompted Soviets to be faced with completely different sets of constraints and consequently distinct optimization functions. The country was tormented by contradictions. For example, capital investment was strongly promoted in heavy industry, yet labor-saving technologies were frowned upon by plant managers. Labor was hoarded to guard against orders to spontaneously increase production, lowering productivity and worker discipline. Besides, more employees meant more clout and higher status for the directors; some S&T research institutes employed thousands, even tens of thousands of persons.

In another example, rewards for output were based, for a long time, on the value of gross output. Therefore, the magnitude of a production operation was determined by the value of output plus the value of raw and intermediate materials (EIU, 1990, p. 32). The greater the value, the more impressive the manager's successes, influencing his rewards such as bonuses and promotions. So managers attempted to utilize the most expensive materials and as many inputs as possible, rather than produce the output at the most resource-efficient level. Waste was the order of the day, with indirect penalties for those who introduced technological advances to increase efficiency and decrease the amount of input per unit output. All this led to productivity decline and all its accompanying aspects.

In the absence of continually growing limitations on the use of personnel or raw materials due to either shortage of reserves or rising costs (only possible with a real price system), a system becomes infected by static inefficiencies that can eventually cripple economic growth and development. The effects reverberate throughout the economy, lulling all sectors to react to the artificial constraints. Therefore, *production amid plenty* in the USSR required technologies to be functional in turning out masses of a particular product regardless of the labor, raw material, or energy inputs needed. As a consequence, the researchers, scientists, engineers, and technicians (producers and developers of the techniques and ideas) were generally subject to the fulfillment of R&D plans based on the relatively simple technical needs. In this way, the USSR was inflicted by the vicious cycle of technological decay; a continuous loop eroding technological progress, except, of course, in sectors of special national interest as defense and space. In most fields of technical change the USSR fell well behind Western industrialized nations. Eventually, the Soviet R&D sector also fell victim to overemployment, inefficient resource use, underutilization, and the outputs were products tailored to the resource-rich nation.

6.1 The Burdens of Abundance

"Too much of a good thing" and "easy money" are figures of speech that quite accurately describe the Soviet-style central planning. The main objective of such a style of government was to eliminate the evils of a market economy. First and foremost, it was seen as an opportunity and a means to prevent the waste of resources resulting from duplication of activities which were said to be characteristic of a competitive environment. In addition, Communist ideology guaranteed a full-employment economy; in fact, all men and 90% of women of working age were employed – on the surface, a haven for equal opportunity. And finally, the Soviet-style CPS was structured to have the potential to generate rapid economic growth on demand from policy makers. This last goal was heavily based on the intensification of raw material and energy use, and amazing escalation of capital investment in relatively unsophisticated heavy industry, particularly iron and steel.

Soviet foreign and trade policies were also strongly anchored to the level of primary industry. The trade relations the USSR conducted with Western industrialized nations were dominated by the flow of exports of fuel and raw materials to the West. In fact, although the extractive industries accounted for only 7.5% of Soviet industrial output in 1979, it generated 52.5% of the total value of Soviet exports (Wright, 1983, p. 617). This business procured 84% of all valuable hard currency earnings for the Soviets in 1980 (Goldman, 1983, p. 623). Manufactured products, chiefly heavy machinery and other engineering products which required energy- and material-intensive production, usually did not meet the quality requirements of Western nations and consequently dominated Soviet exports to developing countries. In exchange, Soviets mainly imported raw materials from these regions. These processes of exchange only further accentuated the Soviet reliance on primary and simple secondary industries; subsequently increasing the obstacles even more to modern, progressive economic growth and development.

The resource-based central planning in the Soviet Union spilled over into its Eastern European neighbors. The Eastern bloc industrial and trade policies closely resembled the directions set out by the USSR for political and economic reasons. *Table 6.1* reveals the significant extent to which the USSR was subsidizing the smaller Communist countries of Eastern Europe with respect to the price and quantity of their energy imports.

Six out of the top 10 importers of Soviet crude oil and oil products were Eastern European nations, and the seventh was Cuba. This group accounted for 74% of the amount imported from the Soviet Union by the top 10 nations, as much as 61% of the quantity demanded by the top 20 importers, and still over 55% of the total Soviet exports of these energy products. The average price per ton charged to the Eastern European six and Cuba was just over 41 rubles, and as low as 37 rubles if Yugoslavia is omitted from the calculation.

In contrast, the average price per ton paid by the Western non-Communist nations that constitute the remainder of the top 20 importers ranged between 62 rubles for Sweden and 113 rubles for France, with the average at approximately 74 rubles – more than twice the price charged to the socialist satellite countries of the USSR in 1976. However, the top 13 Western importers of Soviet crude oil accounted for only a 38% share of the top 20 total imports, which was 34% of the absolute total and 62% of the amount imported by Eastern Europe and Cuba.

The dependency of the smaller Eastern European countries grew as the Soviet Union became more than just the source of a secure and inexpensive supply of energy and raw materials. The large USSR market also became the main customer for Eastern European, low-quality, uncompetitive manufactured goods. One side was inadvertently encouraging economic futility in the other.

Table 6.1. Top 20 importers of Soviet crude oil and oil products, 1976.

Rank	Country	Quantity[a]	Price[b]	Revenue[c]
1	Czechoslovakia	17.2	34	587
2	East Germany	16.8	32	537
3	Poland	14.1	42	591
4	Italy	12.0	65	783
5	Bulgaria	11.9	38	445
6	Finland	9.6	66	638
7	Cuba	8.8	33	288
8	Hungary	8.4	45	377
9	West Germany	7.1	81	577
10	Yugoslavia	4.9	65	319
11	United Kingdom	4.1	68	279
12	France	3.3	113	372
13	Netherlands	2.7	81	220
14	Sweden	2.7	62	167
15	Belgium	2.1	66	139
16	Spain	2.0	64	128
17	Greece	1.9	68	130
18	Denmark	1.6	68	109
19	Austria	1.5	67	99
20	India	1.1	89	98
Total[d]		148.6		

[a]Millions of metric tons.
[b]Rubles per ton.
[c]Millions of rubles.
[d]Includes countries not listed.
Source: Derived from Cole (1984, p. 401).

In fact, only at the 26th Session of the CMEA (in 1985) was a program tabled to address the increasing need to create more favorable economic conditions for improving technological levels to world standards and to consider methods regarding conservation of energy and raw materials (Sobell, 1986, p. 146). The Soviet spokesman encouraged a move away from cooperation in the provision of ever-increasing volumes of raw materials toward cooperation in technological restructuring, which was expected to lead to better processing and allocation of the available resources.

The examples of generous and cheap Soviet supplies to the small nations in Eastern Europe, as well as the Soviet acquisition of their relatively low-quality products, reveal the astounding size of economic gains (profits) the USSR was willing to sacrifice just to secure the diffusion of an ideology that was the basis of the pervasive technologies utilized and the demands of research and development throughout the East bloc. Political compliance with

Soviet-style preferences was the price to be paid for distorted, then attractive advantage that inevitably led to economic decline. Had, for example, the oil been sold in the Western market, then the enormous hard currency revenues could have been used by the USSR to procure foreign technologies, and it would not have fallen so far behind the levels of the industrialized Western nations.

A similar scenario could be drawn for other fuel and nonfuel mineral products from the USSR. Therefore, the highly resource-intense methods of production were rational under the prevailing conditions, and were readily assimilated throughout Eastern Europe.[1] However, this domineering mode of production simultaneously prevented technological evolution driving progressive research and development of innovations as was the situation in Western industrialized economies based on market principles. In addition, the absence of competition between producers provided no incentive for engaging in the risks of technological innovation.

Whether in a domestic or international sense, Soviet industrial policy was molded by the bounteous presence of natural and human resources. In fact, the only time one of the highly rigid five-year plans was abandoned during its term was due to the discovery of new deposits of natural resources (Cole, 1984, p. 42).[2] This was the sixth plan from 1956 to 1960. The problems of planning began and grew because of the inherent inflexibility of administering plans in which the scope was strictly bound, limiting the capacity to adjust to changing conditions, and the increasing complexity of a maturing economy. In the earlier years of the USSR when the activities were few and simple enough to be managed by central directives, the resources were employed to achieve very promising returns and in a relatively efficient fashion.

Nevertheless, beginning already in the 1960s, faced with rapidly increasing economic and technological complexity, the central planning system remained tied to its policy of using original simple technology, high consumption of raw material, and energy- and labor-intensive ideologies causing ever greater misallocations and inefficiencies. In effect, it seems truly unreasonable to believe that it is possible to create an efficient and productive system considering the amount of calculations and data required to formulate the five-year plans of the Soviet economy during the twentieth century. Thirty years ago, a Soviet mathematical economist demonstrated that in 1980 the economy would require 10^{16} calculations to formulate a plan, and that the entire working population of the USSR would be required to work for a total of five years just to formulate the 1981–1985 five-year plan (Cole, 1984, p. 42). It becomes clear that even the great wealth of resources could no longer make up for the inadequacies of planning that led to the lack of necessary technological advance needed to generate more value from the economy for the economy.

6.2 Natural Resources

The Soviet Union covered approximately one-sixth of the land surface on the globe, and controlled the largest share of natural resources, in both variety and volume, of any nation. The resource balance was favorable in both absolute and per capita terms. In fact, resource-policy dominated all other decision making to such an extent that enormous industrial complexes were established in the middle of nowhere, with cities built around them to supply the necessary labor to exploit the reserves. The amounts of centrally directed investments were enormous.

With only a very limited role for prices to stimulate real product or process improvement, the disproportionate growth of heavy industry in the USSR was primarily achieved by systematically increasing the amount of energy and raw material inputs. In spite of the great size of the production sectors, the state of technological development remained relatively low due to the basic interest in setting economic targets in terms of quantity rather than quality. As a result, the bottom-up, or market, response that stimulates the need for R&D in Western economic systems was missing in the Soviet-style command economy.

The advantages of Soviet policy made the country the most impressive producer of primary products, fuels, and semimanufactures in the world. For decades, the USSR was consistently among the top 10, often among the top three, in output of very important and high-value products due to a worldwide limited supply (shown in *Table 3.2* and Appendix 6A).

6.2.1 Fuel resources

Historically, that is, from 1737, when the first 52 hand-dug wells began producing, until 1902, shortly before the Bolshevik Revolution, Russia was the world's largest producer and exporter of petroleum.[3] Unfortunately, the rigid energy policy set forth by the early Communist governments in the five-year plans favored the development of the rich coal reserves. This delayed the exploration and utilization of oil and gas as energy carriers and prolonged the useful life of coal and the old-style industries and industrial processes associated with it. In the 50 years following 1902, so much emphasis was on planning coal expansion that by the mid-1950s coal constituted

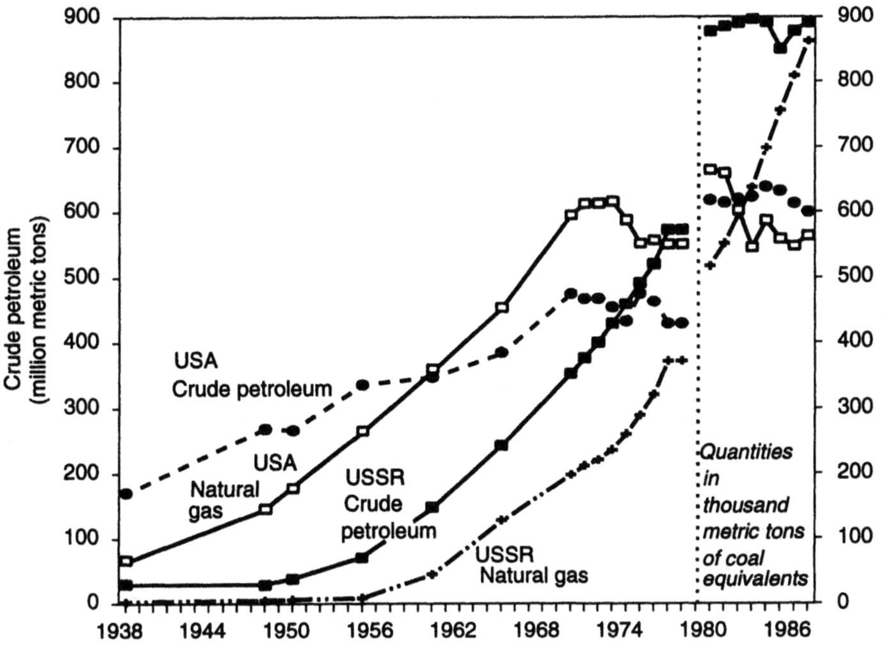

Figure 6.1. Output of crude petroleum and natural gas in the USSR and USA, 1938–1987.

over 65% of Soviet fuel production (based on heat value), while oil and gas barely made up 20% of the total together.

This explains the late and slow growth in the level of oil and gas production shown in *Figure 6.1*. However, since the late 1950s, Soviet energy strategy followed the world trend and began accelerated development and utilization of oil and gas resources, as depicted by the steep up turn in the production curves in the figure. In less than a quarter of a century a significant reallocation had altered the picture of the Soviet energy balance. That is, by 1980 coal output represented only 25.4% of total fuels production; oil accounted for 45.3%; and gas, for 27.1%. Cumulatively the latter two added to 72.4% – a complete reversal of the Soviet energy policy in the early 1950s.

In the global production of energy, the Soviet Union attained a very respectable position in the second half of the twentieth century. In fact, the USSR led all producers in output of natural gas by the 1980s, with 770,000 million cubic meters in 1988 (more than 1.6 times its nearest competitor). It had also become the world's largest oil producer in the late 1970s, with an output of 4,554 million barrels in 1988 (more than 1.5 times its nearest competitor). At least in fuel production, that is, in natural gas and oil, the USSR had finally realized the dreams of most Soviet Communist Party leaders to overtake the United States (refer to *Figure 6.1*). Yet, in retrospect, one now asks whether this was truly such a desirable strategy.

As revealed by the figures in Appendix 6B, the USSR was also among the top three producers of other types of energy; second in the world in electricity output (62% of the global leader); and third in coal production (77% of the global leader).

Earlier in this chapter, the importance of natural resources in the Soviet economy was stressed by indicating that discoveries of new sources have been the only nonmilitary reason for altering the rigid five-year planning system. The role of raw materials, particularly energy resources, was also a pivotal aspect of and consequently came to dominate industrial policy and investment. As the relatively easily accessible primary fuel deposits in West Siberia were depleted in the 1970s, the energy industry moved to the east, north, and offshore. Consequently, centrally directed capital investment was increased to at least 30% to 40% of all investment in industry (EIU, 1990, p. 197), and absorbed as much as 46% of the growth in industrial capital spending.

Because little attention had been paid to successively pressing for advances in technology and management techniques, the extraction industry was plagued by a shortage of innovations and incentives to increase efficiency, improve management, and expand exploration beyond the planned orders. The result was rising costs. Already 20 years ago, the Soviet leadership was obliged to increase the share of energy in total industrial investment to maintain growth in output. In the 1980s, the situation had become desperate. The five-year plan for 1981 to 1985 (inclusive) announced by GOSPLAN stated that energy investment would grow by 50%, making the share of energy in the planned increment of industrial investment an amazing 85.6% (Gustafson, 1989, p. 36). While this looked encouraging, many of the supporting industries were not treated so well.

This again demonstrates the continued neglect of investing in the introduction of innovation in industry that not only could have alleviated some of the pressure on primary industry, but could have simultaneously increased the efficiency of extraction. The data show that, despite the increase in investment growth from 38% between 1971 and 1976 to 48% between 1981 and 1985, the growth in energy output declined from 28% to 13% for the respective periods (Gustafson, 1989, p. 40). So, nearly three times as much investment growth was required to produce and deliver one additional unit of energy in the early 1980s as had been needed a decade or so earlier.

In fact, the 1960s saw one ruble of production in the extraction industry require two rubles of capital investment, while in the 1981–1985 period the same ruble of production required seven rubles of investment (Bradshaw, 1991, p. 9) – an indication of dramatically rising inefficiencies. This was combined with an increased bias toward investment in human and natural resources for the production of military machinery at the expense of civilian machinery under Brezhnev; the latter was responsible for supplying oil- and gas-field machinery. Output problems, essentially shortages, arose as the technologies became obsolete. It had become increasingly difficult to replace them with contemporary innovations because the nonenergy industrial sectors were faced with stagnant budgets and results of R&D at state institutes had gone on largely in isolation of production. This was simply an unsustainable process.

Primarily in the United States, but also in other Western nations, rapid economic growth and expansion in the 1950s and 1960s slowed the previously consistent trend toward improvements in energy efficiencies at the level of the world economy. Nonetheless, the USA and other Western nations were repeatedly faced with oil-price shocks originating in OPEC that caused the accelerated launching of energy-saving and energy-efficiency programs in the last quarter of this century.[4]

In comparison, the Soviet Union was in *energy heaven*; it never faced these external shocks or pressures due to its enormous domestic supply, and lived insulated from world prices. The small Eastern European countries were consequently also insulated. However, in the late 1980s such a shock was becoming a dire reality for the USSR and its socialist partners; decades of living with an overly generous energy policy had taken their toll. The Soviet energy industry began to collapse due to the deterioration of mass-produced, low-quality extraction equipment and machinery built under the quantity-intensive ideologies. The inability to produce sufficient fuel and nonfuel raw material exports reduced hard currency income desperately required for refitting the extraction and transport infrastructure. Thus, the crippling of the most prominent Soviet sector nationally and internationally was a product of the system's own, built-in deficiencies that drew wealth from only this one sector.

6.2.2 Nonfuel resources

As previously mentioned, the Soviet Union was also a leader in the output of nonfuel primary products and semimanufactures. Appendix 6A shows graphically the superior position of the USSR in the output of eight rare and valuable products. The USSR ranked first in the world in the production of lead and iron ore; second in gold, magnesium, zinc and phosphate; third in diamonds (measured in carats); and fourth in bauxite. Most of the arguments expounded for the extensive use of energy carriers in the Soviet Union and Eastern Europe apply just as well to the nonfuel goods.

The Soviet dominance in the production of these goods was partly a function of the sheer size of the industry, exemplified by enormous, vertically integrated enterprises that enjoyed largely monopoly status, and seemingly limitless economies of scale. Yet, in truth, these monstrous production operations were more directly the result of vast reserves of natural resources, both fuel and nonfuel.

On the one hand, geological exploration in search of global fuel reserves in the late 1980s revealed that the USSR had the greatest natural gas resources in the world, the second most voluminous coal deposits, and the fifth largest known oil fields. On the other hand, the extent of nonfuel mineral reserves in the USSR presents an equally impressive picture. *Table 6.2* shows the overwhelming natural advantages of the Soviet Union over Western Europe and the United States with respect to the share of a selected number of basic materials (crucial for industrial production) in the world total. The Soviet numbers are also high in absolute terms, indicating an extended life of known recoverability – otherwise known as plenty of materials for the future.

The availability of minerals was a blessing for Soviet Communist leaders, who wanted to protect the USSR from being dependent on any other nation, especially a capitalist one. Ironically, the Soviet-style politics of self-sufficiency essentially made the smaller Communist countries in Eastern Europe dependent on the USSR, for raw materials, then for industrial development, then for even more raw materials, and finally for products which other industrialized nations were long trying to move away from. However, the immense domestic supply of minerals put the Soviet Union in a unique position for industrial production: virtually no limits (other than man-made ones) that stalled the perceived need for technological change. Out of the 16 minerals listed in *Table 6.2*, the USSR is the most fortunate beneficiary of nature compared with other industrialized nations. In such *valuables* as silver, manganese, and iron it possessed some 30% of world reserves; in others, such as nickel and copper, one-eighth of the global total – figures other industrialized nations could only dream of.

In spite of its clearly inferior natural endowments, or more likely as a result of these, Western Europe has been forced to rationalize and to become as efficient as possible. Due to the physical constraints of not having access to substantial raw materials domestically, and the limitations on funds available for international purchase, Western Europeans and the Japanese had to rely particularly on and invest consequently in advances in technologies that facilitated the sparing use of material resources. Not only were these nations reasonably successful in fulfilling this objective, but they did

Table 6.2. Nonfuel mineral reserves of the USSR, Western Europe, the USA, and the world.

	Quantity of known reserves				
Mineral[a]	World	Western Europe	USA	USSR	USSR as a % of world
Potassium	109	8	n.r.	42	38.5
Iron	96,700	8,500	2,000	31,000	32.1
Manganese	700	n.r.	n.r.	200	28.6
Silver[b]	5,500	n.r.	1,300	1,500	27.3
Asbestos[c]	3.5	n.r.	0.12	0.88	25.1
Nickel	75	n.r.	n.r.	10	13.3
Copper	310	n.r.	85	40	12.9
Sulfur	2,470	60	305	300	12.1
Phosphorus	22,000	n.r.	6,800	2,600	11.8
Lead	95	8	n.r.	10	10.5
Chromium	940	n.r.	n.r.	80	8.5
Zinc	124	14	34	8	6.5
Antimony	4	n.r.	n.r.	0.25	6.3
Aluminum	1,170	38	9	60	5.1
Tin	4.33	n.r.	n.r.	0.21	4.8
Industrial diamonds[d]	630	n.r.	n.r.	25	4.0

[a]Millions of tons, unless otherwise specified.
[b]Millions of ounces.
[c]Production.
[d]Millions of carats.
n.r. = none or few reserves.
Source: Derived and adapted from Cole (1984, p. 104).

so simultaneously expanding the variety and improving the quality of output and raising the general standard of living of the population within their respective borders dramatically more than was achieved by the Soviet-style resource-intensive production.

Even the USA, which is much wealthier than either Japan or Western Europe regarding raw material reserves, has combined strong economic growth and development with increased material saving or natural resource productivity. The changes in the United States have, to a large part, been based on a desire to participate with competitive goods in the world market and on a sound commitment to encourage and support research and development of new products and techniques to enhance the competitive edge.

Table 6.3. Comparison of techno-economic efficiencies measured according to energy and steel intensity in selected Eastern and Western industrialized nations, 1979 and 1987.[a]

	Energy and steel intensity, USSR = 100			
	1979		1987	
Nation	Energy	Steel[b]	Energy	Steel
France	33.7	31.1	9.2	7.1
West Germany	37.9	38.5	12.1	11.2
Italy	44.0	58.5	10.5	13.5
Japan	n.a.	n.a.	7.2	13.0
United Kingdom	55.0	28.1	15.0	8.7
United States	n.a.	n.a.	16.3	8.0
Bulgaria	98.3	64.4	72.4	52.6
Czechoslovakia	86.6	97.8	71.9	90.6
Hungary	71.0	65.2	53.3	48.4
Poland	101.7	100.0	82.1	80.6
Romania	n.a.	n.a.	106.3	116.7
Soviet Union	100.0	100.0	100.0	100.0

[a]Calculations are based on data from the *Economist* Intelligence Unit (1990) for 1979–1980, the United Nations (*Statistical Yearbook* 1987), and the World Bank (World Tables 1991) for 1987. As a result, the magnitudes differ somewhat more dramatically than can be accounted for by increased energy and raw material saving in the West and resource intensification in the East over the eight-year interval. However, the trends and relationships are consistent with and support the arguments presented.
[b]1980.
n.a. = not available.

6.2.3 Techno-economic efficiencies

Discussions on the competitive edge must take into account the concept of efficiency. It has been shown in the example of the energy sector that the efficiency of investment was low and falling at an imposing rate in the USSR over the last quarter century. However, other aspects of resource use also reveal serious inadequacies in utilizing raw materials and energy to their optimal potential, particularly with respect to the standards in Western industrialized countries, though experts have stated that even these are still far from optimal.

The disproportionate growth in heavy industry and the disregard for efficiency in the use of resources in the Soviet Union can be illustrated by the energy and steel intensities. In *Table 6.3*, these are used as indicators to compare the levels of techno-economic efficiency of the USSR with other industrialized countries. From the table it is clear that the Eastern European countries use several times more energy and raw materials to produce a unit of GNP than Western Europe, the USA, and Japan. Among the Eastern European countries, Bulgaria, Poland, and the USSR were battling for the inauspicious title of most inefficient energy user in the 1970s, while Romania was the most inefficient energy user during the 1980s. Czechoslovakia joined Poland and the USSR as the most raw-material-intensive producers in the 1970s based on steel intensity, and Romania was the most inefficient user of raw materials in the 1980s, with the USSR and Czechoslovakia close behind.

For Western Europe, the USA, and Japan, the data in *Table 6.3* disclose no surprises. The United States (and Canada) have steadily been the most energy-intensive countries, while the Western Europeans led by Italy have used more raw materials to produce a unit of GNP as measured by the steel intensity. Although the data from the two selected years are not perfectly comparable, they do indicate that production has gone toward energy and raw-material savings in general, and significantly to a greater extent in Western Europe, the USA, and Japan than in the Soviet Union and Eastern Europe. If the trend over time is reviewed, there is evidence that this energy and raw-materials savings strategy began at least 30 years ago in some countries in Western Europe and has recently grown more rapidly (for a more detailed analysis of the transition of the steel and coal industries see Grübler, 1991).

Russia was already the world's largest iron and steel producer in the early nineteenth century (Goldman, 1983, p. 625). Although this status was lost for more than one century, modern times have seen the USSR acquire this front-running position again. The emphasis on this industry has also filtered to the other smaller Eastern European nations based on the Soviet-style model. Without exception, all Eastern European countries, led by the Soviet Union, were expanding their output of iron and steel until the late 1980s, while Western industrialized countries had long realized the need to switch to a new technological paradigm. North America and Western Europe realized this transition and began several decades ago to concede their market share in total world steel production to the countries that produced just as well and much more cheaply, namely, the NICs and LDCs. The dynamic evolution of the global iron and steel industry implies that the USSR and its neighbors were hanging on and pumping enormous amounts of resources into an industry which they would have been better off to give up in favor of a change to the subsequent techno-economic paradigm or phase of economic growth and development.

In an attempt to summarize all these facts and trends, one must realize that during the early decades of the Soviet Union, the ample supplies of resources facilitated economic growth the easy way. It thwarted or, at least, put off the immediate need for the introduction of technological advances to some future time. Unfortunately, the future caught up with this Soviet-style economic growth and development strategy very quickly. Soon, Soviet technological standards fell behind the levels in Western nations and resource use was intensified and considered a simple and inexpensive way of compensating for the growing void; this policy was certainly easier than planning innovation.

The Soviet Union entered the final stage of decline, simultaneously the initial phase of restructuring, when the holes in the sinking Soviet economy could no longer be patched fast enough. Resource reserves remained large, but always more difficult to extract, and production subsequently declined. The generous returns from the sale and use of easily accessible resources, which insulated against the need to stay at the frontier of nonspecial interest fields for so long, had inhibited the necessary development of the techniques for withdrawing the more inaccessible deposits.

For example, the USSR petroleum-drilling industry traditionally relied on the turbodrill or the rotary drill as its basic exploratory- and development-drilling tools, both known to be ineffective below depths of approximately 2,300 to 3,000 meters (Meyerhoff, 1983, p. 317). The consequent drilling problems (combined with the planned directive for the energy industry) allowed only about 6,000 wells to be drilled in the Soviet Union in 1977. In comparison, 46,479 wells were drilled in the United States and that with just 800 more rigs. As a result, Soviet drilling did not mature nearly as much as North American drilling as shown by the number of known oil and gas fields, 26,200 in the latter and only 2,500 in the former. The solution was sought in importing modern petroleum technology from abroad, despite the ever-increasing shortage of the consequently more valuable hard currency. However, already in the early 1980s some experts predicted it would take up to 20 years to modernize the industry, and much longer without foreign technology (Meyerhoff, 1983, p. 358).

Therefore, as the USSR moved into the last quarter of the twentieth century its political and economic system had cheated the country out of the general economic benefits of consistent R&D-generating innovations, it was reaching the limits of its then technical extraction potential, and the system had left the nation insufficiently prepared for modern-style growth. Inferior technology meant deteriorating fuel and raw materials production in the long term, which in turn meant reduced ability to make up for technological inferiority, at least at the international level – perhaps a blessing in disguise.

Thus, the vicious circle began to close, strangling further development and growth in the economy ruled by central planning. However, mastering the new constraints could liberate previously underestimated, indeed unexpected, growth potential in the successor regions to the Soviet Union.

6.3 Human Resources

For decades, the Soviet Union had been characterized by a prolonged phase of industrialization during which extensive (or wasteful) growth strategies were followed. Within this framework, the predominant objectives were the mobilization of unemployed (or underemployed) production factors (Sobell, 1986, p. 138). The transition to subsequent stages of more modern economic growth distinguished by the diffusion of new technological innovations and greater emphasis on quality and selection and on more intensively generated growth was not achieved as in other industrialized societies of the twentieth century. The cause was an enduring reliance on the extensive forms of old-style industrialization to generate wealth because of the generous availability of latent production factors. One such factor was the supply of labor. Communist belief called for each able person to be employed in the economy in some fashion. Of course, overloading of the employment factor combined with the fundamentals of the Soviet-style political doctrine generated a momentum to slow, even prevent, a move to more efficient, modern styles of economic growth and development in the USSR.

The Stalinist extensive growth strategies demanded more and more labor, in addition to industrial raw materials. Rapid industrial growth and *forced* urbanization came at the expense of rural deprivation; forced collectivization extracted capital from the countryside to fund the construction of steelworks and factories (Bradshaw, 1991, p. 8). All those coming to the new economic/industrial centers were guaranteed employment on the basis of Soviet full-employment ideology. This policy lingered on through the decades of Soviet-style Communist economic growth and development until the disintegration of the USSR in 1991.

6.3.1 Employment and labor productivity

Between 1950 and 1990 the USSR was the third most populated country in the world; China was first; India, second; the United States, fourth; and Japan, seventh. The work forces and numbers of persons employed were correspondingly large and followed the population ranking. *Table 6.4* shows a comparison of the number of employed persons in the Soviet Union and other industrialized or industrializing countries from the West and the South, and the growth over 37 years between 1950 and 1987. The mature economies of Western Europe had very low annual growth in persons employed, ranging between 0.01% in Austria and 0.79% in Italy. Japan's employment growth, 1.35% per annum, was also lower than that in the Soviet Union at 1.46%. Of the industrialized Western nations only the USA had a higher growth rate than the USSR, but the origins of this phenomenon have already been explained in conjunction with the expansion of the science and engineering work force (see Section 4.2.2).

Judging by the growth rate of total employment from 1950 to 1987, the USSR appeared to be a middle-of-the-road country, expanding considerably faster than the average mature Western industrialized economies, but not nearly as rapidly as the newly industrialized countries (NICs) of Southeast Asia, India, or China. Interestingly, of the four most populated countries in the world and Japan (number seven), the USSR registered the largest proportion of employed persons relative to the total population at 51.5%. The two more populous nations, China with 45.8% and India with 38.2%, and the two countries with less inhabitants than the USSR, the USA with 45.2% and Japan with 47.7%, had a considerably smaller percentage of their population employed. These are the first indications that the Soviet Union was employing more people than would have made economic sense, primarily in capitalistic terms but also with respect to the central policies followed in China.

The three columns on the right side of *Table 6.4* give an impression of the relative levels of labor productivity for a selected group of countries including the Soviet Union and the average annual growth rates between 1950 and 1987. For this initial comparison, labor productivity is calculated rather crudely, taking total gross domestic product in international dollars and dividing by total employment.

The level of the general labor productivity indicator rose for each country in the sample over the 37-year period in *Table 6.4*. The annual average growth figures indicate an inverse relationship between the USSR and the industrialized Western countries portrayed by the growth figures for employment: namely, other than two exceptions, each Western industrialized country outperformed the USSR with respect to improvement in labor productivity. Japan led the way with 5.72% growth per year, almost two and a half times the Soviet level. The NICs were closely following the Japanese in growth figures, clearly outdoing the Soviets although the former had about double the annual rate of increase in employment. Even China, with its immense population and yearly employment growth also twice the Soviet level, surpassed the latter's labor productivity growth by 1.5:1.

Again, this evidence would tend to indicate that the Soviet labor policy was to hire as many people as possible disregarding their marginal contribution to output. One reason for hoarding labor was to influence the amount

Table 6.4. Comparison of employment and labor productivity in the Soviet Union and selected nations, absolute totals and growth rates, 1950 to 1987.

	Total employment[a] (mln.)			Labor productivity[b]		
	1950	1987	gr/yr[c]	1950	1987	gr/yr[c]
Austria	3.215	3.226	0.01	4,579	20,610	4.15
Finland	1.959	2.458	0.62	5,342	19,141	3.51
France	19.092	21.269	0.29	6,445	24,806	3.71
West Germany	21.164	25.702	0.53	5,923	23,594	3.81
Italy	18.536	24.819	0.79	5,862	20,757	3.48
Japan	35.685	58.530	1.35	2,616	20,484	5.72
United Kingdom	22.400	24.542	0.25	9,377	21,199	2.23
United States	61.651	111.303	1.61	16,540	29,724	1.60
Soviet Union	85.246	145.972	1.46	4,784	11,535	2.41
South Korea	6.377	15.952	2.51	1,817	11,040	5.00
Taiwan	2.872	9.187	3.19	1,443	10,097	5.40
Thailand	10.119	25.913	2.57	1,255	4,725	3.65
India	161.386	304.227	1.73	800	1,715	2.08
China	184.984	505.775	2.76	999	3,697	3.60

[a]Includes all forms of employment.
[b]GDP in international dollars at 1980 prices divided by total employment.
[c]The average annual growth rate in %.
Sources: Selected from Appendix 3A, growth rates calculated by the author.

of central budget allocations, which was based on number of employed in an enterprise. The result was an abundance of labor, often idle, waiting to be commissioned should there suddenly be an increase in orders by the central plan.

If the comparison of total employment displayed in *Table 6.4* were modified to represent the comparison of the change in the sum of employment in primary and secondary industries,[5] as in *Figure 6.2*, a slightly modified picture results which still substantiates the arguments in this chapter. *Figure 6.2* shows the transformation of the economies in the same group of countries selected for *Table 6.4* over the period from 1950 to 1987. The graphic representation reveals how the mature, Western industrialized nations actually registered a decline in employment in agriculture and industry. This coincided with the rapid expansion of the service sector in these countries, forcing them to face an increasingly limited supply of labor for primary and secondary production. The consequence was a need for increased efficiency based on the utilization of results from research and development for new products and techniques.

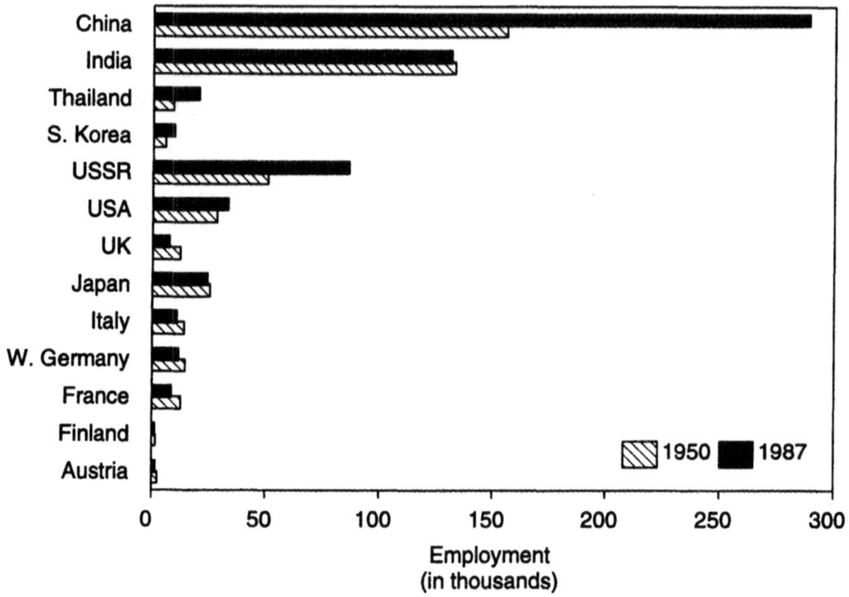

Figure 6.2. Comparison of the change in the sum of employment in agriculture and industry for selected countries between 1950 and 1987.

The Soviet Union, on the contrary, recorded a significantly higher level of employment in agriculture and industry for 1987 compared with the level in 1950.[6] This was also true for the NICs and China, but in their cases this change was due to the growth of the industrial sector which was in its infancy in 1950, employing usually far less than 10% of the total persons employed in the economy. These nations entered a period of remarkable growth in which economic output expanded many times over. However, the Soviet Union did not record any such spectacular growth during these almost four decades. This raises the question: What were all the Soviet employees doing?

If the calculation of general labor productivity (listed in *Table 6.4*) is altered to reflect more precisely the output generated by the economy per person employed in agriculture and industry, then additional support is given to the hypothesis that the abundance of labor combined with Communist ideology obstructed the economic development of the USSR. *Figure 6.3* shows, as expected, that the Western industrialized countries experienced multiple increases in their output per employee in primary and secondary industries. The NICs and China also recorded astounding growth, despite the extremely high rates of annual additions to employment, especially in industry.

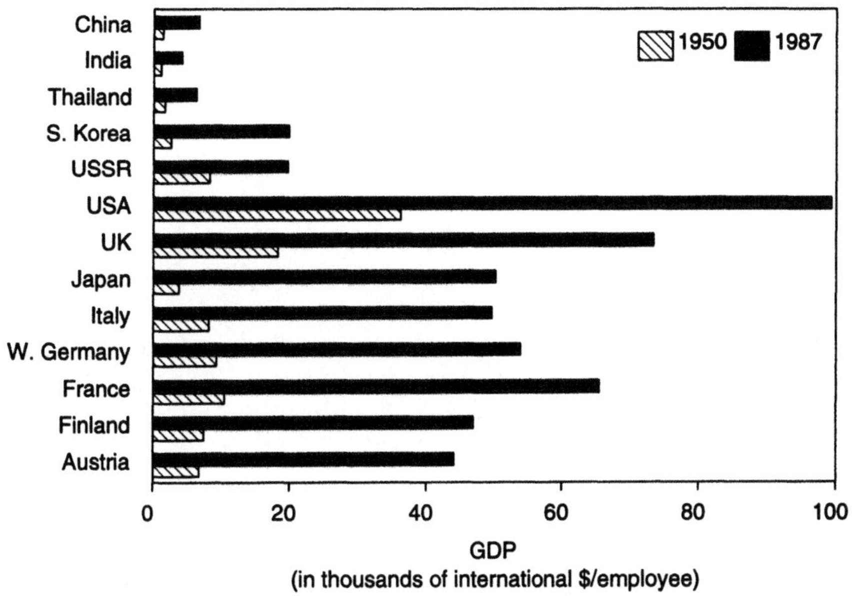

Figure 6.3. Comparison of the change in output (GDP) per employee in agriculture and industry for selected countries between 1950 and 1987.

The Soviet Union's pattern differs from the pattern of any other nation in the figure. Between 1950 and 1987, the USSR registered one of the highest annual rates of increase in employment but the lowest yearly growth in output per employee in primary and secondary industries of the countries in the sample. In fact, the output growth was just 50% of the average of the other nations – verifying that the primary objective of Soviet-style economic policy was employment of production factors, and not their efficient use.

Labor practices in the USSR were the result of the directives from above. Enterprise managers used different labor practices depending on the requirements to secure their income and influence. In the process the managers and the system were losing their grip on the working population after the tough Stalin years. Under Brezhnev, piecework tariff penalties for not achieving planned or commanded output were slack and workers resisted attempts to tighten up on them by operating their own unofficial quotas (Dyker, 1986, p. 155). Therefore, overstaffing became a typical characteristic of the Soviet industrial scene, with enterprise managers who really had very limited powers of dismissal and rarely incentives to do so (rather the opposite). Only as late as 1969 was a new system introduced; in this system some enterprises were permitted to make selected workers redundant (Dyker, 1986). Due to a complicated list of prerequisites, which included releasing someone only subject to finding them another job in cooperation with the local authority, as little as 10% of the industrial labor force was working under the more disciplined system by 1980.

In addition, the low average productivity in many enterprises, especially in engineering, reflected suboptimal scales and low technological levels in auxiliary operations ranging from R&D laboratories to component manufacture. The vertically integrated nature of enterprise structure virtually made each large enterprise self-sufficient in everything from resource acquisition to product distribution. The enormous staff was a substantial barrier and often utilized its lobby against the introduction of managerial or technical innovations that could alter the established procedures to the staff's disadvantage.

6.3.2 Labor productivity and the R&D sector

The general availability of relatively qualified personnel, whether at the R&D level or at the shop-floor level, led to the perseverance of labor-intensive working procedures and to the aversion to introducing more modern, labor-saving technologies. Therefore, the R&D sector was affected in two ways: firstly, by the general overstaffing problem which negatively influenced employee discipline; and secondly, by the lack of demand (if only from above it was at least better than nothing).

Regardless of subordination to the academy, ministry, or enterprise, overemployment at research institutes led to low productivity, inefficiency, and a poor working atmosphere due to underutilization. The excessive stockpiling of labor resources was the result of the managers' or directors' interpretations of distorted signals and commands initiated by the central planning agencies. More precisely, the causes of overemployment included:

- *Hoarding of talent* on the part of institute directors trying to secure a preferred status for their institutes (each institute's achievements influenced the director's future career).
- The desire to fulfill the plans from above, utilizing more employees as a tool in negotiations with superior levels in order to achieve an increase in the wages' fund of a particular institute and to gain the employees favor.
- Protection against the loss of bonuses by being prepared for both unexpected and expected increases in centrally planned demand.
- The pursuit of a relatively comfortable existence by the scientist, which included a rather high status in society, a relatively high wage, extensive fringe benefits, and often not overly strenuous work.

Soviets sought to compensate for their all too often poor, worn out, or simply unavailable instrumentation and equipment by expending countless hours on work which in the West would have been done on computer-controlled instruments. The "do-it-yourself approach" was frequently a product of necessity due to irregular supply or basic unavailability, but required a large staff. This overstaffing solution was no remedy for the shortcomings arising from the lack of more simple but necessary conditions for R&D projects such as adequate clean rooms, state-of-the-art vacuum technology, and computer-aided design systems.

In an attempt to quantify the output and compare the productivity of the Soviet R&D sector with those in other countries, one particular indicator must be chosen. In this chapter, the number of patents has been chosen despite its well-known deficiencies as an indicator of technological innovation. This unit of measurement is seen as imperfect in Western countries because not all inventions or innovations are patented. Many large enterprises use countless other methods to protect themselves from other firms acquiring their technological advances before the firm strategy would allow these to become a tradable good. Market orientation has provided enterprises with alternative modes for appropriating rewards from R&D (including secrecy, lead time, marketing, and entry barriers) and there may be a lesser role for the more formal methods (i.e., copyrights, patents, trademarks) as would be expected *ex ante* (Schneider, 1991, p. 24). In the case of the Soviet-style system, it may appear even more perverse to use patents as an indicator of inventiveness because there have been no intellectual property rights, patents, copyrights, trademarks, or royalties comparable with those in market economies (Schneider, 1991, p. 21).

Nonetheless, patents do provide a sense of the trends in innovative activities. Patents are representative of total inventions in that it is assumed that patented innovations are the same share of total inventions for every year, country of origin, owner, or field of technology that is being compared (NSB, 1985, p. 80). Although it has been accepted that not all patents are of equal significance to technological change, no optimal system of weighting each patent has yet been determined and is consequently not considered in the following calculations.

The data on Soviet patenting have been compiled from NSB (1991). Verification of these numbers are found in the various editions of the official statistical handbooks of the State Committee of the USSR on Statistics (GOSKOMSTAT) in the subsection titled "Science and Technological Progress." This was earlier under the section called "Intensification of Social Production," but was recently moved under the heading of "Development

Table 6.5. Patenting output and productivity in five leading R&D nations, 1989.[a]

	Patents received[b]			Inventiveness of domestic scientists and engineers[c]		
	Domestic	Internatl.	Total[d]	Domestic	Internatl.	Total[d]
Soviet Union	83,308	864	84,172	50.3	0.5	50.9
Japan	54,755	42,109	96,864	130.9	100.7	231.6
West Germany	16,893	30,278	47,171	111.5	199.9	311.4
United Kingdom	4,233	9,107	13,340	42.5	91.5	134.1
United States	50,013	39,663	89,676	60.1	47.7	107.8

[a]Productivity based on gross expenditure on research and development.
[b]Includes only patents received in United States, Japan, West Germany, France, United Kingdom, Italy, Canada, Mexico, Brazil, South Korea, Soviet Union, and India.
[c]Number of patents per 1,000 scientists and engineers engaged in research and development.
[d]Domestic and international.
Sources: Data compiled from Tables 6-21 to 6-31 in NSB (1991).

of Material Production." In fact, the USSR had no patent or other intellectual property-securing system as known in the West, but there was a system of registering inventions; the figures in *Table 6.5* and *Figure 6.4* refer to innovations registered under this system.

At first glance, the Soviet Union looks as though it was a very industrious inventor, producing just slightly fewer registered inventions and patents than Japan, which had the most in 1989, and the United States (see *Table 6.5*). However, Soviet scientists and engineers received almost 99% of their patents domestically and only 1% abroad. Of course, this was a function of their isolation and desire for self-sufficiency, but it required very different R&D management compared with the Western S&E; Americans and Japanese received almost equally as many patents at home as abroad, while Germans and British actually received twice as many abroad as at home. This indicates that the Soviets were scientifically very active at home, but practically invisible abroad.

The three columns on the right-hand side of *Table 6.5* reveal the level of productivity of the R&D sectors of the nations measured in patents per 1,000 S&E engaged in R&D. At the national level, that is, including both domestic and foreign patents received, the Soviet Union was clearly the most unproductive nation. The United States was two times more productive; the UK, almost three times more productive; Japan, almost five times more productive; and Germany, over six times more productive than the USSR. Even more astonishing is that the USSR, with its apparently enormous total of 83,308 domestic patents in 1989, recorded a lower level of domestic

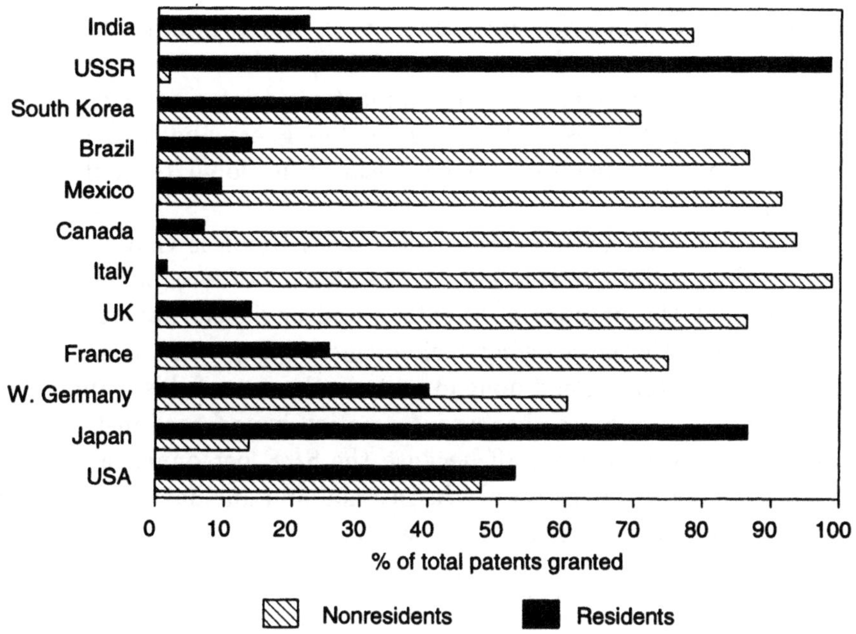

Figure 6.4. Distribution of patents granted to domestic and foreign scientists and engineers in selected countries, 1989.

inventiveness than the other big-spending R&D nations with the exception of the UK. Again, this evidence shows that, in spite of or probably because of the generous availability of scientists and engineers employed in research and development, the Soviet Union was the least inventive of the leading R&D nations in the world.

A key reason for increasing scientific and engineering employment in the USSR was founded in the belief that what could be done abroad could be achieved by Soviet S&E at home. There was a real aversion to the utilization of foreign inventions. In fact, much of the talk of technology transfer has been based on the acquisition of turnkey-style plants, not foreign licenses or patents which could be used and developed further in the USSR. Soviet ideology proclaimed that domestic resources could generate better and more technological advance, primarily based on domestic R&D, than that achieved in the West. *Figure 6.4* reveals that the Soviet Union granted almost no patents to foreigners in 1989 (1.5%). This figure was slightly higher in the distant past but stabilized between 1.5% and 2% in the 1980s.

In comparison, Italy, Canada, and the United Kingdom granted 98.7%, 93.4%, and 86.3% patents respectively to foreigners. Even such strong R&D

nations as West Germany, France, and South Korea granted the majority of patents to scientists and engineers of foreign origin. However, both the United States and especially Japan demonstrate that a country can grant more patents to nationals rather than to foreigners and still be well integrated in the world market and be a leader in global technological and economic growth.

The fundamental consequence in the Soviet Union is that the domestic R&D sector had to fill the void left by the absence of foreign contributions. This meant that the number of scientists and engineers had to be continually increased with the growing technological gap to the West. Internal isolation, lack of interaction among experts in the same fields, supply-driven projects, and an aversion to sharing information have forced institute directors to continue to increase staff because the S&E personnel in practically each laboratory had to perform all the internal and auxiliary functions from secretarial work to constructing their own instrumentation. Of course, some prestige was also involved. The results were low and declining efficiency and real productivity after the 1950s.

The point is that the Soviet policy makers achieved exactly what they had hoped and professed Soviet-style central planning would eliminate – the duplication, misallocation, and waste that was ascribed to be characteristic of competitive, capitalist economies. Many Westerners have cynically stated that the CPS was also not socially optimal because it was only successful in equally distributing poverty rather than wealth among the population. Unfortunately, reality verifies that the consequence was deficient technological and economic growth and development given the potential.

In summary, the abundance of human and natural resources in the Soviet Union clearly influenced policy and the style of economic development. The USSR presents a paradoxical picture: inadequate economic development despite generous reserves of raw materials and slow technological advance in spite of a large, well-trained stock of workers, particularly scientists and engineers. The hypothesis put forth in this chapter has tried to illustrate that the reasons for crisis were *due to* and not *in spite of* the plentiful supply of production factors.

In the case of the productivity and output of research and development, resources were the determining factors both directly and indirectly. The Soviet industrial policy, based largely on extensive, old-style economic growth in which the emphasis was on mobilizing ever greater amounts of inputs in order to generate more output, set the requirements for R&D. Therefore, the demand was essentially already determined in a distorted system and originated in a single consumer – the five-year plan. So, other than a few special sectors, like space and defense, R&D was really geared toward lower technological requirements of an economy stuck in the second gear of industrialization. The R&D sector itself was naturally managed in a similar fashion; subsequently finding such phenomena as overstaffing, wasteful use of resources, and distorted or biased orientation of research projects should not be too surprising.

However, the structure of the CPS in the Soviet Union and its management of the economy does in some way leave much hope for the successor nations of the USSR. With relatively small measures of rationalization, reorientation, and improved efficiency, incrementally much greater advances could be realized for the economies on the whole. This topic is discussed in more detail in Chapter 7.

Notes

[1] In fact, relatively cheap energy before the oil-price shock in 1973 led producers in the West to respond in a similar fashion. The significant energy price increases caused the West to turn to greater efficiency.

[2] Another five-year plan had been aborted before completion 15 years earlier, but this was for military reasons, more precisely the German invasion in 1941.

[3] This and other data in this paragraph are collected from essays concerned with Soviet natural resources in *Soviet Natural Resources in the World Economy* edited by Jensen, Shabad, and Wright. The data are successively on pages 306, 625, 252, and 278. See also Bradshaw (1991, p. 8).

[4] These shocks took the form of embargoes, production cutbacks, and additional strategies by the cartel of oil producers in order to force increases in the world price.

[5] These include agriculture, forestry, fisheries, mining, manufacturing, construction, gas, and electricity and are referred to in this study as agriculture and industry.

[6] However, the cumulative total of employment in agriculture and industry as a percentage of total employment practically did not change between 1950 and 1987, an unusual development in comparison with activities elsewhere.

Appendix 6A

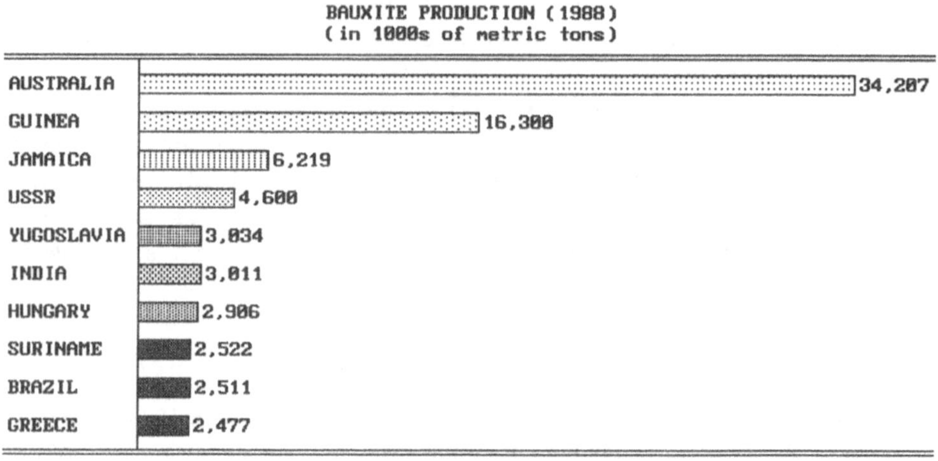

Figure 6A.1. Bauxite production of the top 10 producers in the world, in 1988, in thousand metric tons.

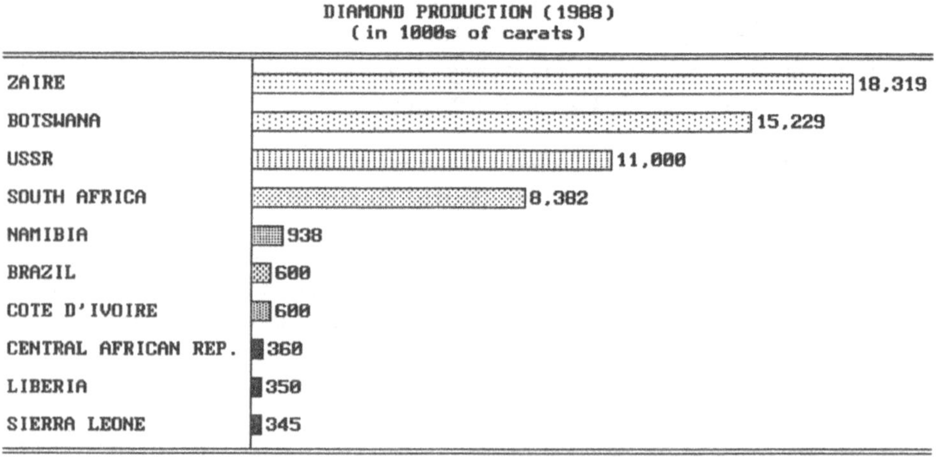

Figure 6A.2. Diamond production of the top 10 producers in the world, in 1988, in thousand carats.

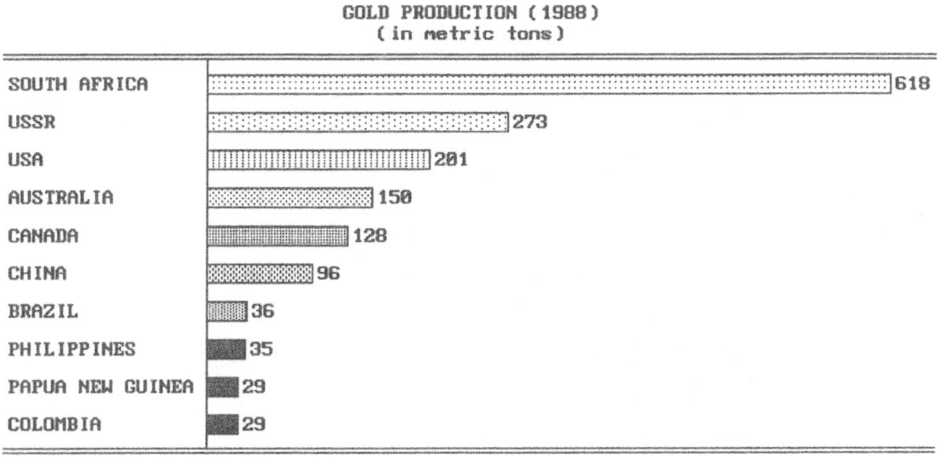

Figure 6A.3. Gold production of the top 10 producers in the world, in 1988, in metric tons.

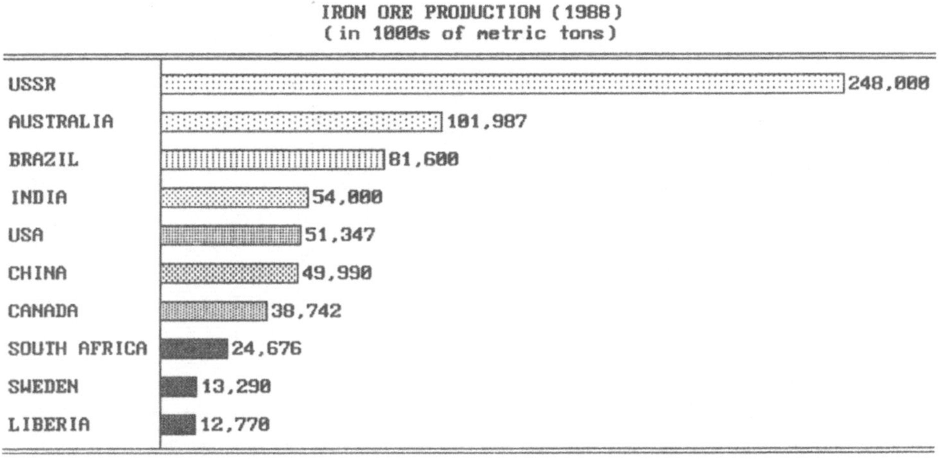

Figure 6A.4. Iron ore production of the top 10 producers in the world, in 1988, in thousand metric tons.

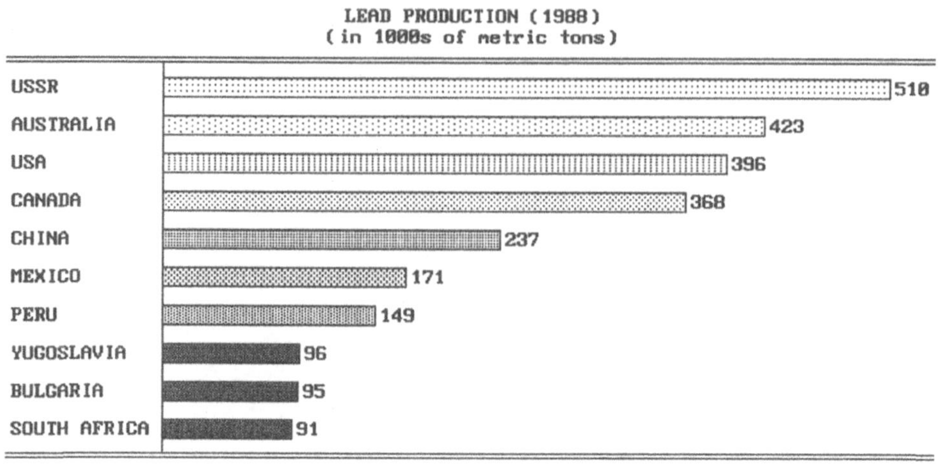

Figure 6A.5. Lead production of the top 10 producers in the world, in 1988, in thousand metric tons.

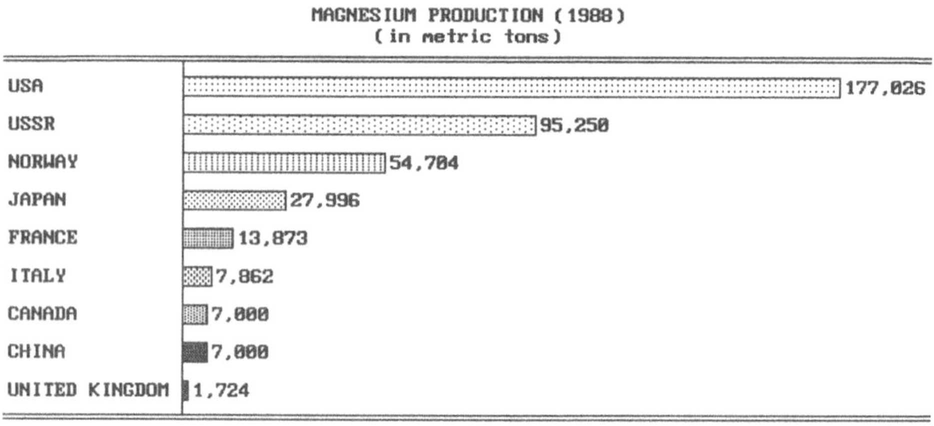

Figure 6A.6. Magnesium production of the top nine producers in the world, in 1988, in metric tons.

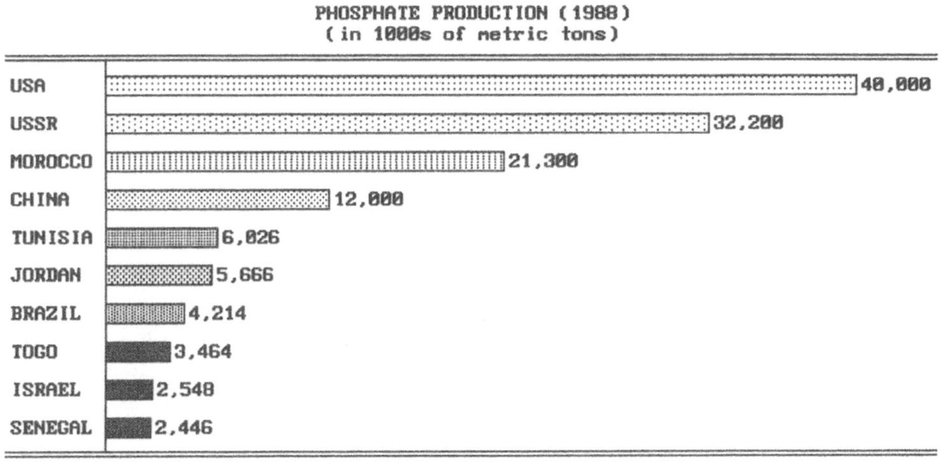

Figure 6A.7. Phosphate production of the top 10 producers in the world, in 1988, in thousand metric tons.

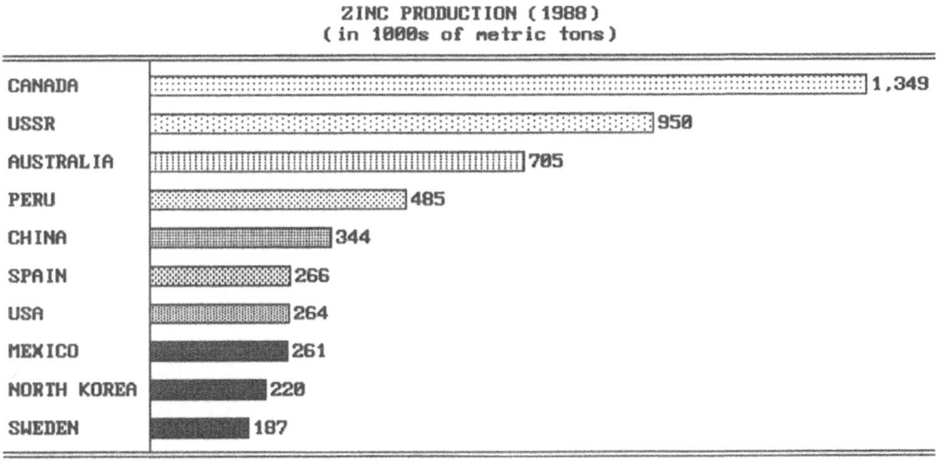

Figure 6A.8. Zinc production of the top 10 producers in the world, in 1988, in thousand metric tons.

Appendix 6B

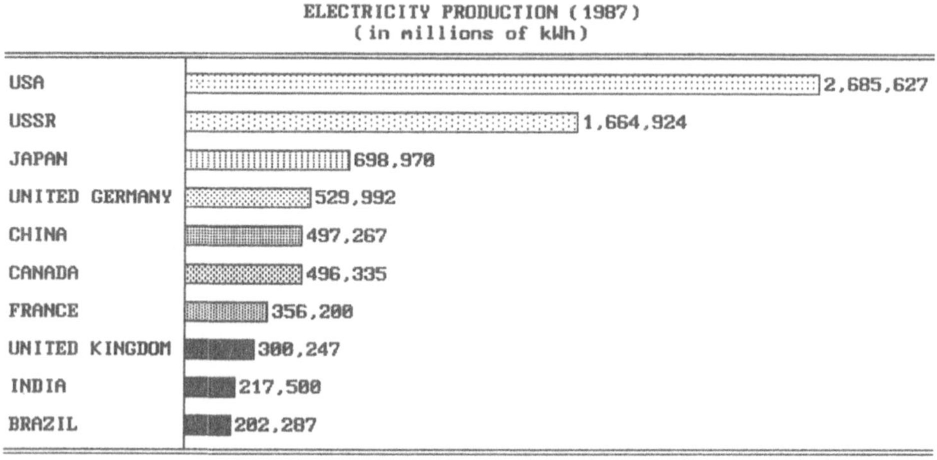

Figure 6B.1. Electricity production of the top 10 producers in the world, in 1988, in million kWh.

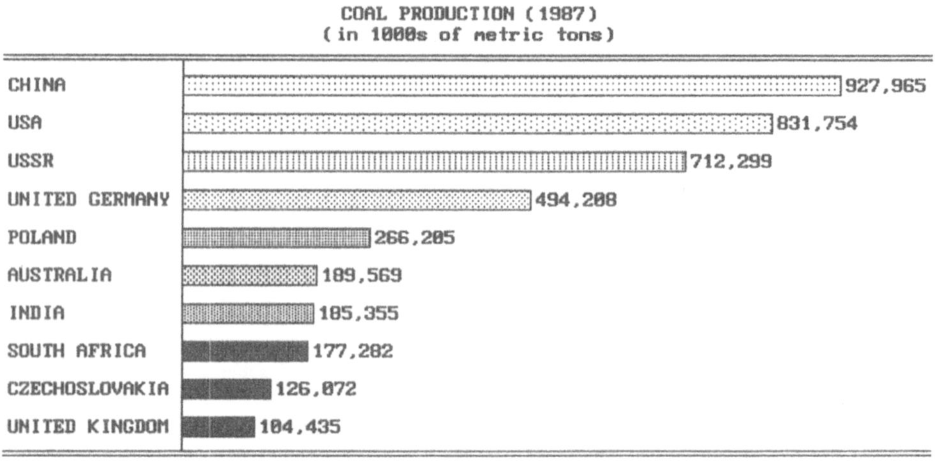

Figure 6B.2. Coal production of the top 10 producers in the world, in 1988, in thousand metric tons.

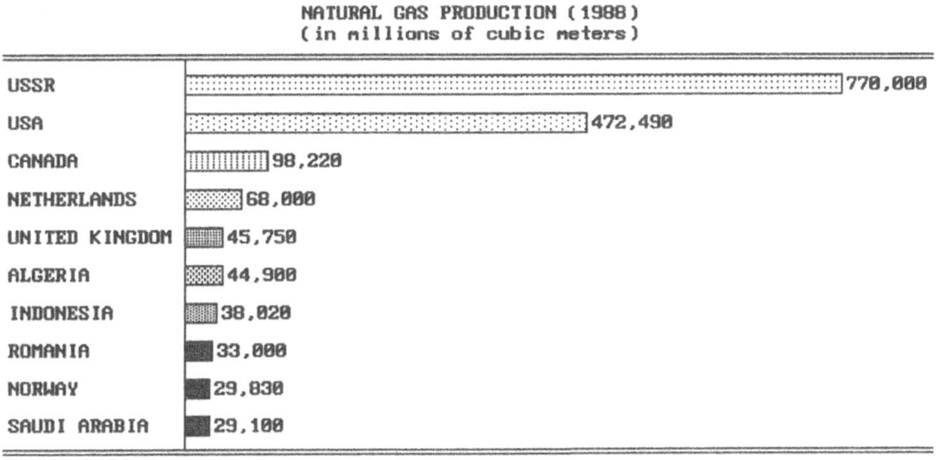

Figure 6B.3. Natural gas production of the top 10 producers in the world, in 1988, in million cubic meters.

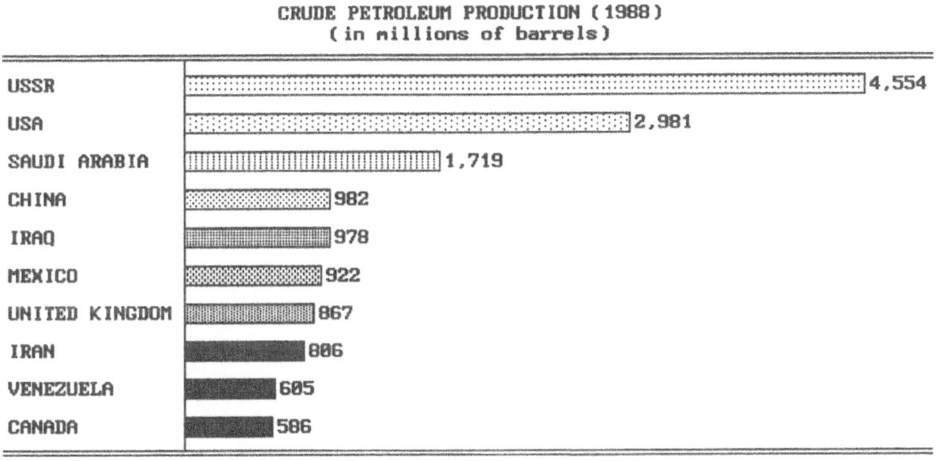

Figure 6B.4. Crude petroleum production of the top 10 producers in the world, in 1988, in million barrels.

Chapter 7

R&D Management in the Transition: From the Soviet Union to Russia

With its large, educated population, more than adequate amount of scientists and engineers, and an abundance of resources, the status of the USSR as one of the world's greatest industrial powers would have appeared to have been assured. This, however, was not the case. The preceding chapters have illustrated and discussed the wealth and potential of the Soviet system, the status of research and development or, more generally, science and technology, and the influence of Soviet-style management on these components and their role as essential catalysts for economic growth and development.

A blending of economic and innovation theories has impressed on us that the social manner of doing things, which implies the absence of individual competition as described in the Arrow model, will make *all* of us better off. Soviet-style socialism did not achieve this. Under no such circumstance did the central planning system prove that it could achieve results superior to those of other systems. In fact, the inadequacies of management techniques based on Communist central planning principles have made the overall successes of capitalist market economies appear even more respectable had the latter not such an opposite example to be compared with.

Studies on the mismanagement of research and development in the former Soviet Union or, rather, the preceding management based on distorted economic signals reveal, however, that there is much room for improvement and future promise. A reorganization of R&D management under new conditions as part of the transition to a market economy could lead to the blossoming of this sector. As a key element of economic growth, the appropriate style of investment in R&D could, in turn, act as a catalyst facilitating and aiding expansion and development, benefiting Russian residents and influencing the status of the successor republics (mainly Russia) of the former USSR in the international scientific, technological, and economic communities.

History has proved time and time again that there is no future without a past. This is no less true in the field of research and development, or in the science and technology sector as a whole, than in any other area – perhaps even more so, due to the value of an accumulated stock of knowledge in the propagation of new innovations. Throughout history, and most accountable since the first industrial revolution of the nineteenth century, the impacts of new innovations have influenced the organization and development of society from technological, economic, and cultural perspectives. Countless major and minor challenges and opportunities have been afforded by developments in new technologies. The potential for new innovation lies in a long-standing commitment to support domestic R&D that cultivates and secures national technological capabilities.

The Soviet Union made such a historical investment. Successful science was part of the cultural pride and identity; in fact, it was anchored in ideology. Today, the USSR no longer exists, but, to a large extent, its science and technology sector, which boasted to have one of if not the largest R&D establishments in the world at the time, lives on for the most part in the new Russian Federation.

The following excerpt from a recent volume on technical change and economic theory emphasizes the requirements of the past for growth and an improved standard of living in the future.

> Previous capital is needed to produce new capital, previous knowledge is needed to absorb new knowledge, skills must be available to acquire the skills and a certain level of development is required to create the scale effects that make development possible. In summary, it is within the logic of the dynamics of technology and growth that the technologically more advanced get richer and the gap remains and widens for those left behind. [Perez and Soete, 1988, p. 459]

Judging by its assets described in the preceding chapters, a large part of the former Soviet Union is not a candidate for being left behind, least of all in research and development. Today, the level of achievement in many fields of scientific endeavor appear to be lagging behind the levels attained in other leading R&D nations. Nonetheless, the achievements in specific areas provide evidence that they are still contenders in global S&T advancement.

During Gorbachev's years of *perestroika* between 1985 and 1991 in the USSR and even more so in Russia today, which is undergoing remarkable changes in all spheres at the hands of courageous reformers, efforts indicate a continuing importance for the role of scientific and technological development. Russia is faced by a dilemma in becoming part of the international S&T community where results and performance determine success: preserving the potential of the enormous S&T establishment (which may in truth be too large for its own good), while attempting to become more efficient and productive by rationalizing and letting the market determine what is needed. As it was, the system could not and would not serve the needs of a modernizing market-oriented economy. However, a scientific-research base is important to a modern economy.

This chapter focuses on the following two themes:

- To emphasize the value of the R&D establishment and accompanying elements created under the former Communist regime in Russia's bid to rejoin the world scientific and economic communities.
- To discuss the requirements of a good R&D organization and its contribution to post-Soviet growth and development.

7.1 Rejoining the World

7.1.1 From the scientific perspective

In the Soviet Union from Lenin to Gorbachev, science and technology, in one form or another, was heralded as the universal remedy for all problems. It was to make Soviets better off at home and the country's position more important internationally. S&T was considered the highest form of culture, the path to social prosperity; it was to serve the masses rather than be exploited for individual profit. The scientific community had fantastic dimensions and enjoyed special status in every sense. The products of scientific endeavor were to be the springboard to technological advance and economic growth superior to that elsewhere, particularly in the Western capitalist countries.

Previously, Soviet science could be proudest of its achievements in military and space technology. Unfortunately, both did little directly for consumer welfare, and even indirect spinoffs were extremely limited (though this should be no surprise considering the deficiency of defense R&D spinoffs in the West). Soviet-style R&D management cultivated a progressively growing technological gap to the West in many scientific fields despite the system's basic natural advantages. These included the capacity to mobilize resources to achieve "mission-oriented" innovations, to train the labor force with the appropriate research and design skills, to acquire specific foreign technology, and to theoretically avoid potential duplication with its centralized determination of innovation, its mandatory enforcement of introduction of innovation, and its centralized investment and materials allocation (Linz, 1992, p. 65).

After hearing for decades that scientific and technological advance would cure socioeconomic decay but experiencing only sparing results, the Russian public has become skeptical of the actual recovery power of R&D investments for economic improvement. In addition, a premise gaining more recognition is that, in Russia today, the central government is acclaimed to be more progressive and reform oriented than the local authorities and often (state) enterprises. This indicates that the Academy of Sciences, some industrial ministries, and special committees will carry much of the responsibility to get a new style of R&D under way. Of course, they will partially be carried by past momentum and significantly by the hordes of scientific and engineering workers and equipment of yesterday.

Perestroika facilitated the introduction of democratization of management and decentralization in existing scientific institutes (for better or worse) in an effort to restructure institutionalization and reorient motivation in the Academy of Sciences, industrial institutes, and government. Evidence from personal interviews with scientists generally documents their continuing belief that scientific activity is value free. Hence, given the right political system and social foundations and the freedom to work without interference, their research naturally would produce great benefits for society (Josephson, 1992, p. 29). Russian policy makers are now in the position to grant the scientific profession such an environment. Some progress has been made and the first results are promising. One example has been that the increase in relative freedoms and flexibilities have facilitated the rebirth of independent professional organizations of scientific experts more than a half century after the Communist Party wiped out such groups (Josephson, 1992, p. 30). Such developments have revealed that characteristics of the Western scientific community can be successfully and rewardingly integrated during the reorganization of R&D management in Russia.

The USSR was plagued by a central planning system that was actually based on bargaining elements which distorted economic signals and led to futile efforts to implement the optimal plan because of the disguised void between plan and reality – the "inefficiency hole." However, the advantages that have become remnants of the former system can catapult Russian R&D and industrial potential to unexpected heights under the conditions characteristic of a new political and economic environment which the reformers are attempting to foster.

Not only will Russian R&D rejoin the mainstream of the international scientific community, but also Russia will rejoin on both economic and technological foundations. One is crucial to the success of the other.

Russian R&D has inadvertently been obliged to become a part of the global scientific and technology system at a time when many of the leading R&D nations are facing similar problems, though to a differing extent, to those that have arisen in Russia's bid to create a market economy. In the West, budget deficits are burdening governments, forcing federal funding cutbacks wherever possible and S&T habitually falls victim to the process; particularly, of course, fundamental science which is most strongly supported by the government in the West. In Russia, reduced funding in basic science could have a substantial human cost due to the large number of scientists and technicians employed in this branch. Of course, the accompanying increase in freedom to change to a job in another institute, field, or completely different sector (as long as experience or education allows), which was previously unknown, may help relieve some of the unemployment and its related social costs. In fact, many persons may finally take the employment they wished to achieve with their education (where possible) rather than the position that was commonly determined for them.

Additionally, R&D in general, but to a greater degree the applied side, is being forced to earn its way in the world. So what the Russians perceive as a result of becoming a market economy is a feature confronting Western applied science (though conventionally rather well supported primarily by the private industrial sector) in an effort to make what appeared to be a good system more cost-effective.

Partly as a result of simple necessity to prevent the R&D sector from completely vanishing, the reorganization of R&D management in Russia began with more urgency after the breakup of the former Soviet Union. Russia, as the largest of the successor states, ceased financing more than 80 central agencies including structures of the former scientific community (Levin, 1992, p. 1). However, within a few months the Russian Academy of Sciences – as it had originally been known from 1917 to 1925 – had been formed, replacing the Soviet counterpart, and several organizations (the former USSR State Committee for Science and Technology, the Russian State Committee for Science and Higher Education, the Committee for Science and Public Education of the Russian Supreme Soviet, and the short-lived Ministry of Science and Technological Policy of the Russian Federation) merged into one unified agency, the Ministry for Science, Higher Education, and Technology Policy of the Russian Federation. Thus, some of the administrative changes have begun, members of the academy are elected in a more democratic fashion, and funding mechanisms are guaranteed but not yet organized. Much is still to be done in the reorganization of R&D management embodied in a new diversified and competitive science policy that is emerging from the transition to a market economy, but a start has been made.

7.1.2 From the enterprise perspective

The changing economic environment in Russia, with reformulated institutional, organizational, and motivational structures, requires modifications of the existing innovation decision-making process. In an effort to integrate in the world economic system and produce goods of international standards for the domestic as well as foreign markets, Russian managers face many new decisions, one of which is considering how to best allocate their R&D budgets. The price they can procure on the market and the diffusion of their product will determine their revenue from which the R&D budget is derived; this is characteristic of applied research in Western market economies. Under such conditions managers can finally truly evaluate rewards and risks of investing in and introducing innovations.

Under Soviet-style research and technology management innovations were often imposed on enterprises from the hierarchical industrial/institutional system. Whenever possible enterprises balked in the face of changes due to the then ruling incentive measures. The gradual reduction in the magnitude of expected punishments for not meeting orders between 1953 and 1982 led to a lack of discipline and enforcement (Ellman and Kontorovich, 1992, p. 10). Managers and directors of enterprises (whether these were research institutes responsible for producing innovations or factories ordered to produce final products) had less motivation to reach output targets. Instead of punishment, superior levels of the hierarchy revised their targets downward resulting in a cumulative brake on technological change.

Yet, as the present reforms continue a major barrier to innovation in the past is significantly shrinking in importance: namely, the supply of inputs to be utilized with the new technology. Under the old system a manager had to mount considerable effort to secure the inputs for the old-style production, suggesting that the introduction of new techniques would have confronted him with a potentially double negative effect – loss of bonuses due to reduced output as a result of retooling and forecast difficulties in the supply of newly required inputs further impeding production. The former distribution system has mostly vanished now. A functional new one has yet to be developed. The doors to input suppliers are open domestically and internationally to whomever can pay the price.

Today, enterprises have essentially two choices with respect to innovation: either they innovate themselves, basing their decisions on consumer demand, supply conditions, costs of inputs, and so on, or they choose to imitate. However, the simple method of imitation utilized in the past will no longer be sufficient; products will have to be developed further by domestic (preferably in-house) R&D personnel to match the specific requirements of local demand. But, the enterprises cannot achieve these results during the transition completely on their own accord. A combination of market signals and government planning is needed to speed economic development and growth (OTA, 1992, p. 11). The latter, as the Soviet Union found out the hard way, cannot replace the advantages of the market and forces of competition.

It is, however, now quite clear that free-market principles based on perfect (or even imperfect) competition provide sufficient incentives to invest in as much R&D as would be socially optimal for a whole nation. This is the argument used to justify government intervention. Examples from Japan, South Korea, and Taiwan, nations that all experienced exceptionally rapid growth, reveal the presence of state intervention to alter but not destroy market signals. Protection of the domestic market and direct funding of R&D were forms of intervention, as were policies to steer low-cost capital, preferential access to foreign exchange, assistance in negotiations with foreign companies for access to technologies, and support of domestic technology development and implementation through a variety of fiscal incentives (OTA, 1992, p. 10). Thus, numerous examples can be given on how to best utilize domestic R&D potential while preserving the drive for entrepreneurship.

Furthermore, should the enterprises prove to be duly successful, then their products will also be sold in the West, in turn influencing the market, prices, and industrial organization there.[1] Evidence from historical developments in other nations, which have been resurrected from rather dismal situations to become economically and socially successful (i.e., Japan, Germany, some NICs), would tend to indicate that imitation will be the initially favored strategy at least for the immediate transitional phase. As world levels of quality and selection come within reach, supported by the very capable domestic R&D sector, the role of innovation will again substantially increase. Of course, the industrial structure will make a difference.

Russia has inherited the industrial structure cultivated by decades of Communist industrial policy. In general, it is one dominated by labor- and capital-intensive industries, but recently there have been signs of at least a willingness to shift to more modern industries along the path of industrial evolution. Countries beginning much later than the USSR on the road to industrialization like Japan, South Korea, and Taiwan have already gone through more shifts. They also began with labor-intensive and moved to capital-intensive industries, moving primarily from light manufacturing and import substitution to heavy and chemical industries. These countries, however, have all gone one step further. They have moved into the knowledge-intensive industries which have facilitated the production of products (i.e., computers) that have allowed the development of downstream industries and consequently promoted economic growth and development.

Although much enterprise activity will be devoted to satisfying the backed-up demand resulting from decades of no selection, the enterprises will be joining the world at the research and technology level, on the one hand, and at the product level, on the other hand. R&D-based technological change (particularly production technology) and diffusion of that technology will contribute to economic growth and the improvement of the standard of living, inevitably making Russian producers and consumers important elements of the world economy.

7.1.3 The international aspect

In today's world, science and technology has become a worldwide phenomenon. The process has been under way for some decades, and international exchange and participation have been crucial to the successes of numerous nations that had to climb back from serious economic and/or technological setbacks. Open borders to scientific exchange, which includes the flow of experts, ideas, experiences, assistance, and supporting materials (such as computers), have served as a catalyst for economic growth and development in the past.

Russia was once no exception. Even as far back as Peter the Great and Catherine the Great, in the seventeenth and eighteenth centuries, respectively, scholars and technicians from many countries including Sweden, the Netherlands, Denmark, and Prussia were invited to practice their craft in Russia, while Russians were sent to England and elsewhere for training and study. It was during the Communist rule in the twentieth century that the Soviet Union turned a cold shoulder to the ever-increasing multilateralization and internationalization of both basic and applied research efforts, not to mention development.

Chapter 5 of this study has been devoted to the internationalization of research and development. Although this process became significant enough after World War II to warrant more serious study, the real thrust to internationalize began in the 1980s and continues today. More and more international scientific associations and consortiums are being established in an effort to spread the risks and costs of research and development, to gain from the pooling of scholars from disparate fields in different nations, and to be assured access to the results of the cooperation. It has become increasingly difficult, costly, uncertain, and less fashionable to *go at it alone.*

In addition, the accompanying advantages of foreign direct investment and multinational corporations' activities are chief determinants in the acquisition of foreign technology. The significance of these elements increases when one considers that much of the newest and most protected Western technology was already being chiefly transferred by multinationals in the late 1980s. In each case the value of the domestic research and development base influences the attractiveness of a particular country for foreign interests and investors. Judging by the stock of scientific resources inherited from the Soviet Union, Russia will have much to offer and will be an attractive partner in international research. Thus, it seems Russia has chosen to return to the world stage of science and technology during a time when more interaction between the players is desirable and much can be gained.

Becoming a part of the world economy and transforming the internal system to a market-oriented style simultaneous to the opening of the S&T sector will facilitate a working environment more conducive to better technological choice and more efficient use of R&D resources. Prices of products, costs of inputs, and returns on investment will finally have meaning in choosing policies and projects. Links to the world will do much for the development of domestic markets to which domestic research and technology must cater and from which demand impulses are expected to aid in guiding reformulation of principles and institutions.

One of the keys to a future for the Russian S&T sector is to sever all links to the former legacy of ideological orientation. Cooperation with other nations, mainly those of the industrialized West, will prove to bear important fruits for the development of Russian R&D, molding it to be a significant factor in economic growth. Benefits can be realized in the procurement of marketing- and technological-assessment infrastructure, policy-setting processes, methods for science management, means for modernizing and retrofitting those branches of industry worth saving, and measures for determining and demonstrating how applied research can be used to make traditional industries competitive (Popper, 1992, p. 114).

It would be incomplete to consider the international aspects of the importance of R&D and technology for economic growth without citing the case of Japan. Notwithstanding the differences, a comparison with Russia today makes the Japanese case especially useful because of the similar historical events. Already in the pre–WWII period Japan had entered a phase of international isolation that extended until the end of the war. Postwar Japan inherited a technological gap to Western industrialized countries and inflated heavy industries (machinery, metals, and chemicals) often associated with the previously extensive military sector.[2] Inward foreign investment was practically prohibited and to compensate for the isolation the state increased the allocation of resources to research and development. This strategy was, however, unsuccessful in closing the technology gap to the Western leaders. If there were no mention of names or dates, this portrait could just as fittingly apply to the late phase of the Soviet Union and the early predicament facing Russia.

One of Japan's most notable solutions to the dilemma was to acquire advanced foreign technology in many ways, with an emphasis on knowledge rather than capital, largely exclusive of inward direct investment (Goto, 1991, p. 10). The Japanese perceived technology as knowledge and information embodied in many forms ranging from persons to equipment. In postwar Japan a vigorous program of personnel exchange with the leading Western nations was initiated and supported in both the enterprise and academic spheres. Japan also imported the *backlog* of technologies developed overseas during the war, and soon moved to new technologies not yet pervasive elsewhere and developed these further at home for both the foreign and domestic markets. The entire process of effectively utilizing imported knowledge and technology to create Japan's own technological base and promote economic growth was helped by the level of indigenous science, research, development, and technology (primarily created during the isolation period) and a well-developed education system. Firms were very active in importing, concluding technological agreements with American and Western European companies, and in sending engineers and managers abroad regularly to search for, find, and return with interesting and useful activities being done elsewhere.

This short account of the postwar Japanese situation was to reveal the benefits of utilizing effective international R&D policy to spur domestic growth. Although there are not too many such examples, it gives a hint of successful measures that can, in one form or another, by useful in the management of Russian R&D during the transition to a market economy. Growth will create a demand for more advanced technology, which promotes more growth. Advanced technology can be produced at home or acquired from abroad. The latter is not an automatic product of the cyclical process described, but requires a deliberate effort on the part of the buyer and the appropriate environment into which it is introduced if it is to be productive.

7.2 The Role of R&D in Russian-style Growth

During the turbulent and often painful times of change in Russia, the following basic question is being raised more frequently: What is the role of modern-style R&D management and technology in a society undergoing rapid social, economic, and political change – a country in transition to a market economy? Of course, there is no single clear, guaranteed answer, but certain precedents do give some indications. Little doubt remains that the stock of knowledge and the ability of a nation to harness it and consistently procure subsequent advances in that stock, which includes cumulative and progressive research and development, influence the rate and style of economic growth.

Since the 1950s, simultaneous to the growth in the world economy, there has been significant acceleration in the pace of scientific progress, in the levels of education, in the numbers and proportions of scientists and engineers in research and industry, in the importance of science-based industry, as well as in many other research- and technology-founded factors exemplified by the industrialized Western economies, and for part of the period by the centrally planned economies of Eastern Europe. Science-based inventions have been a major factor differentiating the products and processes of the twentieth century from the nineteenth century (Nelson *et al.*, 1967, p. 40). Specific and organized research and development directed at opening up new possibilities has replaced chance developments in relevant sciences and biased concentration in individual issues.

In economic sectors or activities singled out as priority areas of the Soviet economy impressive growth was registered based on the research, development, technology, and labor force established and promoted under the former system. A case in point comes from the progress (though inconsistent) in resource development. One of the foremost Western authorities on the Soviet Union provided the following example of the development of the Tyumen oil fields in Western Siberia in a paper written in the early 1980s:

> [The] first petroleum discovery in this desolate, remote area was made only in 1959. The first exploitation of the fields took place only in 1964, when a mere 200,000 tons of oil were extracted. Yet by 1980, despite the mosquitos, swamps, permafrost, and difficult supply conditions, production was 312 million tons, or slightly over half of all Soviet production. Moreover, virtually the entire effort was carried out with existing Soviet labor and technology. [Goldman, 1983, p. 628]

Who is to say that the science, technology, and skilled labor that are largely a product of the former system could not, when united with new market-oriented policies, make similarly significant contributions in other sectors influencing overall Russian growth and development? The proposition adhered to throughout this paper is that a substantial effect can be expected.

Investigations regarding what contributes to growth have identified advances in knowledge (AIK) as a key factor.[3] These advances refer to improvements in the techniques of production, distribution, and business organization that are adopted during a particular period (Denison and Chung, 1976, p. 78). Inherently, they will depend on the level at the beginning of the period; indicating that they depend on past advances. Therefore, introduction of research and development results in both technology and management organization that affect a nation's production is of prime importance.

If the example of postwar Japan is taken as a comparison, there are certainly differences, but strikingly many similarities to post-Communist/post–USSR Russia. In their analysis of why Japan grew so fast Denison and Chung (1976, p. 10) describe some of the postwar Japanese features that resemble the post–USSR Russian situation: namely, the loss of nearly half its land area, repatriation of large amounts of military personnel, shortages of food, clothing, housing, and other daily necessities, agricultural and industrial production reduced to a fraction of what it had been a decade earlier, inflation, large government deficits, and so forth. Finally an economic reform package was introduced that laid the foundation for recovery and growth. The expansion was then determined by numerous factors, but none so singly significant as advances in knowledge.

In Japan, the contribution of AIK clearly helped to close the technology and productivity gaps, and turn the postwar lag with respect to other Western countries into world leadership 40 years later. It had more influence than economies of scale or reduction of international trade barriers. The Japanese growth rates of most of the crucial sources of growth identified by Denison and Chung were greater than their counterparts in many of the leading Western nations including the USA, Canada, Belgium, Denmark, France, West Germany, Italy, the Netherlands, Norway, and the UK between 1953 and 1971. The category AIK was no exception: Japan secured more growth from AIK than any other country in the world, and in so doing moved closer to the technological and managerial frontier (Denison and Chung, 1976, p. 49).

So, the process in Japan was successful, but the number of such examples is still quite limited (i.e., the United States and a number of Western European countries in the nineteenth century, West Germany after World War II, South Korea in the 1980s, and some others; see Abramovitz, 1979; and Maddison, 1969, 1982, 1987). The purpose here is not to suggest that Russia will become a global technological leader (though it may possess some of the necessary attributes), but to illustrate that significant growth could be achieved in the appropriate environment based on the nation's vast research and development resources. However, one can only speculate at this time, but, should the economic and political framework facilitate a growth-compatible environment, then the Russian research, science, and technology sectors would certainly give the AIK category much influence as a source of that growth. Overly strong commitments to past or existing technologies, levels of employment, or management structures can hamper a potential bid to catch-up.

The advances in knowledge are rarely portrayed as sources of growth in isolation. Most frequently these are linked to productivity; essentially the initial gaps between actually existing and potentially possible productivity (Abramovitz, 1979, p. 17). Studies devoted to the productivity growth of the Soviet Union have revealed that during certain periods the rates were high enough (in fact, higher than in Western nations) to close the technological gap (Bergson, 1978, 1983; and Gomulka, 1971). Unfortunately, these rates never persisted for a sufficient length of time. After attaining rates during the post–WWII years close to those required to narrow the gap to the Western leaders, the USSR growth rates dropped to a level significantly lower than those in the so-called industrial latecomers like Japan and Italy. A *latecomer* is said to be in a position to achieve faster growth than the technological leader for a certain period due to the access to the leader's technology (Poznanski, 1987, p. 53). The amazing aspect about the post–WWII growth in the USSR is that it occurred largely without access to foreign technology.

Nonetheless, the initial gap in productivity levels, which have to a great extent been attributed to technological lag, will not absolutely shrink if the latecomer does not develop its own capability to produce original technology. Originally, the Soviet-style system of R&D management was successful in generating technological innovation that, when used in the CPS, raised total factor productivity and enhanced growth. By 1975, statistical reviews of the levels of Soviet productivity revealed that the ability of the domestic R&D sector declined in attempts to produce sufficient original technology to reduce the productivity gap and a phase of equilibrium technology gap was reached.[4] However, the presently changing economic and political environment in Russia may prove to be the necessary remedy for the systematic weaknesses existing in the old Soviet system. It could launch the resource- and talent-rich Russian R&D sector into a phase of effective technological catch-up, stimulating rapid productivity increases, accompanied by faster overall economic growth and development.

The central planning, Soviet-style economic system was successful in turning, in many ways, a historically backward, technologically lagging, and to a large extent virgin land into an industrial powerhouse by the 1960s and world superpower for most of the twentieth century. Therefore, if the economic and political situations are modified to become somewhat more democratic and market oriented, future gains in economic growth and development would seem to be assured. The newly industrialized countries, for example, have attained astounding achievements in technological advance and economic growth, but they began from a much more technologically inferior position than the situation Russia finds itself in today. The NICs have continuously complemented and offset their domestic production of technology, by innovation or imitation, with extensive imports of foreign technology. As Russia becomes a more integrated element of the world economy this option becomes increasingly viable and could support a new growth strategy.

7.3 Prospects and Prescriptions for R&D Management and Technological Advance in the Transition to a Market Economy and Beyond[5]

7.3.1 Reform, transition, and R&D

The presentation of R&D in the Soviet economy in the previous chapters reveals the enormity and complexity of the task to appropriately manage this factor. It has particular relevance due to its position at the core of the relationship between science and technological growth. Management of research and development in the USSR was characterized by a conflict between political, national, and historical priorities (competing at all levels of science and technology), and countless distinct cultural and regional peculiarities. Although the economic transition has been recognized as necessary, the existing influences appear to adhere to an excess devotion to maintain all institutions and employment in R&D, including the applied area. Different solutions are required in both the basic and applied areas. Since the breakup of the Soviet Union in late summer 1991, the processes of transformation in Russian science administration and policy have been accelerated, but have yet to be successfully concluded.

Two factors have differentiated Eastern and Western R&D systems:

- *The origin of basic research*: A great portion of R&D was conventionally done in the special research institutes of the Academy of Sciences rather than in the higher education institutions. In this sense, the Soviet system resembled the French system most of those in the West. Generally, there are different mixes in the West, but determining the precise mixture for the Russian R&D community is, perhaps, not the most crucial issue at present.

- *The role of the enterprises*: In the planned economic system, industrial R&D was not the responsibility of enterprises' management. If *perestroika*, in its new form under the Russian reform-oriented leadership, proceeds and competition is successfully established through demonopolization and privatization, the present system will prove to be infeasible and the number of free-standing or independent industrial research laboratories will diminish because the industrial enterprises will themselves take up the research. Building a R&D laboratory into the enterprise allows the firm to work effectively and in a proprietary fashion with the laboratory to reduce the actual needs for formal legal instruments (such as patents) in order for companies to best appropriate their returns.

The organization of science often reflects the organization of the economy. The differentiation and separation between fundamental and applied science is a crucial policy issue. This has direct implications for the distinction between basic and commercial R&D. The latter depends not only on the quality of R&D personnel. In a market economy, resources for applied R&D are primarily allocated by the market mechanism in a decentralized manner responding to market forces. Resources for basic research are largely supplied by the government. Thus, a review of the experiences and literature on the integration of science and technology in a market economy would seem in order before considering policies that can propagate a simple division of R&D activities into nonprofit (fundamental) and commercial (applied).

Research and development, like the general situation in the USSR, was confronted with a lack of interactions between users at economic, societal, and regional levels. In analyzing Soviet R&D, a number of criticisms can be distinguished that have not been uncommon in the West:

- Technological progress in the USSR has been characterized as proudly originating essentially in its own roots. This influenced the manner in which scientists and engineers solve problems, often far from economic reasoning, particularly in the short term, as it is unnecessary to start most investigations for new innovations or inventions from scratch in today's international scientific community.
- Science has habitually neglected the market influence of society's demands. Science and technology appeared to be more imposed on society

in the centrally planned economies than in the West. S&T was based on social integration much more in Western nations than in socialist societies. It is considered by some a paradox that a capitalist-based system has led to a better quality of life.

- A major problem was the branch system or monopoly, which has been previously discussed in this book. While management of S&T in the Soviet Union is rapidly becoming increasingly obsolete causing significant inefficiencies and unproductiveness in the economy, the advanced Western industrialized countries are building new systems with technological growth potential.

The Russian science and technology policy, which is being developed parallel to the other measures for economic transition, could have a more relevant and applied perspective for dealing with issues concerning the management of R&D if the following initiatives are undertaken:

- Conversion of the defense-oriented R&D to concentrate more on civilian issues. This is, at least to a some extent, beginning to happen. In fact, some specific branches within the military industrial complex (MIC) were already responsible for producing certain civilian goods in the 1980s under the still Communist leadership. Additionally, there is a need for simultaneous commercialization and privatization of the state MIC that can make conversion effective.
- Directing a portion of the scientific effort toward specific areas that are less sensitive to short-term price changes so that valuable resources and potential will not be lost.
- Closer interaction with other policy areas. Science does not operate in a vacuum, so it should not be isolated from but integrated into society and the economy, facilitating the liberation of creativity and the encouragement of exchanges and reviews.
- Closer ties with user needs. These make R&D effective and commercializable. If R&D is linked to industry in a more competitive environment, it is consequently tied to user needs.
- Actual integration of R&D into industry in order to link it more closely to the production process and eliminate administrative and bureaucratic inefficiencies and barriers. This implies a need for the development of more in-house research.

With regard to the time horizon of R&D activity, an increased devotion to short-term projects causes the squeezing out of relevant long-term research. Furthermore, the question concerning the portfolio of R&D has been a contentious issue in the West; this was also true in the final phases of

Soviet reform and is still the case now and will continue to be so in the Russian reform of R&D policy. The rise of the independent industrial research laboratory owned by a firm in the West was to separate some of the scientists and engineers from short-term work. A typical example of the structure is a central laboratory (dealing with long-term issues) and decentralized laboratories that are close to production, doing short-term, demand-oriented work. A final note related to timing: the R&D community in the former USSR and now especially in Russia is struggling to accommodate economic reform and not the other way around.

In order to make valuable contributions when proposing alternative measures for change, good and reliable statistics must be available. Numerous questions have arisen in the discussion surrounding the reform of Soviet/Russian R&D management and the science and technology sector as a whole with respect to the availability of representative statistics, their value, reliability, comparability, and meaning. The information available indicates a need for major restructuring in the field of R&D statistics in Russia. Before any policy decisions are made, it is crucial to have a clear and undistorted picture of the existing situation (i.e., R&D performance and potential). There is a need for modern and comparable statistics because the historical data collected are the product of the old institutional structure and were normally presented in isolation. The new style in the last years of the USSR and in the first years of the Russian Federation is to rely heavily on surveys. But, whether these generate the best results, particularly because so much depends on the respondents to the questionnaires, is uncertain.

As a result of traditionally inflated numbers coming from the Soviet Union, there is much interest in the precise definitions of the measures reported. For example, whether only full-time workers are included in R&D employment, who is actually classified as a scientist,[6] what precisely distinguishes a higher educational institution, what should or should not be included in material and technical resources, and so forth. The meaning of certain indicators must also be clarified. For example, the age of equipment leads to questions of whether they were state of the art when purchased; or an increase in graduate students may not have as positive an increase as first thought if, as in the USA, there is a strong influx of foreign students (indicating that the number of domestic students may actually be decreasing while the total is increasing). Finally, the key will be a successful restructuring of R&D categories to allow the best domestic analysis and international comparisons (possibly on a value basis). A first step may be to compare the definition of former Soviet categories or indicators with those defined in the Frascati manual and routinely used in OECD countries.

7.3.2 The survivability of R&D

Western experts often question why and how the Soviet science and technology sector was able to grow so large in the presence of such formidable obstacles. Obviously, there were political and ideological goals at the foundation, not those of the economy or the market.

The recent decline of R&D financing must be seen as a process of weaning the R&D sector from full state dependence. Market forces inevitably result in a dilemma; no success without failure. But, the uncertainty incorporating the risks of failure and the benefits of success provide precisely the incentives required for competition. On the whole, Soviet state enterprises did not show sufficient initiative. Thus, private entrepreneurs may do better in striving for survival. In the case of computers, for example, it appears that a great market for specialized and tailored software existed in the USSR. However, the best technology is only one requirement needed to achieve market share; other requirements are development, service, marketing, and so on.

Science and technology is a mixed system in most Western economies. The key is to move the research into an innovation quickly so that it can enter the market soon in order for the benefits of the product to be available. In the steel industry, for example, the producers themselves develop the research because of interindustry competition (this is referred to as suicidal R&D; if they do not do it, their competitor will). While the decrease in Soviet state funding was been accompanied by an increase in contract funding, the quantity of research contracted out in the West is kept to a minimum. The Western combination of in-house and external R&D is a perfect example of the mix of market and planned economics: internal R&D is more part of the planning rather than part of the market because the risk is high, uncertainty often makes contracts unenforceable, and once much has been invested in a project there is a desire to preserve that continuity.

Soviet policy makers should proceed with caution when attempting to directly apply present Western standards with respect to R&D management in any industry or sector because many of these standards are undergoing transitions in the West. It would be preferable to aim for long-term goals rather than short-term advance that would only approach a current level that may prove to be obsolete by the time it is attained.

7.3.3 (Pre-)Conditions for successfully restructuring R&D

The Soviet economy appeared to be the most monopolized of industrialized nations. Soviet innovation was a function of the bargaining process and was associated with rising inflation. In comparison, Western innovation has been identified with falling prices as a result of reduced costs brought about by the diffusion of the innovations.

The following four factors are essential to successful innovation in the West and could, to varying extents, contribute to improved R&D management in Russia:

1. Industrial R&D is largely financed by firms and performed in the industrial laboratories owned by firms. The R&D must be done in facilities that are directly responsible to management.
2. A competitive approach to technological change is required. Russian S&T experts have identified the domination of monopoly power (the failure to have a competitive industrial structure) to have hindered innovation. Thus, there is a need to restructure the system in order to encourage competition. A look at the industries with great growth and clear technological progress in the West reveals that they have all been characterized by avid competition. A diversity of approaches to technological change developing simultaneously is an essential element that generates technological change in a market economy. Competition is required to provide incentives (i.e., the threat or risk of failing, not to mention the sweet taste of success).
3. Scientists and engineers enjoy freedom to move. Mobility is essential for creativity. Communication is required in generating a proper structure conducive for innovation. Of course, too much mobility is deleterious for the firm's innovative activity for proprietary reasons.
4. University research plays an important role in industrial innovation in the West. The usual mechanism is people in industry identifying the needs that would be profitable and then looking to science for the answers; thus, it is need and demand driven rather than science driven, though science facilitates finding the solutions.

The Russian Federation cannot now simply look toward contract research to solve the nonmarket problems of the S&T sector. Toward the end of the Communist era in the 1980s, when reform had become an inevitable requirement for survival, contract research was frequently identified as a favored route to achieve market orientation in research and development. More emphasis should be accorded to the need for a move toward in-house research. The fact that Soviet R&D laboratories were and have remained, in a way, disconnected from manufacturing presents a real problem. A possible solution may be to divide them up by assignment and subsequently allow the market to direct the labor to those fields in demand.

Some of the problems that previously plagued the R&D community in the USSR and continue to burden it under Russian authority are not unique and, therefore, should not be viewed so pessimistically. Inevitably, due to the market environment that is at its basis, Western science does not have an overall, coherent, concentrated, and organized unified quest for truth; rather, there is an intense individual sense of competition. This competition may not be without costs. But the advantages of dissemination of scientific results are very great in the West, and thus it is actively inspired. From this perspective, the results of a recent survey investigating R&D managers' behavioral reaction to the reform of R&D organization, which revealed that managers generally favored decentralization, private ownership, mobility, and other aspects of reform, are encouraging and display courage and ambition on their part. On these grounds, the outlook for Russian S&T becomes more positive.[7]

The area of international technology transfer is important and will gain in importance as the process of transition to a market economy continues. An entire chapter in this book has been devoted to this subject. The emphasis on the export of technology is understandable due to the need for hard currency, but a more appropriate policy orientation would place the emphasis on technology imports. This will bring the necessary results for long-term modern economic growth if the surrounding environment is receptive.

The current need for foreign currency should be secondary to the effort to build up internal welfare based on domestic economic growth. Some experts contend that the more technologies can be imported, the faster the economy will grow, assuming that the domestic research and technology levels are at least sufficiently compatible to facilitate easy and useful assimilation. The technological balance of payments will be negative, but the trade balance could be running a large surplus (as in Japan, Germany, South Korea, Taiwan, and others). Other problems (including hard currency shortages) will be solved in the long run, but some strategic vision from the state on R&D imports can be helpful immediately (particularly where problems may arise with respect to the financial limitations of enterprises).

7.3.4 Areas for restructuring R&D

One of the first places to begin restructuring with some of the greatest potential rewards is the monstrous, until recently well-financed military industrial complex. Conversion of the military industry is a common and widely discussed topic in Western industrialized economies. Countries like Japan or the USA have gone through quite extensive conversion programs in the past.[8] The conversion can come from above in the guise of a centrally planned conversion, or it can come from below when each enterprise seeks its own destiny. The latter, decentralized manner was typical in the USA. In

Japan, conversion was sudden, but goals of the ensuing policies were to facilitate competition with an early emphasis on serving the world market with domestically developed products. Conversion from below is usually more successful because it produces products and technology that the civilian sector is demanding. The reorientation from the defense to the civilian sector has great potential due to the big backlog of demand for civilian products which has arisen during the decades of concentrating on military production.

The Russian Federation has many assets that can be provided through conversion and the transition to a market economy. Many firms of the defense ministry are already producing a number of civilian products, primarily because no civilian firms are engaged in such production. Also, this great nation has a very well-educated and highly trained population, particularly in the fundamentals. The West will need to provide assistance in certain areas such as education (exchange of students, scholars, managers, etc.) and technological agreements. Knowledge is more important than equipment (and much cheaper because it requires less foreign exchange) in the long run when the purpose is to build up domestic S&T potential.

In developing the appropriate environment for progressive R&D there is an essential need for the construction of legal support for innovative activities. The law is to be a facilitator of rather than a barrier to R&D. It is difficult to provide a complete legal structure for research, development, innovation, and diffusion. This structure must be adaptable and flexible as more is understood about the innovative process. Of course, providing model forms of contracts and legislation is valuable, but scope must be provided for adaptation and evolution of such documents.

Preservation of the rights of individual scientists is very important. The individual inventor may not play a big role alone in developing innovations, but his role in an R&D enterprise is and will be crucial. There is a definite need for support for the intellectual labor market. There is no question that the concept of property rights must be clarified. In the West, different industries use different methods in appropriating rewards from R&D such as secrecy, lead time, patents, and others. Market orientation gives enterprises alternative modes for appropriation and there may be a smaller role for the more formal methods (i.e., copyrights, patents, trademarks) as would be expected, *ex ante*.

It is ironic to observe that in the transition of the Soviet Union to a market economy, it is Lenin's question that we face: *What is to be done?* This section attempts to move us a considerable distance in thinking about this question.

There seems to be general agreement among both experts of Soviet/Russian R&D and scholars of Western R&D systems that basic, fundamental R&D will need support during the transition to a market economy in Russia and thereafter. There is no economy which relies entirely on private funding in this area. It is the nature of basic research that it investigates not directly profit-making areas, in which firms (profit oriented in a market economy) tend to underinvest. Applied research should be primarily funded by the private sector with the exception of private R&D that is aimed at or tailored to specific national preferences (i.e., defense) and areas where goods are not really traded in the market (i.e., health, environment, ecology, and others).[9]

Funding becomes a key issue in the transition as there may be inadequate demand for applied R&D during this stage of development. The danger of insufficient private sector demand is the potential loss or destruction of valuable human capital (research teams, etc.) that may be very productive in the future Russian economy. These may need to be the beneficiaries of some transition (temporary) subsidies.

As stated earlier, a diversity of organizational forms is ultimately desirable. The same organizational form is not necessarily appropriate for all types of S&T activities. Many Western experts are strong advocates of the view that the market should select appropriate organizational forms, but the market can only achieve such a solution with a decentralized style of laboratories and institutions with a variety of alternatives. Therefore, some science and/or industry might be quickly integrated into a new system, while others may stand alone for some time.

Even if one believes that R&D done within the manufacturing enterprise will become the dominant organizational form, engaging the existing laboratories in contract R&D activities is likely to be a viable route during the transition if market forces are allowed to operate in full. It may prove to be tough for laboratories to be absorbed into firms, because they may want to enter manufacturing directly. The latter activity is just another route the market provides. For market purposes, it is irrelevant whether the laboratories buy enterprises or vice versa.

In returning to the problem of inadequate demand for R&D products during the transition, it appears that the applied field will face more difficulties than the basic area, though both will need some forms of support. It may prove to be unavoidable to continue a similar magnitude of (only) financial support from the state budget to basic science as was the case in the recent past. This must be accompanied by simultaneous, substantial changes with respect to establishing principles of competition for funding, competing sources, peer review, expert assessment for determining national priorities, and so on.

Applied research presents a more formidable problem. Assistance will be required in the interim, but if it is too generous it can deter and defer the development of competition, innovation, and the benefits thereof. Transitional subsidies may make sense, but a new tax might accomplish the same results. The operation of the tax should be studied more closely to determine whether rules that govern the tax distort, in any way, the laboratories' or enterprises' choice of organizational structure. Experience has shown that it is preferable to avoid taxes that create an incentive to promote stand-alone research laboratories or solely contract research. Any tax scheme is required to be neutral, while providing adequate funds for investment and development.

Finally, there is a fundamental dependence of scientific and technological reform on legal and economic reform. In the legal sphere, the central issue is the establishment of property rights of all forms (intellectual and material). The more quickly an appropriate legal framework is in place, the more rapidly the transitional problems will disappear.

In the economic sphere, it is clear that for rational technological assessment at the enterprise and national levels one needs the right prices (those that reflect the market-determined supply and demand). De-monopolization is essential to allow competition to drive R&D investment. There are two separate benefits to de-monopolization:

- Some competition will turn out to be better than no competition.
- In terms of increased size of total private resources invested in R&D, de-monopolization and consequent competition will facilitate an improvement in the functioning of the selection process (the moving toward more desirable organizational forms).

Labor mobility is also very important in the economic sphere. S&T workers must be free to choose their employer and vice versa. To restrict labor mobility is to exclude a large fraction of the potential benefits of economic reform.

Notes

[1] We are reminded of the shift of certain types of production to newly industrialized countries as in the cases of steel, chemicals, or automobiles. The specific advantages of these nations drew these manufacturing industries to their soil, and these industries have in a number of situations been further developed, subsequently helping these nations to become substantial exporters of the resulting products themselves. Simultaneously, a reorientation is required in

those more mature nations from which the manufacturing initiatives originally came.

[2] The percentage of heavy industry production in total manufacturing output was 79% in 1944 (Goto, 1991, p. 6).

[3] The most thorough and renowned studies on this topic have been completed by Edward Denison and his colleagues; see the References and Chapter 2.

[4] Numerous authors have come to the same conclusion regarding this fact. Ellman and Kontorovich (1992) state that technological progress in the USSR slowed down significantly in the 1970s, retarding economic growth. The slowdown in technological progress was due in part to the degradation of the research and development sector (pp. 9–10). See also Poznanski (1987, p. 54).

[5] The views and propositions made throughout this section are based on personal discussions with leading experts and policy makers from Russia and Western nations who participated at an IIASA conference on "Research and Development Management in the Transition to a Market Economy" in Moscow in July 1991.

[6] In the United States, only 35% of scientists are directly employed as R&D personnel, while 45% are employed in related activities. They are involved in marketing, communication, exchange programs, and so on. These related activities make an essential contribution to research development and growth without being immediately associated with R&D.

[7] This refers to the survey concerning managers' interpretations of R&D organization and structure within the framework of the economic reform program. This study was presented by Leonid Kosals at the IIASA conference "R&D Management in the Transition to a Market Economy" in Moscow, July 13–15, 1991.

[8] In 1945, the USA had to undergo a much larger conversion than that facing the Soviet Union. At that time, approximately 40% of US GNP was devoted to defense. In Japan the large military sector, which was built up during WWII, disappeared overnight after the war.

[9] This is representative of the organization of R&D funding in most market economies.

Chapter 8

Summary and Conclusions

8.1 Summary of Major Points

The purpose of this study is to conduct an up-to-date review and international comparison of the structure, organization, management, and performance of the Soviet research and development sector, subsequently deducing the potential and form of its remnants in Russia's transition to a market economy and bid to rejoin the global mainstream scientific and economic communities. This is a substantial task by any means, but a rewarding one. Rewarding in that the results reveal the ominous size and significant devotion of Soviet planners to promote R&D, despite their inefficient use of it. Russia, the largest successor republic of the former Union, is heir to most of these voluminous resources accumulated over the decades, though also to the administrative burdens. The potential for a progressive future looks positive if accompanied by appropriate management reforms.

In Chapter 2, the importance of research and development for economic growth is reviewed from the theoretical and empirical perspective. Findings have shown that little doubt remains with respect to the fact that R&D is one key source of economic growth. The discussion also reveals that, in theory, under more or less free market economic conditions the incentives to both competitive and monopoly industries to undertake R&D are less than the potential social benefits. Consequently this causes a tendency to underinvest in a purely market economy, and portrays a socially managed or planned economy as more capable of achieving the optimal (meaning most profitable and least wasteful to maximize social benefits) level of returns for society using the optimal level of investment in R&D.

In addition, the theory of market structure has led some experts to hypothesize that only large firms with large profit potential, high market shares in large secure markets, and the possibility of achieving economies of scale in their R&D departments will engage in the risky operation and financing of R&D and that too many firms doing research may generate unnecessary repetition and a low productivity research process at the industry level. But centrally planned economies have been dominated by immense, vertically integrated firms. Thus, by such theoretical rationale, the planned societies should have reached far superior levels of economic growth, development, and living standards than those nations with more market-oriented economies. These theoretical suggestions, however, have *not* been verified by reality; the course of history, particularly recent decades, has *actually proved the contrary* with respect to the Soviet Union.

Chapter 3 explicates the links between R&D and technological development and growth in the Soviet context. After describing the participation and status of the Soviet Union in the world economic and technological community, the chapter continues with an introduction to Soviet science and technology as it was. The review indicates that Soviet-style socialism has proved to be incompatible with rapid technological innovation. A number of characteristics are listed as evidence, including:

1. Firms had to make a considerable effort to overcome supply difficulties.
2. Process innovations dominated over product innovations.
3. Financial incentives for research, development, and implementation were small, if not negative.
4. Enterprises' priorities were more inclined to emphasize the quantity rather than the quality of output.
5. There has been a long time lag between invention and innovation; subsequent diffusion was also slow.

A closer analysis of the structure and management of the R&D sector reveals long-standing ideological foundations and a severe mismatch between the established institutions of the Soviet science community and the need for technological change and accompanying factors. The Soviets themselves recognized the need for change, but the introduction of any alterations under the old regime led to more complications, inefficiencies, and inequalities rather than less.

Chapter 4 provides an account and international comparison of the inputs into the R&D sector under seven decades of Soviet leadership, and clearly shows the magnitude of the R&D sector and its significance with respect to the total global scientific resources. Statistics indicate that the general *educationalization* of the Soviet Union took place within a fairly limited period of time, allowing the nation to subsequently draw on a strong educational base. The commitment to considerable and consistent financing for education continued. Yet, the arrangement and variety of schools, the indirectly dictated areas for individual specialization, and the almost complete absence of R&D activity conducted in institutes of higher education have left many questions of whether the investment has served to continually improve the level of education for R&D. With the globalization of research, technology, industry, and business, the need arises to modify the requirements of the higher education system and its associated research function as well as redefine the university/industry interface which has been intensified in recent years in the Western nations. Russia's opportunity for sweeping change is now.

Chapter 4 continues with a description of R&D personnel. By setting yearly plan targets higher, the Soviet Union created a mega work force of scientists and engineers numbering in excess of 1.5 million in the late 1980s, the most in any single nation in the world. Unfortunately, there was largely an organizational separation of science from production, and a sort of separation of R&D from the different ruling scientific institutions. Thus, the stock of available human resources was increasing though their actual utilization may not have been increasing as quickly, or at all for that matter. Immobility, specialization, special benefits, and lack of information about the activities of others provided plenty of disincentives to contemplate a move elsewhere, would it have been possible. Consequently, the overall management of the R&D institutes and the large institutes' internal policy were thwarting creative developments (which are generally said to accompany growing employment of university graduates) and squandering scientific potential.

The final part of Chapter 4 deals with R&D financing. The figures verify a continual strong budgetary commitment to research and experimental development activities. This emphasis was partly the result of a desire to maintain a lasting tradition of promoting science as Marx had said it should be done, and partly for the more practical reason that progress in science and technology would yield solutions to economic and social problems. Essentially, all financing was from the state. No one, however, from the science and technology sector, or any other sector for that matter, was *directly* involved in the budgetary process. Money automatically allocated from the GKNT was considered "easy money" and frequently led to low-quality R&D and the free-rider problem. As a consequence, funds were wasted on research studies that had little or no commercial value and were often antiquated. Nevertheless, the financing process made it easy for the Soviet scientific community to continue to grow and did secure numerous impressive results, particularly in the technical sciences (although these priorities differed significantly from those in the nonsocialist countries of the Western industrialized world).

The material in Chapter 5 covers the extent and form in which Soviet R&D management was linked to the world S&T community, and what the consequences were. For many decades, the Soviet Union (naturally including its R&D sector) was characterized by partially self-imposed and partially inflicted isolation from the industrialized Western world. So, it could neither benefit from nor contribute to the developments and advances made in the non-Communist West. Attempts were made within the CMEA to establish a cooperative group of socialist nations to counter their exclusion from Western activities. This, however, did not prove to be very fruitful. The opening of the Soviet Union to the world in the late 1980s revealed the true level of scientific achievements. Although there were some fields that did have something to offer, many others (particularly in the civilian sector) were seriously lacking. Russia seems to be rejoining the world scientific, technological, and economic communities just when internationalization and globalization are coming into full swing. This and the factors associated with it could help rejuvenate R&D in Russia, especially since there is such a strong domestic S&E base which is favorable for attracting foreign R&D interests.

Chapter 6 leaves the specifics of R&D management and describes the economic environment that has accompanied the development of the R&D sector during the decades of Soviet Communist Party leadership. The central planning system and bargaining economics determined everything in the economy: from the priorities of and the resources for research and development of innovations, to the needs for and objectives of scientific activities, to the technologies used for production, to the prices and quantity of output of all products, and to whom these would be distributed. However, the enormous supply of labor in the full-employment economy and the access to an undervalued and seemingly bottomless pit of raw material resources negated the demand for more advanced, efficiency-enhancing, and input-saving technologies.

Therefore, as stated in Chapter 6, "production amid plenty" in the USSR required technologies to be functional in turning out masses of a particular product regardless of the needed labor, raw material, or energy inputs. As a consequence, the researchers, scientists, scholars, engineers, and technicians (producers and developers of the techniques and ideas) were generally subject to the fulfillment of R&D plans based on the relatively simple technical needs. In this way, the Soviet Union was inflicted by the vicious cycle of technological decay: a continuous loop eroding technological progress, except, of course, in sectors of special national interest such as defense and space. In most fields of technical change the USSR fell well behind Western industrialized nations. Eventually, the Soviet R&D sector also fell victim to overemployment, inefficient resource use, and underutilization; the outputs were products tailored to the resource-rich nation. Nonetheless, the future need not seem bleak in light of these events. With a moderate investment in resource saving, a much greater advance in productivity growth can be attained in the successor republics of the former USSR than can be achieved with the same investment in a mature market economy.

The final chapter of the study discusses R&D management in the transition to the future: from the Soviet Union to Russia. The mismanagement of research and development in the former Soviet Union or, rather, the preceding management based on distorted economic signals leaves much room for improvement and future promise. The value of an accumulated stock of knowledge and experience in R&D is crucial in the propagation of new innovations. Russia now has this stock, although it also has its deficiencies. Therefore, if the economic and political situation is modified to become somewhat more democratic and market oriented and to facilitate a reform of R&D management, organization, and structure, future gains in economic growth and development for Russia would seem to be assured. Some thoughts on the management of R&D and technological advance in the transition to a market economy are also given; these include such essential items as:

1. Directing a portion of the scientific effort toward specific areas that are less sensitive to short-term price changes so that valuable resources and potential will not be lost.
2. Closer ties with user needs.
3. Closer interaction with other policy areas.
4. Actual integration of R&D into industry.
5. Conversion of defense-oriented R&D to civilian-oriented R&D.

8.2 Concluding Remarks

The Soviet-style central planning model has demonstrated that it may be possible, at least for a while, to reasonably plan production (supply) and even to steer the desires of the public depending on the ideology underlying the political system in order to plan consumption (demand). Yet, Soviet-style socialism in all aspects of the economy, including the management of research and development, particularly in comparison with the principles ruling a market economy, has proved that it is incapable of planning innovation to achieve the conditions corresponding to modern economic growth and development.

Innovative activities, that is research and development, are creative, dynamic, and evolutionary processes that depend on an economic environment that will provide:

- The financial support when it is warranted and required to realize and introduce an idea for commercialization that will increase overall social welfare.
- The rewards that result in the continued interest of individuals and various types of public and private groups (institutes or companies) to engage in R&D and make technological change a cumulative process.

As Schumpeter emphasized, innovation is spontaneous (though ultimately founded on previous achievements) and occurs at a nonlinear rate over time. Thus, truly productive research and development, which supports the progress leading to the successfully and continually transforming societies in which the standard of living reaches the level residents in Western industrialized nations have become accustomed to, can only really flourish where economic policy has laid the foundations of a market system; a system in which the consumers' desires reverberate all the way to the researchers and scientific experts who must respond, and for whose investigations, experiments, and developments certain forms of free and secured financing is always available but not automatic. Only potential success in a competitive arena can procure the necessary resources to generate success. Of course, as is evident in Western examples, this does not preclude the presence of some strategic government intervention to aid the cause, not to interfere with but rather to support the functions of an R&D market.

Although this may be thought of as wasteful at first, it is really a method for improving efficiency. Less valuable resources are discarded on worthless prospects, or at least not before their time has come. In addition, the actors are endeavored to inevitably provide the optimum currently available in an effort to stay ahead of any competitors. The resulting choice made by consumers starts the process all over in a continuous, dynamic fashion.

In the former Soviet Union, the entire economic system was in a static state – no dynamism, no change, no evolution. Like the dinosaur, it did not alter its characteristics, behavior, habits, or relations with other components of the changing system in order to accommodate the modifications in the environment. And, like the once mighty and feared dinosaur, the technological strength of the former Soviet Union is confronted with potential demise. The implementation of appropriate R&D management in the transition to a market economy is a necessity if the fate of the scientific and technology communities is to be rescued. There must be competition, demand responsiveness, and international support and exchange, as well as cleverly directed government policy.

In the past, a number of economists have frequently called attention to a tendency to underinvest in R&D in the private sector: that is, firms devote too few resources to the development of new technology (for example, Mansfield, 1980; and Rosenberg, 1980). There are several reasons for this. R&D is a risky activity, and many firms appear to be rather risk averse. But even more important are the short-term time horizons within which business operates that make it difficult for firms to appropriate the benefits that society receives from new technology. In addition, some industries or even specific R&D activities are characterized by certain indivisibilities such as economies of scale or industrial fragmentation which prevent some, often small organizations from undertaking them efficiently (Mansfield, 1980, p. 139). As a result, several of the experts contend that a more extensive system of government subsidy is needed to better articulate society's legitimate long-term R&D needs and to strengthen the incentives of business in technology development involving more distant payoffs (Rosenberg, 1980, p. 129). Considering all these difficulties in enabling productive and efficient R&D for the general benefit of society under market economic conditions, central planning may look like an attractive alternative at first glace.

In fact, Soviet-style central planning as it was formulated in the 1930s and 1940s was based on numerous principles that could have solved the potential problems in a market structure. The Soviet scheme for R&D management was expected to be accompanied by many benefits, including the effects of large-scale production, the potential to eliminate duplicate work, the extension of time horizons, and the selection of projects according to social (not private) rates of return.

While this style of management originally satisfied at least the planners' requirements, the increasing inability to detect all the rapidly growing needs of both society and producers led to inadequate quantity and quality of output in both the R&D and manufacturing sectors despite the overly abundant growth rate in inputs. Indeed, during the extensive-growth policy environment of the 1950s and 1960s, the planners' demand for innovation focused on technologies that increased the quantity of output, rather than on cost- or resource-saving technologies that were the key to a modern-style growth future (Linz, 1992, p. 68). Therefore, the same political and economic conditions that promoted a valuable and enormous R&D sector (as inefficient or unproductive as it has been accused of being) also created an environment where this sector was essentially detached from the production and consumer sectors. The real demand was lost in the R&D management process.

By the end of the Communist leadership in the Soviet Union, the R&D sector had become riddled with issues that were reasons for concern when anticipating the future. On the education side, the rate of total graduates began to fall. The isolation aspect not only prevented domestic students from going abroad (though there were additional reasons like the lack of hard currency and others), but also kept the number of foreign students very low. In the United States, for example, rising numbers of foreign students make up for the decreasing number of domestic students. On the whole, rigidities and lack of breadth in certain educational areas hindered the expansion of fields when they were growing in importance on the world scientific stage.

Simply stated, Soviet scientists and engineers were engaging in R&D activity in an overburdened bureaucratic environment. Bureaucratic barriers to communication and low scientific mobility added to the isolation of R&D workers from their domestic peers in addition to their relative international solitude. There was generally a rather low level of sophistication of equipment and supplies, and especially a lack of access to computers that could have made scientists' and engineers' work many times more efficient. The age structure of leading Soviet researchers led to a dominance of the old (in ideology and age) directors of institutes who were against change. A bargaining style of politics developed that caused the acceptance of scientific overemployment at the expense of underutilization.

But rather than continue to describe the problems of Soviet R&D, more enthusiasm should be shown for the positive aspects: the achievements of scientists and engineers under difficult working conditions in Soviet laboratories. The Soviet system did have some virtues that deserve attention. These begin with the enhanced level of prestige afforded the scientist on ideological grounds; until the relatively recent past, their annual income was higher than that of firm managers – quite contrary to the situation in, for example, the USA. In general, the Soviets were devoted to consistent long-term approaches to problem areas and the use of proven techniques.

Even the low level of sophistication of equipment and instruments had its positive side. It fostered craftsmanship and creativity, and a low technician to researcher ratio. This, however, resulted in numerous scholars, particularly younger ones, having functions very different from those they had been trained for. Combined with a relatively high standard level of idleness, this indicates that a considerable amount of the educated capacity was not utilized in a productive manner. Yet, such a phenomenon was not specific to the input side of the R&D sector, but also typified the output side. A high proportion of research work was left unused (or incomplete) and firm inventories were full of noninstalled domestic and foreign new machinery. Communist leaders of the former Soviet Union recognized this problem and repeatedly voiced their concern at various party congresses since the early 1940s regarding the large quantity of scientific discoveries and important inventions that lie around for years or even decades without being introduced into practical applications (Berliner, 1987, p. 72). Who knows what the potential impact would be if only a portion of the idle capacity were harnessed?

The possibilities seem endless. Particularly today, when Russia is undergoing the transition to a market economy and the economic, institutional, and ideological foundations upon which the scientists' and engineers' working environment was predicated for so long have finally been all but swept away. The former official Western discrimination and the parallel reluctance of the East to become too dependent on the West are no longer barriers to Russia's opportunity for rejoining the global mainstream in research, technology, and economics. Science and technology establishments in Russia are well endowed with qualified personnel and other factors (R&D expenditure taking a proportionately larger share of national income for many decades under Soviet leadership than was and is usual in the West), and are, contrary to others in Central and Eastern Europe, substantial as far as the world scientific community is concerned. The concentration of scientists and engineers in the R&D institutes could provide an ideal environment in which the giant S&E work force can be introduced to the functions and characteristics of a market economy with respect to science and technology. Russia does not have to fall into the position of a product-cycle follower as many of its neighbors might. During the transition and possibly for some time afterward, imitation may be the dominant style of technological advance, but innovation should soon become more significant.

Therefore, in a nutshell, Soviet-style R&D management resulted in an unproductive and inefficient use of and a low if not negative social rate of return in the long term on the enormous resources going into the promotion of scientific and technological activity. Under new management methods, such as those characteristic of a country as Russia attempting to complete the transition to a market economy, much of the R&D resources created under the former regime could be effectively used to generate crucially needed growth in the economy. This growth could lead to an improvement of the Russian economy and renewed prominence for the Russian S&T community, but based on market principles and not the plan. As a consequence, Russia's position in the world market would change. There is the potential for a global impact that can affect many nations, both R&D leaders and followers, and international economic relations will once again need to be adjusted.

References

Abramovitz, M., 1979, Rapid Growth Potential and its Realisation: The Experience of Capitalist Economies in the Postwar Period, in: E. Malinvaud, ed., *Economic Growth and Resources – Vol. 1: The Major Issues*, Macmillan, London, UK.

Aganbegyan, A., 1988, *The Challenge: Economics of Perestroika*, Hutchinson Education, London, UK.

Ageev, A.I., and Kuzin, D.V., 1991, Responsiveness of Soviet Economy to Scientific and Technical Innovations: Comparisons with World Experience, Paper presented at an IIASA Conference on R&D Management in the Transition to a Market Economy, in Moscow, July 13–15.

Ayres, R.U., 1990, CIM: Driving Forces and Applications, in: W. Haywood, ed., *CIM: Revolution in Progress*, IIASA, Laxenburg, Austria.

Beckler, D.Z., 1988, Science and Technology in Presidential Policymaking: A New Dimension and Structure, in: W.T. Golden, ed., *Science and Technology Advice to the President, Congress, and the Judiciary*, Pergamon Press, New York, NY, USA.

Bergson, A., 1978, *Productivity and the Social System: The USSR and the West*, Harvard University Press, Cambridge, MA, USA.

Bergson, A., 1983, Technical Progress, in: A. Bergson and H. Levine, eds., *The Soviet Union Toward the Year 2000*, Columbia University Press, New York, NY, USA.

Berliner, J., 1987, Organizational Restructuring of the Soviet Economy, in: Joint Economic Committee, eds., US Government Printing Office, *Gorbachev's Economic Plans Vol. 1*, Washington, DC, USA.

Berliner, J., 1988, *Soviet Industry: From Stalin to Gorbachev*, Edward Elgar Publishing Company, Aldershot, UK.

Bertsch, G.K., 1986, Technology Transfers and Technology Controls: A Synthesis of the Western-Soviet Relationship, in: R. Amann and J.M. Cooper, eds., *Technical Progress and Soviet Economic Development*, Basil Blackwell Ltd., Oxford, UK.

Boguslavskii, M.M., ed., 1992, *Joint Ventures in the Soviet Union*, I.B. Tauris & Co. Ltd., London, UK.

Bornstein, M., 1984, Pricing Research and Development Services in the USSR, *Research Policy 13*, Elsevier Science Publishers, Amsterdam, Netherlands.

Bradshaw, M.J., 1991, Introduction: Industrial Restructuring and Soviet Regional Development, in: M.J. Bradshaw, ed., *The Soviet Union: A New Regional Geography?* Belhaven Press, London, UK.

Braunstein, Y.M., Baumol, W.J., and Mansfield, E., 1980, The Economics of R&D, *TIMS Studies in the Management Sciences 15*, North-Holland Publishing Company, Amsterdam, Netherlands.

Bright, J.R., 1964, *Research, Development, and Technological Innovation*, Richard D. Irwin, Inc., Homewood, IL, USA.

Brooks, H., 1991, Educating and Training the US Work Force for the Twenty-first Century, in: D.S. Zinberg, ed., *The Changing University*, Kluwer Academic Publishers, Dordrecht, Netherlands.

Chesnais, F., 1988, Technical Co-operation Agreements between Firms, *STI Review, No. 4*, OECD, Paris, France.

Chiang, Jong-Tsong, 1990, *Management of Technology in Centrally Planned Economy*, WP 3130-90-BPS, Alfred P. Sloan School of Management, Cambridge, MA, USA.

Chirot, D., ed., 1989, *The Origins of Backwardness in Eastern Europe*, University of California Press, Los Angeles, CA, USA.

Cole, J.P., 1984, *Geography of the Soviet Union*, Butterworths, London, UK.

Coombs, R., Saviotti, P., and Walsh, V., 1987, *Economics and Technological Change*, Macmillan, London, UK.

Crawford, M., 1986, Soviets Pin Hopes on Technology, *Science* **238**.

Dembinski, P.H., 1991, *The Logic of the Planned Economy: The Seeds of the Collapse*, Clarendon Press, Oxford, UK.

Denison, E.F., 1967, *Why Growth Rates Differ: Postwar Experience in Nine Western Countries*, Brookings Institution, Washington, DC, USA.

Denison, E.F., 1974, *Accounting for United States Economic Growth 1929–1969*, Brookings Institution, Washington, DC, USA.

Denison, E.F., 1985, *Trends in American Economic Growth, 1929–1982*, Brookings Institution, Washington, DC, USA.

Denison, E.F., and Chung, W.K., 1976, *How Japan's Economy Grew So Fast: The Sources of Postwar Expansion*, Brookings Institution, Washington, DC, USA.

Dicken, P., 1986, *Global Shift: Industrial Change in a Turbulent World*, Harper & Row Publishers, London, UK.

Dosi, G., and Soete, L., 1991, Technnological Innovation and International Competitiveness, in: J. Niosi, ed., *Technology and National Competitiveness*, McGill-Queen's University Press, Montreal and Kingston, Canada.

Dyker, D.A., 1986, Soviet Planning Reforms from Andropov to Gorbachev, in: R. Amann and J.M. Cooper, eds., *Technical Progress and Soviet Economic Development*, Basil Blackwell Ltd., Oxford, UK.

ECE, 1989, *Economic Survey of Europe in 1989–1990*, Secretariat of the Economic Commission for Europe, Geneva, Switzerland.

The Economist, 1992a, Pity the Typists, *The Economist*, January 18.

The Economist, 1992b, Business this Week, *The Economist*, April 11.

EIU, 1990, *Eastern Europe and the USSR: Economic Structure and Analysis*, Economist Intelligence Unit Limited, London, UK.

Ellman, M., and Kontorovich, V., 1992, *The Disintegration of the Soviet Economic System*, Routledge, London, UK.

Fabricant, S., 1954, *Economic Progress and Economic Change*, in: *34th Annual Report of the National Bureau of Economic Research*, New York, NY, USA.

Falkus, M.E., 1972, *The Industrialization of Russia, 1700–1914*, Macmillan, London, UK.

FAO, Statistics Division of the Economic and Social Policy Department, 1989, *FAO Yearbook: 1988 Production, Vol.42*, Food and Agricultural Organization of the United Nations, Rome, Italy.

Flora, P., Kraus, F., and Pfenning, W., 1987, *State, Economy, and Society in Western Europe 1815–1975*, Campus Verlag, Frankfurt, Germany.

Fortescue, S., 1987, *Recent Developments in the Administration of Branch Ministry Research*, in: C. Sinclair, ed., *The Status of Soviet Civil Science*, Martinus Nijhoff Publishers, Dordrecht, Netherlands.

Fortescue, S., 1990, Soviet Science Under Gorbachev, *Prometheus* **8**(2).

Fortescue, S., 1992, Science and Technology, in: T. Konn, ed., *Soviet Studies Guide*, Bowker-Saur Ltd., London, UK.

Freeman, C., and Soete, L., 1987, Factor Substitution and Technical Change, in: C. Freeman and L. Soete, eds., *Technical Change and Full Employment*, Basil Blackwell Ltd., Oxford, UK.

Galbraith, K., 1952, *American Capitalism*, Houghton Mifflin, Boston, MA, USA.

Gamota, G., 1987, Soviet Science and Technology: A Crosscutting Overview, in: C. Sinclair, ed., *The Status of Soviet Civil Science*, Martinus Nijhoff Publishers, Dordrecht, Netherlands.

Garrett, T., 1989, Science and the Spark of Perestroika, *New Scientist*, 11 March.

Glaziev, S., 1991, Prospects of Soviet R&D Restructuring, Paper presented at an IIASA Conference on R&D Management in the Transition to a Market Economy, in Moscow, July 13–15.

Glenny, M., 1986, Soviet Congress Wants Science to be the Savior, *New Scientist*, 13 March.

Goetz, P.W., ed., 1988, *The New Encyclopaedia Britannica*, Encyclopaedia Britannica, Inc., Chicago, IL, USA.

Gokhberg, L., and Mindely, L., 1991, Soviet R&D Resources: Basic Characteristics, Paper presented at an IIASA Conference on R&D Management in the Transition to a Market Economy, in Moscow, July 13–15.

Goldman, M.I., 1983, The Changing Role of Raw Material Exports and Soviet Foreign Trade, in: R.G. Jensen, T. Shabad, and A.W. Wright, eds., *Soviet Natural Resources in the World Economy*, University of Chicago Press, Chicago, IL, USA.

Goldman, M.I., 1987, *Gorbachev's Challenge*, W.W. Norton and Company, New York, NY, USA.

Gomulka, S., 1971, *Inventive Activity, Diffusion, and the Stages of Economic Growth*, University of Aarhus, Aarhus, Denmark.

Gomulka, S., 1986, *Growth, Innovation, and Reform in Eastern Europe*, Wheatsheaf Books Ltd., Brighton, UK.

GOSKOMSTAT (The State Committee of the USSR on Statistics), multiple issues, *The USSR in Figures*, Finansy i Statistika Publishers, Moscow, Russia.

Goto, A., 1991, Technology Importation: Japan's Postwar Experience, Paper presented at an IIASA Conference on R&D Management in the Transition to a Market Economy, in Moscow, July 13–15.

Grant, J., 1979, Soviet Machine Tools: Lagging Technology and Rising Imports, in: *Soviet Economy in a Time of Change*, United States Congress Joint Economic Commitee, US Government Printing Office, Washington, DC, USA.

Gregory, P.R., 1982, *Russian National Income 1885–1913*, Cambridge University Press, Cambridge, MA, USA.

Griliches, Z., 1958, Research Costs and Social Returns: Hybrid Corn and Related Innovations, *Journal of Political Economy* **66**.

Griliches, Z., 1964, Research Expenditures, Education, and the Agricultural Production Function, *American Economic Review* **54**.

Griliches, Z., 1973, Research Expenditures and Growth Accounting, in: B. Williams, ed., *Science and Technology in Economic Growth*, Macmillan, London, UK.

Griliches, Z., 1975, Return to the Research and Development Expenditures in the Private Sector, Paper presented at the Conference of Income and Wealth.

Grübler, A., 1991, Technology Diffusion in a Long-Wave Context: The Case of the Steel and Coal Industries, in: T. Vasko, R.U. Ayres, and L. Fontvieille, eds., *Life Cycles and Long Waves*, Lecture Notes in Economics and Mathematical Systems, Springer-Verlag, Heidelberg, Germany.

Gustafson, T., 1989, *Crisis amid Plenty: The Politics of Soviet Energy under Brezhnev and Gorbachev*, Princeton University Press, Princeton, NJ, USA.

Hagedoorn, J., and Schakenraad, J., 1991, *The Economic Effects of Strategic Partnerships and Technology*, MERIT Research Memorandum 91-003, Maastricht, Netherlands.

Hanson, P., 1981, *Trade and Technology in Soviet-Western Relations*, Columbia University Press, New York, NY, USA.

Hentze, J., and Wiechers, R., 1991, East-West Joint Ventures: A Tool for Technology Transfer, in: E. Razvigorova and G. Wolf-Laudon, eds., *East-West Joint Ventures: The New Business Environment*, Basil Blackwell, Inc., Cambridge, MA, USA.

Hough, J.R., ed., 1984, *Education Policy: An International Survey*, Croom Helm, London, UK.

IMF (International Monetary Fund), The World Bank, Organization for Economic Co-operation and Development, and European Bank for Reconstruction and Development, 1991, *A Study of the Soviet Economy*, Vols. 1,2, and 3, OECD, Paris, France.

INFOBRIEF Luxembourg SARL, 1990, *Research and Technology*, Siegfried Neumann, Luxembourg.

Jensen, R.G., Shabad, T., and Wright, A.W., eds., 1983, *Soviet Natural Resources in the World Economy*, University of Chicago Press, Chicago, IL, USA.

Josephson, P.R., 1992, Science and Technology as Panacea in Gorbachev's Russia, in: J.P. Scanlan, ed., *Technology, Culture, and Development: The Experience of the Soviet Model*, M.E. Sharpe Inc., New York, NY, USA.

Kahn, A.E., and Peck, M.J., 1991, Price Deregulation, Corportization, and Competition, in: M.J. Peck, and T.J. Richardson, eds., *What is to be Done? Proposals for the Soviet Transition to the Market*, Yale University Press, New Haven, CT, USA.

Kamien, M.I., and Schwartz, N.L., 1975, Market Structure and Innovation: A Survey, *Journal of Economic Literature* **13**.

Kiselev, S.I., and Voskoboy, A.S., 1991, International Transfer of Technology, Paper presented at an IIASA Conference on R&D Management in the Transition to a Market Economy, in Moscow, July 13–15.

Kneen, P., 1989, Soviet Science Policy Under Gorbachev, *Soviet Studies* **4**(1).

Kontorovoch, V., 1992, Technological Progress and Research and Development, in: M. Ellman and V. Kontorovich, eds., *The Disintegration of the Soviet Economic System*, Routledge, London, UK.

Kosals, L., 1991, R&D Organization and Innovation in Industry in the Transition to Market, Paper presented at an IIASA Conference on R&D Management in the Transition to a Market Economy, in Moscow, July 13–15.

Kulichkov, Y.N., 1991, Defense Research and Designing Institutes in the State's Program of Conversion, Paper presented at an IIASA Conference on R&D Management in the Transition to a Market Economy, in Moscow, July 13–15.

Lall, S., 1984, Transnationals and the Third World: Changing Perceptions, *National Westminster Bank Quarterly Review*, May.

Lane, D., 1985, *Soviet Economy and Society*, Basil Blackwell, Oxford, UK.

Levin, A.E., 1992, *Changes in Russian Science Administration and Policy*, Mimeograph, University of Maryland, College Park, MD, USA.

Linz, S.J., 1992, Innovation Strategies in Centrally Planned and Transition Economies, in: J.P. Scanlan, ed., *Technology, Culture, and Development: The Experience of the Soviet Model*, M.E. Sharpe Inc., New York, NY, USA.

Maddison, A., 1969, *Economic Growth in Japan and the USSR*, George Allen & Unwin Ltd., London, UK.

Maddison, A., 1982, *Phases of Capitalist Development*, Oxford University Press, Oxford, UK.

Maddison, A., 1987, Growth and Slowdown in Advanced Capitalist Economies: Techniques of Quantitative Assessment, *Journal of Economic Literature* **25**.

Maddison, A., 1989, *The World Economy in the 20th Century*, Development Centre of the OECD, Paris, France.

Mansfield, E.W., 1968, *Industrial Research and Technological Innovation*, W.W. Norton, New York, NY, USA.

Mansfield, E.W., 1969, Industrial Research and Development: Characteristics, Costs, and Diffusion of Results, *American Economic Review* **59**.

Mansfield, E.W., 1980, The Role of Technological Change in US Economic Growth, in: C. Bliss and M. Boserup, eds., *Economic Growth and Resources – Vol. 3: Natural Resources*, Macmillian, London, UK.

Mansfield, E.W., 1984, Economic Effects of Research and Development, the Diffusion Process, and Public Policy, in: R.A. Goodman and J. Pavón, eds., *Planning for National Technology Policy*, Praeger Publishers, New York, NY, USA.

Mansfield, E.W., 1989, How Economists See R&D, in: D.E. Chubin and E.W. Chu, eds., *Science Off The Pedestal: Social Perspectives on Science and Technology*, Wadsworth Publishing Company, Belmont, CA, USA.

Mansfield, E., Rapoport, J., Romeo, A., Wagner, S., and Beardsley, G., 1977, Social and Private Rates of Return from Industrial Innovations, *Quarterly Journal of Economics* **91**.

Matcheret, G., 1987, The Academy of Sciences and the Restructuring of R&D in the Soviet Union, in: C. Sinclair, ed., *The Status of Soviet Civil Science*, Martinus Nijhoff Publishers, Dordrecht, Netherlands.

Meyerhoff, A.A., 1983, Soviet Petroleum: History, Technology, Geology, Reserves, Potential and Policy, in: R.G. Jensen, T. Shabad, and A.W. Wright, eds., *Soviet Natural Resources in the World Economy*, University of Chicago Press, Chicago, IL, USA.

Mickiewicz, E., 1973, *Handbook of Soviet Social Science Data*, The Free Press, New York, NY, USA.

Mikerin, G., and Kozlova, O., 1991, Technological Assessment Problems in the Transition to Market Economy, Paper presented at an IIASA Conference on R&D Management in the Transition to a Market Economy, in Moscow, July 13–15.

Mikulinski, S.R., and Richta, R., eds., 1983, *Socialism and Science*, Academia – Publishing House of the Czechoslovak Academy of Sciences, Prague, CSFR.

Minasian, J.R., 1969, Research and Development, Production Functions, and Rates of Return, *American Economic Review* **59**.

Motor Vehicle Manufacturers Association of the United States, 1991, *World Motor Vehicle Data*, Public Affairs Division of the Motor Vehicle Manufacturers Association of the United States, Inc., Detroit, MI, USA.

Motorygin, B., and Glaziev, S., 1991, Economic Reform Impact on Soviet Research and Development, Paper presented at an IIASA Conference on R&D Management in the Transition to a Market Economy, in Moscow, July 13–15.

Mytelka, L., 1990, New Modes of International Competition: Case of Strategic Partnering in R&D, *Science and Public Policy* **17**.

Narin, F., and Whitlow, E.S., 1990, *Measurement of Scientific Co-operation and Co-authorship in CEC-related Areas of Science*, Commission of the European Communities, Brussels, Belgium.

Nelson, R.R., 1980, R&D, Knowledge, and Externalities: An Approach to the Puzzle of Disparate Productivity Growth Rates Among Manufacturing Industries, in: C. Bliss and M. Boserup, eds., *Economic Growth and Resources – Vol. 3: Natural Resources*, Macmillian, London, UK.

Nelson, R.R., 1987, *Understanding Technical Change as an Evolutionary Process*, Elsevier Science Publishers, Amsterdam, Netherlands.

Nelson, R.R., 1992, National Innovation Systems: A Retrospective on a Study, Paper prepared for an IIASA Conference on Industrial R&D Management in the Transition to a Market Economy, in Laxenburg, March 27–28.

Nelson, R.R., and Winter, S.G., 1982, *An Evolutionary Theory of Economic Change*, Harvard University Press, Cambridge, MA, USA.

Nelson, R.R., Peck, M.J., and Kalachek, E.D., 1967, *Technology, Economic Growth, and Public Policy*, Brookings Institution, Washington, DC, USA.

Nove, A., 1986, *Marxism and "Really Existing Socialism,"* Harwood Academic Publishers, Chur, Switzerland.

Nove, A., 1989, *An Economic History of the USSR*, Penguin Books, London, UK.

NSB (National Science Board), 1985, *Science Indicators: The 1985 Report*, US Government Printing Office, Washington, DC, USA.

NSB (National Science Board), 1987, 1989, 1991, *Science and Engineering Indicators*, US Government Printing Office, Washington, DC, USA.

O'Brien, M.P., 1964, Technological Planning and Misplanning, in: J.R. Bright, ed., *Research, Development, and Technological Innovation*, Richard D. Irwin, Inc., Homewood, IL, USA.

OECD, 1989, *OECD Science and Technology Indicators Report: No. 3 – R&D, Production and Diffusion of Technology*, OECD, Paris, France.

OECD, 1991a, *Main Science and Technology Indicators*, OECD, Paris, France.

OECD, The Technology/Economy Programme (TEP), 1991b, *Technology in a Changing World*, OECD, Paris, France.

OECD, 1992, *Science and Technology Policy: Review and Outlook 1991*, OECD, Paris, France.

OTA (Office of Technology Assessment), 1992, How Free is Free: America's Competitors Have Few Doubts About Managing Markets, *NE-MW Economic Review*, March.

Parrott, B., 1987, Information Flows in Soviet Research and Development, in: C. Sinclair, ed., *The Status of Soviet Civil Science*, Martinus Nijhoff Publishers, Dordrecht, Netherlands.

PC Globe, Inc., 1990, *PC Globe*, Tempe, AZ, USA.

Pearce, R.D., and Singh, S., 1992, *Globalizing Research and Development*, Macmillan, London, UK.

Perez, C., and Soete, L., 1988, Catching up in Technology: Entry Barriers and Windows of Opportunity, in: G. Dosi *et al.*, eds., *Technical Change and Economic Theory*, Frances Pinter, London, UK.

Peterson, W., 1971, The Returns to Investment in Agricultural Research in the United States, in: W. Fishel, ed., *Resource Allocation in Agricultural Research*, University of Minnesota, USA.

Piskunov, D., and Saltyko, B., 1991, Transformation of Basic Structures and Operating Mechanisms of Soviet Science, Paper presented at an IIASA Conference on R&D Management in the Transition to a Market Economy, in Moscow, July 13–15.

Popper, S.W., 1992, Science and Technology in Eastern Europe After the Flood: Rejoining the World, in: J.P. Scanlan, ed., *Technology, Culture, and Development: The Experience of the Soviet Model*, M.E. Sharpe Inc., New York, NY, USA.

Porter, M.E., 1990, *The Competitive Advantage of Nations*, Macmillan, London, UK.

Poznanski, K.Z., 1987, *Technology, Competition, & the Soviet Bloc in the World Market*, Institute of International Studies, University of California, Berkeley, CA, USA.

Razvigorova, E., and Djarova, J., 1991, Dynamics of East-West Economic Relations and the Role of Joint Ventures, in: E. Razvigorova and G. Wolf-Laudon, eds., *East-West Joint Ventures: The New Business Environment*, Basil Blackwell, Inc., Cambridge, MA, USA.

Rich, V., 1983, Soviet Applied Research: Broader View Demanded, *Nature* **303**.

Rich, V., 1986, Soviet Education: University Shake-up Canvassed, *Nature* **321**.

Rip, A., 1989, Opening the Black Box of Technological Development, in: D.E. Chubin and E.W. Chu, eds., *Science Off The Pedestal: Social Perspectives on Science and Technology*, Wadsworth Publishing Company, Belmont, CA, USA.

Román, Z., 1982, *Productivity and Economic Growth*, Akadémiai Kiadó, Budapest, Hungary.

Rosegger, G., 1980, *The Economics of Production and Innovation: An Industrial Perspective*, Pergamon Press, Oxford, UK.

Rosenberg, N., 1980, The Role of Technological Change in US Economic Growth, in: C. Bliss and M. Boserup, eds., *Economic Growth and Resources – Vol. 3: Natural Resources*, Macmillian, London, UK.

Rosenberg, N., and Birdzell, L.E., 1990, Science, Technology and the Western Miracle, *Scientific American* **263**(5).

Ryan, M., 1990, *Contemporary Soviet Science: A Statistical Handbook*, Edward Elgar Publishing Company, Aldershot, UK.

Sakwa, R., 1990, *Gorbachev and his Reforms 1985–1990*, Philip Allan, Hertfordshire, UK.

Scherer, F.M., 1965, Invention and Innovation in the Watt-Boulton Steam Engine Venture, *Technology and Culture* **6**.

Schneider, C. M., 1991, *On Research and Development Management in the Transition to a Market Economy*, WP-91-44, IIASA, Laxenburg, Austria.

Schumpeter, J.A., 1934, *The Theory of Economic Development*, Harvard University Press, Cambridge, MA, USA.

Schumpeter, J.A., 1943, *Capitalism, Socialism and Democracy*, Harper & Row, New York, NY, USA.

Semeria, M., 1987, Information Channels for Science and Technology, in: C. Sinclair, ed., *The Status of Soviet Civil Science*, Martinus Nijhoff Publishers, Dordrecht, Netherlands.

Shaw, D., 1991, Restructuring the Soviet City, in: M.J. Bradshaw, ed., *The Soviet Union: A New Regional Geography?* Belhaven Press, London, UK.

Sinclair, C., ed., 1987, *The Status of Soviet Civil Science*, Martinus Nijhoff Publishers, Dordrecht, Netherlands.

Smith, G.B., ed., 1980, *Public Policy and Administration in the Soviet Union*, Praeger Publishers, New York, NY, USA.

Smith-Morris, M., ed., 1990, *Vital World Statistics*, The Economist Books Ltd., London, UK.

Sobell, V., 1986, Technology Flows within COMECON and Channels of Communication, in: R. Amann and J.M. Cooper, eds., *Technical Progress and Soviet Economic Development*, Basil Blackwell Ltd., Oxford, UK.

Solow, R.M., 1957, Technical Change and the Aggregate Production Function, *Review of Economics and Statistics* **39**.

Stoneman, P., 1983, *The Economic Analysis of Technological Change*, Oxford University Press, Oxford, UK.

Terleckyj, N., 1974, *Effects of R&D on the Productivity Growth of Industries: An Exploratory Study*, National Planning Association, Washington, DC, USA.

Thirtle, C.G., and Ruttan, V.W., 1987, *The Role of Demand and Supply in the Generation and Diffusion of Technical Change*, Harwood Academic Publishers, Chur, Switzerland.

United Nations, Department of International Social and Economic Affairs, Statistical Office, 1990, *Statistical Yearbook: Thirty-sixth Issue*, United Nations, New York, NY, USA.

WIIW, Wiener Institut für Internationale Wirtschaftsvergleiche (Vienna Institute for Comparative Economic Studies), 1990, *COMECON Data 1989*, Macmillan Academic and Professional Ltd., London, UK.

Wright, A.W., 1983, Soviet Natural Resource Exports and the World Market, in: R.G. Jensen, T. Shabad, and A.W. Wright, eds., *Soviet Natural Resources in the World Economy*, University of Chicago Press, Chicago, IL, USA.

Yakovets, Y.V., 1991, Technological Crisis and Conversion of Military Industry, Paper presented at an IIASA Conference on R&D Management in the Transition to a Market Economy, in Moscow, July 13–15.

Zwick, P.R., 1980, Soviet National Policy: Social, National, and Political Aspects, in: G.B. Smith, ed., *Public Policy and Administration in the Soviet Union*, Praeger Publishers, New York, NY, USA.

The International Institute for Applied Systems Analysis

is an interdisciplinary, nongovernmental research institution founded in 1972 by leading scientific organizations in 12 countries. Situated near Vienna, in the center of Europe, IIASA has been for more than two decades producing valuable scientific research on economic, technological, and environmental issues.

IIASA was one of the first international institutes to systematically study global issues of environment, technology, and development. IIASA's Governing Council states that the Institute's goal is: *to conduct international and interdisciplinary scientific studies to provide timely and relevant information and options, addressing critical issues of global environmental, economic, and social change, for the benefit of the public, the scientific community, and national and international institutions.* Research is organized around three central themes:

- Global Environmental Change;
- Global Economic and Technological Change;
- Systems Methods for the Analysis of Global Issues.

The Institute now has national member organizations in the following countries:

Austria
The Austrian Academy of Sciences

Bulgaria
The National Committee for Applied Systems Analysis and Management

Canada
The Canadian Committee for IIASA

Czech and Slovak Republics
The Committees for IIASA of the Czech and Slovak Republics

Finland
The Finnish Committee for IIASA

Germany
The Association for the Advancement of IIASA

Hungary
The Hungarian Committee for Applied Systems Analysis, Hungarian Academy of Sciences

Italy
The National Research Council (CNR) and the National Commission for Nuclear and Alternative Energy Sources (ENEA)

Japan
The Japan Committee for IIASA

Netherlands
The Netherlands Organization for Scientific Research (NWO)

Poland
The Polish Academy of Sciences

Russia
The Russian Academy of Sciences

Sweden
The Swedish Council for Planning and Coordination of Research (FRN)

United States of America
The American Academy of Arts and Sciences

GPSR Compliance

The European Union's (EU) General Product Safety Regulation (GPSR) is a set of rules that requires consumer products to be safe and our obligations to ensure this.

If you have any concerns about our products, you can contact us on ProductSafety@springernature.com

In case Publisher is established outside the EU, the EU authorized representative is:

Springer Nature Customer Service Center GmbH
Europaplatz 3
69115 Heidelberg, Germany

Batch number: 10725973

Printed by Printforce, the Netherlands